PETROCARIBE

THE PROSECUTOR SPEAKS

JEAN SENAT FLEURY

ISBN 979-8-90528-024-5 (Paperback)
ISBN 979-8-90528-025-2 (Ebook)

Inquiries and Book Orders should be addressed to:
Leavitt Peak Press
17901 Pioneer Blvd Ste L #298,
Artesia, California 90701
Phone #: 2092191548

"As for the people I am accusing, I do not know them, I have never seen them, and I have no rancor or hatred against them. They are for me only entities, spirits of social malfeasance. And the act I am doing here is only a revolutionary way to hasten the explosion of truth and justice."

I have only one passion, that of light, in the name of humanity that has suffered so much and who has the right to happiness. My fiery protest is only the cry of my soul. So, let's dare translate me into the Assize Court and let the investigation take place! I wait."

Émile Zola. "I Accuse…!"

"Revisiting history: it is not the privilege of a few, or a negotiable right poorly granted or challenged by the State. It is, first, a necessity. It is also the inescapable current brought by the evolutionary points of view of the successive generations. It is, at the same time, an indispensable step if one wants to keep alive the memory of the People.

Jules Roy, *The Trial of Marshal Pétain*

Contents

Acknowledgements

My sincere thanks as well as all my gratitude go to Dr. Willy Lubin, Prosecutor General at the Court of Appeal of Rennes, who wrote the preface, also to Danielle Saada, retired French magistrate, Malachie Azémar and Guy Jacques, who revised the manuscript. I also extend my sincere and profound thanks to engineer Luckner Bayas, Anne-Edline François, jurist, the sociologist Jacques Arnaud Démézier, Dr. Jean Élifaite Gué, researcher, professor at the State University of Haiti, Dr. Josué Pierre, sociologist-researcher, and Mr. Harold Gresseau, who kindly agreed to write a commentary published at the end of the book. Finally, I thank Professor Amerigo Bernadel, who helped me in editing the text and provided me with useful advice and guidance.

Jean Sénat Fleury

Preface

In 2008, Erick Maurel, currently Attorney General at the Court of Appeal of Basse-Terre (Guadeloupe), wrote in the preface to his book entitled Portraits of Prosecutors, that *"the prosecutor is first and foremost terrifying... It is fear that he must inspire, it is fear that must emanate from the accused in the face of this man -necessarily - austere, angry and threatening, who looks down on you since, thanks to an alleged carpenter's mistake, he sits at the same level as the judges, thus gaining in height without losing in blood ties... It was therefore essential to lift this robe that he wears, a distant sign of the clerk he once was, to see a heart beating there."*

It is because of his extensive experience working with many prosecutors during his distinguished career as a judge that Jean Sénat Fleury gives them the floor in this book, "*Petro Caribe: The Prosecutor Speaks*".

Jean Sénat Fleury learned that some cases transcend the simple framework of a financial scandal. They become symbols. They embody the betrayed hopes of a people, the unfulfilled promises of a state, and the demands for justice of a society.

The Petro Caribe affair undoubtedly belongs to this category.

Initially, the Petro Caribe program held a promise: energy and financial cooperation that could provide Haiti with the resources to support infrastructure projects, strengthen public services, and improve the living conditions of millions of Haitians. In a country marked by profound economic and social difficulties, this initiative had raised many hopes.

However, over the years, these hopes have turned into questions, then into disappointments. Official reports and investigations by oversight bodies have raised serious concerns about the use of funds from this program. Amounts were committed without any transparency, some projects remained unfinished or were fictitious, and the management mechanisms were riddled with irregularities.

These revelations have sparked widespread outrage among the population. Citizens, civil society organizations, and concerned journalists have demanded explanations.

A fundamental question has emerged in the public debate: where did the Petro Caribe money go?

This question is not only financial. It is also moral, political and institutional. It touches on the relationship between the state and the citizens, the responsibility of public leaders and the capacity of institutions to guarantee transparency and justice.

However, despite the scale of the alleged facts and the importance of the issues at stake, the judicial process related to this case remains uncertain. Responsibility still appears to be scattered. Expectations of justice remain high, while institutional responses in this crisis-stricken country are nonexistent.

It is in this context that Jean Sénat Fleury's work is situated.

Rather than offering a simple narrative or descriptive analysis of events, Jean Sénat Fleury adopts an original approach, which is becoming his specialty: the simulation of a trial. He does not claim to replace the competent courts or pronounce a real verdict. His approach is intended primarily as an intellectual and civic exercise, a way of staging the arguments, the facts, and the potential responsibilities. In order to better illuminate the public understanding of this case, he chooses to give a voice to representatives of society.

Thus, Jean Sénat Fleury offers a particularly fruitful framework for this objective. In a trial, the facts are presented, the evidence examined, and the arguments confronted. Both the prosecution and the defense have the opportunity to present their interpretation of events.

However, by only reproducing the role of the prosecution, even in a simulated way, this book manages to give the reader the necessary tools to think for themselves. It invites them to explore the different dimensions of the case, to weigh the arguments, and to consider the potential responsibilities involved.

This narrative choice also has an educational value. It allows for a better understanding not only of the facts related to the Petro Caribe affair, but also of the role of the prosecutor in the functioning of the justice system.

Because, beyond this particular scandal, a broader question arises: that of a culture of accountability in the management of public affairs. A democracy is not measured solely by the holding of elections, but also by the capacity of its institutions to be held accountable and to ensure that public resources are used in the general interest. The prosecutor's office must ensure this.

This book is therefore part of a process of remembrance and reflection. It contributes to a collective effort to prevent oblivion or indifference from erasing the essential questions for Haiti's future. By revisiting the events in the form of a mock trial, it reminds us that the search for truth is a process that belongs to every society.

Jean Sénat Fleury invites the reader to enter the imaginary courtroom to discover the complexities of a case in which the prosecutor must take responsibility, in the name of the Haitian people.

But above all, it will make him think. Each reader becomes a witness and a symbolic juror of history.

The pursuit of justice is not limited to the courts. It is also fueled by public debate, citizen vigilance, and the work of remembrance.

Jean Sénat Fleury's book contributes to this reflection, to enlightening consciences and to reminding us that the management of public resources is, above all, a responsibility towards an entire nation.

Willy LUBIN,
Doctor of Private Law and Criminal Sciences
Deputy General, Near the Court of Appeal of Rennes

Note

What if justice finally speaks?

Inspired by one of the biggest financial scandals in Haiti's contemporary history, the book " *Petro Caribe: The Prosecutor Speaks* " stages a fictional trial before an Assize Court where law, history and national conscience intersect.

Between 2008 and 2016, billions of dollars from the Petro Caribe program – intended for Haiti's economic and social development – were embezzled, squandered, or mismanaged. Through a powerful judicial reconstruction, former investigating judge Jean Sénat Fleury transforms audit reports, public inquiries, and political controversies into a grand literary trial where the accused must answer for malfeasance, embezzlement, fraud, overbilling, abuse of power, and corruption.

A career magistrate, teacher, and writer, Judge Fleury brings to this work his profound knowledge of Haitian law and criminal procedure. His writing, both rigorous and committed, analyzes:

- The mechanisms of the misappropriation of Petro Caribe funds.
- The alleged responsibility of high-ranking Haitian state officials and private companies.
- The persistent culture of impunity in Haiti.
- The role of the prosecutor in the society.

At the crossroads of legal novel, political essay and historical testimony, this work echoes Émile Zola's famous "*Accuse*" and poses a fundamental question: can justice restore the confidence of a people?

More than a book, " *Petro Caribe: The Prosecutor Speaks* " is a profound reflection on governance, public responsibility, and the institutional destiny of Haiti.

This is an essential book for anyone interested in Haitian politics, the mechanisms of international corruption, financial scandals, and the contemporary history of the Caribbean.

Petro Caribe: The Prosecutor Speaks is a fictional trial based on administrative reports from the Court of Auditors, reports from the Latortue/Beauplan Senate Commissions, and other facts related to investigations into the management of the Petro Caribe program.

Prologue

During that entire night, Me. Antoine thought about the opening of the trial, which would begin the following morning at the Port-au-Prince courthouse. He reflected on the responsibility he bore in prosecuting some sixty defendants in the Petro Caribe case. This was without mentioning the fifty of them who would not appear before the Assize Court and against whom a judgment in absentia would be rendered. The task was colossal, and obtaining the conviction of those implicated in the squandering of funds, in the name of the Haitian people seeking justice, was a laudable objective that demanded every sacrifice.

As he reviewed his notes for the umpteenth time, his mind was absorbed by the case file. He had spent weeks preparing the facts in consultation with several others prosecutors who would help him build the case. Leaning over the desk piled high with law books and the new penal code, he pondered, his eyes half-closed. Stacks of files reached almost to the ceiling. A desk lamp illuminated a heap of documents. A photograph of his grandfather, a career magistrate, hung on the wall. It was 4:30 in the morning. Outside, the sound of motorcycles and the calls of the market women, " *madan sara,* " could already be heard as they headed to sell their wares at the Salomon market.

The lawyer is eager for the dawn to break. He has long dreamed of this hearing. His ambition has always been to write his name in the annals of Haitian justice, to have his portrait in the gallery of great Haitian jurists: Rodrigue Casimir, Joseph C. Nerette, Hyppolite Thermitus, Rock Raymond, Myrbel Jean-Baptiste, Gérard Gourgue,

Jean Vandal, André Villejoint, Théodore Achille, Dantès Colimon, Maurice Vilaire, Roger Ancion, Noé Fourcand, Michel Donatien, Webert Michaud, Boniface Alexandre, Clémenceau Thomas, and others.

He memorized the closing argument of former Commissioner Rodrigue Casimir, who brilliantly presented the case against Frantz Leroy and his associates in the Stamp Affair. In 1975, a sensational trial took place that made headlines. The legal profession, academic circles, and the entire Haitian society witnessed a criminal trial of exceptional quality, technically and judicially, as well as oratorically.

Fifty-one years later, he finds himself in the same role: presenting the prosecution's case against the accused. One of the most positive consequences this trial could have is undoubtedly the renewed confidence of the Haitian people in the judicial system.

Me. Antoine slammed his right fist on the table: "Let's bring justice to Haitian people. Let's begin the work with the Petro Caribe trial."

Introduction

From underdevelopment to entrapment, Haiti's socio-economic situation worsens daily. Although the country receives significant foreign aid, this assistance has never had a tangible impact on improving the lives of Haitians. In May 2006, Haiti joined the Petro Caribe program. The agreement represents a breath of fresh air for the Haitian economy, characterized by high vulnerability and a persistent security crisis. Established on June 29, 2005, Petro Caribe is the result of a market development strategy aimed at selling Venezuelan petroleum products. Venezuela sells oil on favorable terms to a group of Caribbean countries; a portion of the payments is reinvested in their national development.

Haiti received its first oil shipment in early 2008. The country purchased oil from Venezuela and resold it to local Haitian oil companies. These companies paid their invoices within 30 days. The Bureau for the Monetization of Development Assistance Programs (BMPAD), a public institution under the supervision of the Ministry of Economy and Finance (MEF), had 90 days to pay 40% of the debt to Venezuela. The remaining 60% constituted a long-term debt payable over 25 years at a 1% interest rate. The profits were intended to finance social development projects.

Corrupt Haitian officials sabotaged the program. Between 2008 and 2018, funds estimated at between 4 billion and 4.2 billion US dollars were misappropriated or mismanaged. The Petro Caribe fund embezzlement is the most significant corruption case recorded in the annals of fraud and misappropriation of public funds ever perpetrated in the history of the Republic of Haiti.

The scandal is a crime of such ignominy that it reaches the heights of indecency and greed. Billions of dollars intended for Haiti's economic and social development were embezzled, and what little remained was deliberately mismanaged to conceal the extent of the squandering. This vast embezzlement involves heads of state, prime ministers, ministers, directors general, as well as actors in the private and public sectors and foreign firms. The case has sparked profound outrage and given rise to massive protests.

Inspired by this unprecedented scandal, Judge Fleury writes – *Petro Caribe: the prosecutor speaks.* – In this work, the author invents a fictitious trial during which the case is presented before an Assize Court where the accused are tried for embezzlement, misappropriation of funds, abuse of office, fraud, forgery of public documents, overbilling, bribes, abuse of office, money laundering, influence peddling, corruption of national/foreign agents and officials of international organizations, and many others.

Chapter 1

THE OPENING OF THE TRIAL

(The first day of the hearing)

Monday, June 8, 2026. The Government Commissioner visited the National Penitentiary of Port-au-Prince early this morning. Knowing the extreme anger of the people who have been gathering for days around the prison, he wanted to ensure the effectiveness of the security protocol for transferring the defendants to the Assize Court. In a rectangular cell in the prison, the accused were gathered. The space was cramped, oppressive. The heat was terrible. The smell was foul. A bare lightbulb hung from the ceiling, casting a yellow light. Filtered through the thick walls, one could hear the distant beat of drums and, in waves, the muffled chants of the crowd: "Kot kòb Petrokaribe a!" (Where is the Petro Caribe money?). There are thousands of Petro Challengers out there. Some carry ropes and others brandish batons. They are waiting for the defendants, those accused of misappropriating Petro Caribe funds, to be dragged to court.

The Port-au-Prince courthouse, a hub of legal eloquence where professionals gather to debate legal issues, is teeming with an enthusiastic crowd, excited by the prospect of the historic "*Petro Caribe Trial.*" The rhythm of life seems to have ground to a halt. In homes and on the streets, the only event dominating conversations and making headlines is the verdict for those accused of misappropriating Petro Caribe funds. This momentous trial, dubbed the "trial of the century," has relegated all other national and international news to the background.

The event is receiving such extensive media coverage that it's even overshadowing the opening of the 2026 World Cup in North America. This global and historic event will see the participation of 48 countries, including the Haitian national football team, which valiantly qualified after playing several matches abroad. The match between the Grenadiers and the Brazilian national football team on June 19, 2026, at Lincoln Financial Field in Philadelphia, is one of the most anticipated events worldwide. It's already being called a battle between Goliath and David. On the Brazilian side, names like Vinicius, Rodrygo, Raphinha, Alisson, and Danilo are being mentioned, while on the Haitian side, Placide, Nazon, Guerrier, Pierrot, Bellegarde, and Izidor are being named.

A large crowd filled the courthouse. People from all walks of life were present: lawyers, students, historians, journalists, sociologists, human rights activists, economists, accountants, and political and religious leaders. All were eager to follow the proceedings closely. In neighborhoods of Port-au-Prince and in provincial cities, the government, in agreement with the municipalities, installed giant screens on almost every street corner to allow people to follow every moment of the trial live. The idea of defeating corruption permeated everyone's hearts, minds, and words. Several million people were interested in learning the facts.

Beyond the thick walls of the courthouse, an entire people symbolically stand in the dock. In remote rural areas, in working-class neighborhoods, in the diaspora, ordinary citizens listen, observe, and comment.

Some remember the promises made regarding the use of Petro Caribe funds, others think of the unfinished construction projects, the roads never built, the hospitals announced but never constructed. Many are unfamiliar with the intricacies of the law or the complex financial mechanisms, but they all understand one thing: the squandered money is theirs.

The case is of considerable interest. It is very rare in Haiti for state officials to be tried for acts of corruption. With around one hundred people indicted and some fifty private firms prosecuted for embezzlement and money laundering, this case far surpasses, in its scope, the Consolidation Trial (1903-1904), which had generated immense interest at the time.

The Consolidation trial and the Stamps trial show that this is not the first time that the Haitian justice system has initiated proceedings against high-ranking state officials. History, discreet and persistent, preserves the memory of these two previous trials where hope briefly illuminated the judicial scene before fading away.

Each generation has experienced its anticipated moment of truth, often followed by a brutal return to impunity. It is in light of these precedents that we can measure the gravity of the present moment. The past is never far away; it watches silently, waiting to see if it will be repeated or finally contradicted.

The Consolidation Trial took place under the government of General Nord Alexis. On November 28, 1904, the trial opened with accusations of fraud, theft, and forgery of bonds issued under the government of Tiresias Simon Sam around 1900-1901. These bonds bore the signature of the Minister of Finance at the time, and the transactions were carried out in accordance with a duly passed law. Numerous high-ranking officials were implicated.

The Consolidation Trial was a major legal event. A decree adopted on March 21, 1903, established an administrative inquiry and audit commission tasked with examining the various operations carried out under different administrations and also with auditing public finances amidst the current crisis. Despite the enormous publicity surrounding the case, given its importance and implications, the trial was ultimately considered a failure. While the fraudsters were indeed prosecuted, tried, and convicted, they all soon found themselves at the helm of state affairs. Some of those convicted were pardoned by Nord Alexis himself, despite having initiated the trial. Others benefited from the clemency of his successor, Antoine Simon. Cincinnatus Leconte, pardoned in 1909 by President Antoine Simon, became president in 1911. Tancrède Auguste, convicted in absentia and pardoned, became Nord Alexis's Minister of the Interior. He became president in 1912 with 99 votes out of 114 from the National Assembly. Vilbrun Guillaume Sam, sentenced to forced labor for life, benefited from a pardon decree on December 31, 1905. He became president in 1915.

This historic conclusion hangs in people's minds like a threat. Even then, it embodied the specter of total impunity, of a judicial farce. Somewhere along the way, a clear-sighted and bitter observer might wonder if, in twenty years, an unborn child will read in their history book that today's accused, or their protégés, had become ministers, senators, or had founded powerful economic dynasties. Can justice be anything more than a brief theatrical interlude between two acts of plunder? The crowd, for its part, rejects this idea. It wants to believe that this time will be the last, that the iron cycle has finally been broken. Its massive presence is an act of faith, or perhaps the last gasp of a people who still hope to liberate Haiti.

The Petro Caribe case, considered the trial of the century, attracts far more attention than the Stamp Trial, which took place in 1975 under the regime of Jean-Claude Duvalier. Described as memorable and historic for its educational and didactic significance, it brought twelve defendants before the Assize Court in Port-au-Prince.

Several months of inquiries and investigations uncovered sufficient evidence against individuals suspected of being perpetrators and accomplices in the "Audubon Birds" counterfeit stamp affair. At the end of August 1975, the government of Jean-Claude Duvalier, through the Minister of Justice, Aurélien C. Jeanty, organized the trial, considered one of the most remarkable hearings ever held before a Haitian Assize Court.

As the public prosecutor, Rodrigue Casimir told the court: "This trial is very serious. It calls into question the prestige of a country, the values of a society, and the principles of social education. The accused must be tried publicly so that those present can see and understand. We have no interest in hiding the facts..."

This statement, made decades earlier, seems to transcend time to resonate at the heart of the Petro Caribe affair. The words change little, the stakes remain the same.

Judging publicly is not just a legal act; it is an educational, almost civic act. To show, to explain, to expose: all these verbs reflect the hope that justice will not only be served, but understood.

Even today, this requirement applies to the prosecutor's office.

Haiti has already experienced two major corruption trials, but these seem almost insignificant compared to the Petro Caribe affair, which exposes the crimes and malfeasance of six successive governments. Unlike the Consolidation case or the Stamp Affair, the Petro Caribe affair represents a major turning point in the history of financial scandals in Haiti. Indeed, several officials from both the Haitian public and private sectors are implicated in acts of corruption and abuse of power. In total, six governments are accused of embezzling funds estimated at between 4 and 4.2 billion US dollars. The Court of Auditors' audit report lists numerous irregularities in the execution of the projects. It notably highlights administrative discrepancies, anomalies in the implementation of the projects and related activities, as well as shortcomings in compliance, legality, validity, and integrity of the operations carried out. The report also examines the control and traceability of released funds, the actual disbursements, the management mechanisms used, and the levels of responsibility of the various managers involved. Corrupt officials abused their power and unscrupulous businesspeople used their connections to embezzle billions of dollars.

Two former Haitian senators, Youri Latortue and Evalière Beauplan, investigated the irregularities. In two reports, they methodically outlined the numerous anomalies observed. The Commissions examined a dozen contracts signed in 2011 by the Haitian government with an initial firm, J&J Construction, which was dissolved on September 27, 2010, and noted that a number of them were signed without the certificate from the National Commission for Public Procurement (CNMP).

The report of the Special Senate Commission of Inquiry was presented to the Senate for adoption in October 2017. It indicates that the firm COMPHENER SA, headed by Mr. Jovenel Moïse, signed a contract for the supply and installation of 65 streetlights in the localities of Savanette and Mon-Organisé. The contract was awarded without competitive bidding on January 11, 2013, between the Bureau of Monetization of Development Assistance Programs (BMPAD), the agency managing Petro Caribe funds, and COMPHENER SA. This contract lacked the approval of the Court of Auditors and did not have a certificate of no-objection from the National Commission for Public Procurement (CNMP). The contract amounted to 4,949,389 gourdes. This cost was deemed excessive for the installation of 65 streetlights, since the average price per unit was 76,144 gourdes for this project. The overbilling appears all the more evident given that, in a similar project, the average cost of the same type of street light was half as much.

More than a dozen contracts were signed in 2011 with the general partnership Milfort Augustin & Co, formed by Josselin Mifort and Jackson Augustin, known as J&J Construction.

This firm oversees the construction projects awarded to Secosa. These two companies received the largest number of contracts. The investigation was not able to establish the basis on which

J&J Construction's services were selected, nor could it determine the reasons for choosing Secosa as the contractor. The percentage allocated to supervision is also higher than the industry standard, exceeding 10% of the total value between the project owner and the contractor.

For example, the amendment relating to the Lycée National de Pignon represented 99.16% of the value of the initial contract, whereas an amendment cannot legally exceed 30% of the amount of the contract.

J & J CONSTRUCTION

CONTRACT	Enforcement firm	Amount (excluding tax)	Supervisory Firm	Amount (excluding tax)	Percentage Supervision
National High School of St Raphael	SECOSA	46,485,885	J&J Construction	5,650,000	12.15%
Ranquitte National High School	SECOSA	48,485,885	J&J Construction	5,000,000	10.31%
National High School of Maïssade	SECOSA	36,105,931.36	J&J Construction	4,000,000	11.08%
Pignon National High School	SECOSA	55,463,488	J&J Construction	5,600,000	10.10%
Amendment to the National High School of Pignon	SECOSA	55,000,000			
Gressier National High School	SECOSA	55,463,488	J&J Construction	5,600,000	10.10%

Cerca-Carvajal National High School	SECOSA	148,457,665	J&J Construction	21,000,000	14.14%
New National High School of Hinche	SECOSA	60,463,488	J&J Construction	Cost not determined	

The J&J Construction contracts were signed between January 2011 and August 2011 by Prime Minister Jean-Max Bellerive, while the general partnership did not exist, having been dissolved in 2010. A publication in *Le Nouvelliste* attests to the dissolution of said entity, therefore the contracts were not valid.

This announcement, published on December 24, 2010 in *Le Nouvelliste,* reads as follows:

"*Le Nouvelliste* – Classified Ad/Dissolution of the General Partnership J&J Construction 2010-12-24/The Augustale Law Firm informs the general public and interested parties in particular that the general partnership J&J Construction, whose corporate name is "Milfort-Augustin & CO," with a share capital of one hundred thousand gourdes (100,000 HTG), managed by partners Josselin Milfort and Jackson Augustin, is dissolved by deed of dissolution dated September 27, 2010, and filed with notary Jean A. Lamothe on November 8, 2010. For the firm: Margarette B. Augustave, Attorney. Gérald Augustave, Attorney."

Furthermore, the signatory, Hérode Thélusma, representing J&J Construction, had no authority to represent the company. No documents were found in the files, no references, and no way to contact him, even for follow-up. Despite an arrest warrant, the investigating judge was unable to locate Mr. Thélusma to obtain further information. The investigation is focusing on a system of nepotism where individuals in positions of authority grant favors to family members or friends based on personal connections. The signatories orchestrated a scheme to facilitate irregular disbursements to a group closely linked to the contract awarding structure organized by former Premier Bellerive.

The misappropriation of Petro Caribe funds began well before the January 12, 2010 earthquake. From 2008 to 2010, the government of former President René Préval managed the funds as if they were private assets, without any management structure or accounting mechanisms. The disbursed sums were not taxed and were entirely at the disposal of the presidency, which used them as it saw fit, in total violation of the principles of governance, ethics, and transparency. The embezzlements attributed to Préval's inner circle are well documented. Among the best-known cases are the US$ 197 million, partially misappropriated in 2008, and the US$ 163 million mismanaged in 2010 through no-bid contracts awarded to those close to the government.

*****

JUDGMENT BY APPOINTMENT

On Monday, June 8, 2026, at 9:00 a.m., the sixty defendants involved in the Petro Caribe affair arrived at the courthouse in ten vehicles belonging to APENA (the National Penitentiary Administration). Handcuffed, shackled, and heavily escorted, they were taken to the First Chamber of the Civil Court of Port-au-Prince. One by one, they took their places in the dock set up specifically for the trial.

The presence of chains and handcuffs does not go unnoticed. They are not merely security devices: they embody a powerful message that is difficult to ignore. In a society where so many defendants have long evaded justice, visible restraint becomes a symbol.

For some, it is a necessary humiliation; for others, a belated reminder that the authority of the state can still be exercised. The silence in the room reflects this ambivalence: neither triumph nor compassion, but a heavy, almost incredulous expectation.

The procession is silent and humiliating. Each step the accused take toward the dock tolls like a death knell. A few years earlier, some of these men would have crossed these same streets in motorized convoys, greeted by guards, fawned over by courtiers. Today, escorted by APENA agents, they are nothing more than numbers in a legal proceeding. The clinking of handcuffs and chains marks their fall. The crowd, behind the barriers, stares at them mercilessly; in their eyes, there is no longer fear, but a cold, patient thirst for redress. The dock is not a seat, but a modern-day pillory.

The trial, however, does not dwell on appearances. It moves forward.

At 10:00 a.m., the court entered. On the order of the court usher, the audience rose. The presiding judge signaled for the public to sit down and declared the first day of the trial open.

This simple gesture of the hand, inviting the audience to sit down, is laden with a reversed symbolism. For decades, it was the people who had to remain silent, efface themselves, and accept. Today, it is justice – or at least its most accomplished semblance – that takes its place and marks the beginning of the trial.

In the silence that falls after the rustling of robes and the scraping of chairs, echoes resonate with all the stifled words, all the buried reports, all the ignored complaints. The opening of the trial is less a beginning than a reopening, that of a case never truly closed in the Haitian soul. Thus begins the first day, under the seal of form, an indispensable prerequisite to substance.

In the controlled silence of the courtroom, all eyes turn to the area reserved for the prosecution. There, another dimension of the trial unfolds: that of public discourse tasked with representing the general interest. The role of the public prosecutor is not merely to accuse, but to present, explain, and support the course of justice on behalf of society as a whole.

The prosecution is led by Guy Antoine, the government commissioner attached to the Port-au-Prince Prosecutor's Office, assisted by a team of deputy prosecutors. This expanded team reflects the scope and complexity of the case. Each deputy prosecutor supports a portion of the prosecution's case. In a trial where the events span several years and involve exceptionally complex financial and administrative mechanisms, this shared responsibility is essential.

Before the court, the public prosecutor is thus preparing to support a collective, methodical accusation, intended to unfold over time.

The president proceeds to question the defendants about their identity. He calls them individually to state their name, surname, age, profession, place of birth and address. The accused answer one after the other.

Once this formality was completed, the dean ordered the reading of the arrest warrants, which had remained unfulfilled, against a number of defendants who were absent from the hearing. At that moment, those present learned that several defendants named in the committal order were not in the dock.

A ripple of murmurs rippled through the courtroom. The physical absence of some defendants, along with the presence of others in handcuffs, raised questions. Where were they, the Petro Caribe embezzlers absent from court? Hidden away in locked Florida residences, relying on the protective magic of their spare passports? Their flight was yet another insult, a telling one. It confirmed what the trial wouldn't even need to establish: the cowardice and guilt of the absent defendants. It brought to light the other side of this transnational crime: siphoning off millions and making them disappear into foreign banks with offshore complicity. The dock was empty, but the courtroom was full of ghosts, those who recognized themselves in these fugitives, who had made off with the state's money.

These accused individuals, summoned three times, did not respond either themselves or through their lawyers, so the dean declared:

— "Prosecutor, you have the floor to present your closing argument."

Me. Antoine rises with calculated calm. As the government commissioner, he embodies procedural rigor and the discipline of the prosecution. His demeanor is measured, his gaze focused, aware that every word spoken before this Assize Court engages not only his function as public prosecutor, but the very authority of the State. He briefly consults the file spread out before him.

A seasoned courtroom veteran, Me. Antoine begins his plea with confidence. His calm, firm voice cuts through the silence of the courtroom:

- "Your Honor, the public prosecutor, acting as counsel for society, requests the court to note the absence of the accused and to rule in accordance with Article 366 of the Code of Criminal Procedure."

The petition, beneath its apparent technicality and formal dryness, conceals a particularly stringent procedural rigor. The default judgment is its most blatant expression. This is not simply a failure to appear. It reveals a deliberate will to evade the authority of the Nation and reflects an ultimate contempt for its institutions. By acknowledging this, the court performs an initial act of sovereignty: that of judging despite the void left by the fugitives. This approach recalls the old legal principles according to which a criminal who flees is considered to have confessed guilt. In the diaspora, watching on television, many must recognize familiar names, sometimes self-proclaimed benefactors of their associations. The verdict rendered in absentia also begins, symbolically, to strip them of this fabricated respectability.

By requesting the application of Article 366 of the Code of Criminal Procedure, the public prosecutor is not speaking in his own name. He is endorsing the abstract, but demanding, voice of society.

This voice does not call for vengeance, but simply states the facts. It demands that the law acknowledge reality and draw the necessary legal conclusions.

The silence that follows the requisition marks the transition from words to decision.

The prosecutor, while adjusting his glasses, resumed his seat.

The dean dictates his judgment, which the court clerk puts in writing.

— "The Court: In the name of the Republic,

— Given the absence of several defendants in court and given the prosecution's indictment.

— Whereas, at the hearing, these persons accused of corruption, theft, criminal association, embezzlement, overbilling, and misappropriation of funds to the detriment of the Haitian State, did not respond despite the notification of the indictment order duly made to them, and their absence was noted.

— Whereas in criminal matters, there can be no default judgment regarding the application of criminal law; that if the accused has been apprehended, he is detained according to the arrest warrant in the final judgment; that if, on the contrary, he escapes the investigations of justice and if he has not appeared within ten days of the aforementioned notification, proceedings are brought against him by the law on contempt of court.

- Whereas, in accordance with Articles 366 and 367 of the Code of Criminal Procedure (CIC), it is appropriate to order that the absent defendants be required to appear within ten days, with the legal consequences.

- For these reasons, the Court orders that the defendants who are absent and named in the committal order and in the indictment appear within a new period of eight days from this date; otherwise they will be declared rebels against the law and suspended from the exercise of their rights as citizens; says that their property, in this case, will be sequestered during the investigation of the contempt; that any legal action will be prohibited to them during the same time; says that any person will be required to indicate where they are; says that this order will be published and posted at the door of their home, at that of the justice of the peace and at that of this court.

- Given that, under no circumstances, shall the absence of an accused person prevent or delay the judgment of the accused persons present; the court decides to continue the hearing.

At this stage, the prosecutor intervenes and requests a suspension of the hearing.

The president:

- "The hearing is suspended and will resume tomorrow at 10:00 AM."

Chapter 2

SPECIAL DEBATES

(The second day of the hearing)

The trial has generated considerable interest. The courthouse is experiencing unprecedented crowds. Many civil servants have left their offices to attend the hearings. Across the country, citizens can be seen glued to their radios, following the proceedings with rapt attention. In homes with televisions, families gather around the screen. Outside the courtroom, tens of thousands of demonstrators, placards in hand, are massing, eager to see justice prevail. For some, the goal is to secure indictments; for others, to eradicate the systemic corruption that plagues public institutions. Together, they demand justice and reparations.

Slogans such as "Kot kòb PetroKaribe a" (Where is the Petro Caribe money?) and "Pote kòd pou mare vòlè" (Bring ropes to tie up the thieves) could be seen. Some protesters carried ropes, while others held up photos of Dutty Boukman, Cécile Fatima, Toussaint Louverture, Jean-Jacques Dessalines, Henri Christophe, Capois-La-Mort, Marie-Jeanne Lamartinière, and others. "Where did the Petro Caribe money go?" was the rallying cries as protesters gathered in front of the courthouse to denounce the misappropriation of funds and demand the heads of the accused.

At that precise moment, the crowd was no longer simply a mass of people. It became a living memory. Each chanted slogan carried the weight of years of frustration, broken promises, schools never built, and hospitals that remained mere plans. For many, this trial transcended the legal sphere: it touched upon their very existence. The people were not only demanding convictions, but also recognition of their suffering and proof that justice could still speak on their behalf.

The portraits brandished like banners are not mere images; they are reminders of the order of history. They serve as a reminder that Haiti's history is marked by struggles against injustice and arbitrary rule. Dutty Boukman calls for a break with the past, Dessalines for sovereignty, Toussaint for the organization of the state. By invoking the founding fathers, the demonstrators recall the nation's original principles and contrast them with the current reality. They thus establish a symbolic link between the ideal of justice embodied by these historical figures and this contemporary trial, where the adversary no longer comes from elsewhere, but is lodged at the very heart of the institutions. This invocation signifies that the current fight against corruption is directly in line with the struggles for freedom and dignity. The ropes, symbols of a popular and swift justice, engage in a strange dialogue with the serene faces of the ancestors. This is where the Haitian paradox is revealed: an almost sacred respect for the fathers of the nation, mixed with an indignation that pushes some to consider the most extreme responses to the failure of those who claim to follow in their footsteps.

Members of the Association of Youth United for the Development of the Central Plateau, a grassroots organization of the *Movement to Reclaim Charlemagne Peralte* (MRCP), are present in the area reserved for protesters. For several years, these young people have been leading a mobilization campaign in Hinche to demand the arrest of all those involved in the embezzlement of public funds. They have gathered in the public square opposite the courthouse, carrying signs and posters, to denounce the administrative mismanagement that prevails within the Haitian public administration. Today, they are historical witnesses to the trial organized to judge and convict criminals involved in theft and waste—a trial that many thought would never take place.

"We are in front of the Port-au-Prince courthouse. We are searching for the Petro Caribe funds. It is time for justice to prevail and for accountability. It is unacceptable that a small group within the state can unite against the people," declared Juno Pierre, Secretary General of the OJRDPC (Association of Youth United for the Development of the Central Plateau).

Another member of the group adds:

"We are at war with all those involved in the misappropriation of Petro Caribe funds. We represent the people of Hinche and the entire Central Plateau in denouncing the administrative chaos that reigns within public institutions in Haiti. That is why we demand the conviction of the accused. They are appearing today before the Assize Court of Port-au-Prince to answer for their management of the country."

It is 10:00 a.m. Tuesday, June 9, 2026. The dean opens the second day of hearings. An even larger crowd than the day before fills the courthouse. Inside, the session begins. Outside the courtroom, the usual excitement reigns. Police officers are stationed throughout the corridors. Alongside the police, soldiers and civilians with earpieces, openly carrying their weapons, provide security for the building. Some carry armored cases intended to serve as shields in case of an attack. Snipers are positioned on the roof. Gigantic stone blocks are placed in front of the courthouse to block vehicles crossing the area. Traffic is prohibited on the surrounding streets, forcing motorists to detour onto Rue Monseigneur Guilloux and Rue de La Réunion. The École Normale Supérieure, located next to the courthouse, is temporarily closed to students. Given the importance of the event, silent cameras are exceptionally permitted in the courtroom to record the proceedings.

In the dock, the defendants remain motionless, their heads tilted as if to avoid the weight of the stares. On their faces, one can discern the brutal clash of reality, and in their eyes, an irrepressible fear surfaces like a shadow that can barely conceal itself.

This posture of defeat, these bowed heads, these averted gazes, already carry the weight of justice. The country's usual order is overturned: those who once decided the fate of millions, heads held high, can no longer meet the people's gaze. This avoidance becomes the silent admission of their downfall.

A palpable tension is revealed in their eyes: these are men who see their world crumbling in real time. The self-assurance of a caste that believed untouchable is disintegrating before their very eyes, taking with it the privileges that had long protected them and the impunity that had shielded their actions, however criminal and devastating they may have been for the country. The fear that grips them can no longer be concealed; it rises to the surface like an involuntary confession. And this fear, now visible, is nothing other than a reflection of the fear they themselves imposed for so many years.

Among them, one of the accused stares at an invisible point in front of him. He's no longer really listening. His mind wanders to the years of opulence, the hastily affixed signatures, and the meetings where anything seemed permissible. He suddenly realizes that what was once abstract to him — the law, accountability — now has a face, a voice, a place. And that place is this courtroom where he stands today to face justice. A justice he has so long scorned, mocked, and ridiculed.

The public interested in the case is just as large in the diaspora. Millions of people are closely following the trial on social media. Many Haitians living abroad have traveled specifically to attend the proceedings. In the United States, France, Canada, Brazil, Chile, Nicaragua, Mexico, the Dominican Republic, and Belgium, Haitians are mobilizing en masse to demonstrate. "DOWN WITH

CORRUPTION," "LONG LIVE JUSTICE!" chanted a group of activists gathered in front of the United Nations headquarters in New York.

Major international media outlets: *New York Times* , *Washington Post, Boston Globe* , *Miami Herald, Guardian* , *Telegraph* , *Le Figaro, Le Devoir* , *RFI, L'Équipe, Listin Dario, Le Parisien, Jeune Afrique, Le Journal de Montréal*, Le *Monde Voice of America* , *Journal la Diaspora,* feature headlines like:

"HAITI: THE PETROCARIBE TRIAL. FINALLY, JUSTICE IS TAKING ITS TOLL AGAINST THE GUILTY."

The main national and international television networks are also present on site: *CNN* , *FOX* , *TV5* , *TF1* , *Canal+* , *France 24* , *CBC* , *BBC* , *CNBC* , *MSNBC* , *El Jazeera* , *Univision* , *Télé Haïti, Télé Nationale, Télé Métropole, Télé Guinen* and *Télé Caraïbes* ...

Several international media outlets are covering the case. Mediapart, a French news website, published an article on September 9, 2019, entitled "Petro Caribe, the development scam that is outraged in Haiti." The journalist devotes a significant portion of the article to explaining the nature of the oil financing, the Venezuelan program granted to Haiti. He highlights the voices of citizens, describing the scale of the mobilizations and repeated demonstrations held to obtain answers and demand a trial.

On August 17, 2020, *France 24* devoted an entire article to the case, titled: "Petro Caribe Scandal: In Haiti, the Court of Auditors Slams the Government." In this article, the news outlet reported on the Haitian government's financial misconduct. It also highlighted the lack of legal proceedings against President Jovenel Moïse for embezzlement.

On August 20, 2020, *RFI* (Radio France International) highlighted the demands and protests of Haitians with the headline: "Petro Caribe

Funds: Haitians Demand Accountability from the Political Class." A segment was then dedicated to the issue, outlining the grievances, discontent, and incomprehension of the Haitian people.

In Canada, the French-language news site LaPresse.ca devoted an entire page to the subject. Under the headline "Corruption: The Court of Auditors Slams the Haitian Government," the site details and analyzes the Court of Auditors' first report on Haiti. It highlights the government's "catastrophic" management and the involvement of several political figures in this scandal. This accountability movement, which began on social media, has been amplified by various communication channels. This extensive media coverage, both in Haiti and abroad, has had a positive influence, contributing to the organization of these criminal trials held in Port-au-Prince.

Before opening the proceedings, the president paused briefly. In that imperceptible moment, he took stock of the weight resting on the Court. He knew that every decision would be scrutinized, commented on, and dissected, not only by legal experts, but by the entire nation. He remembered that a judge is never as alone as when rendering a decision awaited by all.

At precisely 10 a.m., the president opened the proceedings. A heavy silence filled the room. Shortly after, the senior judge's deep voice rose to address the members of the defense and the civil party.

— "Lawyers, please stand."

One after another, Me. Vilaire, Rocourt, Georges, Coicou, Annibal, Justin, Noël and Lauture...about thirty lawyers rise. They request acknowledgment of their presence; some for the accused and others for the civil parties.

Addressing the members of the defense, the president made this recommendation:

— "Gentlemen of the Defense Council, while acknowledging your position, I warn you, in accordance with Article 245 of the Code of Criminal Procedure, that you may not say anything against your conscience or against the respect due to the laws, and that you must express yourselves with decency and moderation."

— "We take note of this recommendation," the older members of the council replied in unison, while the younger ones, Messrs. Coicou, Annibal, Noël, Lauture, Sainvil, Casimir, Lambert, Apollon, Amistral, and Justin, were content with a simple nod of approval before sitting down.

The presiding judge, now addressing the defendants who are standing up, declares:

— "Accused, pay attention to what you are about to hear."

Then, turning to the clerk, the president adds:

— "Clerk, please read the committal order and the indictment."

The reading takes place in a heavy, almost oppressive atmosphere. Faces are closed, focused, and certain passages provoke reactions of astonishment, visible in gestures and glances. At times, a lawyer leans forward to whisper a few words to one of the accused, briefly breaking the silence.

The court clerk, Mr. Aurélien Bayard, reads the committal order and the indictment.

The moment is almost religiously solemn. The reading of the indictment drawn up by the Public Prosecutor's Office is the moment when the investigative report, long pondered in the secrecy of the chambers, is poured into the public sphere for the first time. Each word carries the weight of evidence and the scope of consequence. The accused, who were familiar with the contents of the case file because they had been questioned about the indictment, now hear it formalized, proclaimed, and brought to the attention of the nation and the world. It is the transformation of suspicion into accusation, of the investigative report into a legal instrument.

The investigating judge's committal order largely reiterates the information contained in the Court of Auditors' audit reports concerning the management of Petro Caribe funds. Following a resolution dated February 1, 2018, the Senate Assembly requested the Superior Court of Accounts and Administrative Disputes (CSCCA) to conduct an audit of the management of Petro Caribe funds by those responsible for authorizing them for the period from September 2008 to September 2016, in accordance with Article 200 of the Constitution and the decree of November 23, 2005, amending that of November 4, 1983.

In its investigation, the Court examined the effectiveness of public spending related to fund disbursements, analyzed procurement procedures, contractual commitments, and the management of projects financed by these funds. It identified shortcomings inherent in the execution of the funded projects and activities. It also noted administrative discrepancies, irregularities, and anomalies in project implementation and assessed the level of compliance, legality, validity, and integrity of the operations carried out within the framework of the financing. It audited the disbursed funds as well as the accuracy and reality of the disbursements. Finally, based on the project management mechanisms, it determined the levels of responsibility of the managers.

Having finished reading, Master Firmin asks to speak:

— "Your Honor, I request the floor."

The president:

— "You have it."

—“Your Honor,” declared Attorney Firmin, “I hereby acknowledge my status as a civil party on behalf of the Haitian State, represented by the Director of the General Directorate of Taxes (DGI).”

The president:

— “Prosecutor, you have the floor on this request for an investigative act.”

The public prosecutor’s office:

— “No objection.”

The president:

— “The Defense Council has the floor on the request for action.”

One of the lawyers stands up and declares:

— “No objection.”

The president addresses Me. Firmin directly:

“The request for the document is accepted.”

The lawyer for the Haitian state, very calm, resumes his seat. Me. Vilaire then rises and asks to speak:

“Your Honor, I request the floor.”

The president:

— “You have it.”

Mr. Vilaire:

— "Magistrate, I request that my appearance be recorded on behalf of the Petro Challenger collective, nicknamed the "kot kòb Petro Caribe a" collective (where is the Petro Caribe money), which is joining the proceedings as a civil party under Article 50 of the Code of Criminal Procedure."

The president:

— "Prosecutor, you have the floor on this request for an investigative act."

Master Laraque (one of the deputies):

— "No objection."

The president:

— "The Defense Council has the floor on the request for action."

After a few minutes of exchanges from the defense, Me. Guilbaud takes the floor:

— "Your Honor, the Defense Council opposes this request from the Petro Challenger collective, which has decided to intervene as a civil party in the trial. It also rejects the request of all other parties who wish to become civil parties. We maintain that the Haitian State is already represented as a civil party in the trial by the Director General of the DGI."

Me. Guilbaud continues:

> — "More than sixty Haitian citizens, united within the collective "kot kòb Petro Caribe a" (where the Petro Caribe money is), have filed a lawsuit as civil parties. They claim to be victims of the fact that the Republic's budget allocates more than nineteen billion gourdes for repaying the debt

to the Venezuelan government, using taxes levied on members of the population. In addition to the repayment of the Petro Caribe debt through their taxes, they justify their status as civil parties by the fact that their fundamental rights guaranteed by the constitution, such as the rights to life, health, education, and training, have been violated by the misappropriation of these funds."

"If the reasons given allow every Haitian citizen to become a civil party in this trial, one can imagine that there would never be a Petro Caribe trial; because millions of people would make the same request."

The Defense Council continues:

- "Your Honor, this question has already been raised and resolved by a ruling of the French Court of Cassation since August 29, 1834.

—Indeed, Article 50 of the Code of Criminal Procedure, used by the plaintiffs to become civil parties, stipulates: "Any person who claims to be harmed by a crime or offense may file a complaint and become a civil party before the investigating judge, either of the place of the crime or offense, or of the place of residence of the accused, or of the place where he may be found."

- This article reproduces verbatim Article 63 of the former French Code of Criminal Procedure:

  "Any person who claims to be harmed whether that person experiences the harm themselves or experiences it through the person or property of individuals whose safety is as precious to them as their own. Harm is therefore essential for one to have the right to file a complaint. If harm is not established, the complaint must remain a simple denunciation, and the judge continues the investigation without the plaintiffs. A direct interest and an actual right are required to be admitted as a civil party. The general interests presented by the plaintiffs do not imply a direct, personal interest, but rather a collective one."

Me. Guilbaud continues:

- "The good faith of these citizens is commendable. They did, after all, move the case forward. But in the application of the law, there must be no room for sentiment. They must all be excluded from the trial for lack of standing."

The defense attorney resumes his place in a theatrical gesture.

Me. Vilaire then stood up to say:

- "Your Honor, is there any impediment preventing the Petro Challenger collective from joining the proceedings as a civil party? The lack of transparency from the Haitian government regarding the management of the Petro Caribe program has led to a chain of demonstrations throughout the country and also within the Haitian diaspora."

- It all began in August 2018, when Haitian filmmaker Gilbert Mirambeau Jr. launched the hashtag #PetroCaribeChallenge on Twitter. The intention behind this campaign was to question the management of public funds, administered by the Haitian state, within the framework of the Petro Caribe program. An instant movement erupted in Port-au-Prince on July 6 and 7, 2018, followed by similar movements in various foreign countries. This wave of denunciation went viral on social media, and very quickly the movement spilled into the streets in the form of popular demonstrations.

- In Haiti, people are protesting against rising fuel prices. This movement has resonated with young Haitian intellectuals, who have mobilized on social media to denounce the misappropriation of Petro Caribe funds by corrupt Haitian leaders and demand justice. From this emerged a citizens 'movement called Petro Challenger, led by courageous figures. "Let us build our Haiti," pleaded Petro Challenger leader Emmanuela Douyon before the U.S. Congress.

- Your Honor, the mass protests of 2018-2019 transformed Petro Caribe into a scandal. Haitians took to the streets, denouncing mismanagement and corruption, the embezzlement and squandering of hundreds of millions of dollars. The affair became a global issue. The movement became a powerful source of hope for Haiti, prompting reflection on the extent of the corruption revealed by the Petro Caribe scandal. This vehement denunciation by the population of the waste, contempt, and irresponsibility of its elites represents the people's determined demand for the moralization of public life. The "country lockdown" is precisely the struggle aimed at preventing the return of a system of governance based on tolerance and impunity. This type of power has plunged Haiti into a continuous decline in living conditions, a rise in violence, and the gradual collapse of its institutions.

- One thing is clear: without this pressure, the trial we are witnessing today would never have taken place. This is where the main lever for change lies. Hence, the need for a strong social movement that denounces corruption and impunity, and demands both the reimbursement of the squandered funds and the reparations owed to the Haitian people.

- Your Honor, these committed citizens are demanding accountability from the authorities of the time. Today, these high-ranking officials and their accomplices are being brought before the criminal court to stand trial. The young people of the Petro Challenger collective, with the slogan "Kot kòb Petro Caribe a" (where is the Petro Caribe money?), forced an administrative inquiry, which led to the arrest of several offenders. These young university students contributed through their courage and determination to opening this chapter of history. They held vigils, organized sit-ins, and took to the streets carrying placards to make their voices heard.

- These academics—true patriots—mobilized within the Petro Challenger collective, not only have the right to demand accountability, but they also have the right to compensation. This is why the collective has decided to become a civil party in the trial. The Haitian state, under the administration of those accused, has transformed into a truly predatory state. While billions have been squandered by unscrupulous leaders, the honest Haitian citizen no longer even has enough to live on. People are currently dying of hunger in the country. There are no schools, no hospitals, and no road infrastructure. Nothing... Nothing...

Me. Vilaire's voice is transformed. It is no longer that of a lawyer arguing a procedural point, but that of the spokesperson for a defrauded generation. By listing all that is lacking—no schools, no hospitals, no roads—in light of the billions squandered, he is not merely stating the harm; he is drawing up the moral indictment of the trial. This "nothing" is the true charge, far more serious than those listed in the code of criminal procedure. It places the court before its ultimate responsibility: will it be merely the accountant of embezzlement, or the witness to a crime committed against the future of an entire people?

Me. Vilaire glances towards the accused and continues:

- "Your Honor, Haiti has been the most corrupt country in the Western Hemisphere for decades. An example must be set. The time has come to punish those responsible, who must finally be held accountable. The time has come for them to reimburse the funds squandered from the Haitian state. The Petro Challenger collective, whom I represent, is here to claim damages. That is why, Your Honor, I reiterate my request to be formally recognized as a civil party in this trial on behalf of the Petro Challenger collective."

The president:

— "The prosecution has the floor."

Me. Saintilus:

— "Your Honor, the prosecution requests that the court dismiss the defense's objection as frivolous. The group of Haitian citizens gathered within the Petro Challenger collective has the right to become a civil party in accordance with Article 50 of the Code of Criminal Procedure (CIC). Therefore, we request that the court acknowledge Attorney Vilaire, acting on behalf of the Petro Challenger collective, as a civil party in the proceedings."

A round of applause greeted the prosecutor's remarks. He returned to his seat under the admiring gaze of several student members of the Petro Challenger group present at the hearing.

The defense is preparing to respond. The president rings his bell, saying:

- "The incident is closed. The hearing is adjourned and will resume tomorrow at 10 a.m."

The suspension of the hearing does not ease the tension. It merely shifts it. In the corridors, on the courthouse steps, in the surrounding streets, everyone is replaying the trial in their own way. The approaching night promises to be long filled with debates, analyses, and a glimmer of hope. For now, a line has been crossed: justice cannot longer back down without betraying itself.

Chapter 3

THE FACTS OF THE ACCUSATION

(The third day of the hearing)

The hearing, suspended the previous day after the prosecution's closing arguments, resumed at 10:35 a.m. The public, eager to know the truth, was even larger at the courthouse. Comments were flowing freely when, suddenly, a voice rang out:

— "The Court," declares the bailiff, ringing his bell.

The entire courtroom leaped to its feet. The presiding judge and the ten members of the public prosecutor's office took their seats. The audience was asked to sit down, and the judge consulted the code of criminal procedure before declaring:

- "In the name of the Republic,

— Whereas the civil party is the person injured by the crime or the offence and the person who, by application of art. 3 of the Code of Criminal Procedure (CIC), exercises the civil action at the same time and before the same judge as the public action.

- Whereas at this stage of the proceedings, the Petro Challenger collective, through its representative Me Vilaire, requests to intervene as a civil party, on the grounds that the interests of the group have been harmed by a series of fraudulent and criminal actions committed by the accused;

- Whereas it is necessary to establish a distinction between the interests of the Haitian State and the interests of the group; that the embezzlements have harmed the interests of the State certainly as a public entity, but have also harmed the interests of each Haitian citizen as an active member of society, as well as each group and each organization, as entities separate from the State;

- It should be a general principle that any party may become a civil party when it meets the following conditions:

1) That the crime or offence caused him personal harm;

2) That this damage is real and current;

3) That this person or the representative of the injured organization is capable of taking legal action; that once these conditions are met, this person or organization can become a civil party.

- Given that the group of citizens gathered within the Petro Challenger collective meet these conditions.

- For these reasons, the court admits the Petro Challenger collective as a civil party in the proceedings; and acknowledges Me. Vilaire's appointment to represent the collective's interests.

The president's decision falls not as a mere procedural judgment, but as a palace revolution. By admitting the collective, the court officially recognizes that civil society is not a spectator, but an injured party, a legal actor. It is a retrospective validation of all the marches, all the sit-ins, all the tweets. The law often perceived as the tool of the powerful, turns for once to endorse popular pressure. A slight tremor, mixed with relief and determination, ripples through the bench where the Petro Challenger youth sit. They are no longer at the gates of justice; they are at the table, facing those who have mortgaged their future. The trial has just gained depth: it is no longer simply a matter of judging individuals, but of acknowledging the breakdown of the pact between the State and its youth.

The president continued:

— "Prosecutor, you have the floor to present the facts of the case."

The entire courtroom is gripped by emotion when the prosecution takes the floor. As a key figure in the trial, he is well aware of the impact of his closing argument. He knows that every word he speaks will resonate far beyond the courtroom walls. His words will be repeated, commented on, sometimes even distorted. But he also knows that this trial demands a firm, structured, and unambiguous statement.

He is no longer simply society's advocate; at this precise moment, he becomes its high priest and its surgeon. The burden on his shoulders is not merely to prove guilt, but to articulate a national tragedy in legal language. Before him, the dock forms a map of fallen power. Behind him, the held breath of the courtroom represents a nation's expectation. Between the two, his words must build the fragile, yet necessary, bridge between crime and punishment, between the cynicism of some and the desperate hope of others.

With the assurance of a seasoned magistrate, Attorney Antoine presented the facts. The audience hung on his every word. The public had invested so much mentally and emotionally in this moment. Haitians were placing so much hope in this trial, which held so much promise for a Haiti where leaders had too often demonstrated dishonesty, corruption, and indifference toward their own people. The audience remained silent. Everyone cherished the hope that this trial would mark a turning point in the country's history, a point of no return.

"Your Honor, as a public official charged with conducting criminal proceedings and ensuring the application of the law, my fellow deputy prosecutors and I have decided to carry out our duties with all the rigor that characterizes our office. Our mission is to safeguard the general interests of society before the courts. Our primary task before this Assize Court is to support the prosecution against the defendants charged in the misappropriation of Petro Caribe funds."

- We act on behalf of the company, as the prosecuting party, and it is on behalf of this company that we present the facts of the case. As legal professionals, we ensure that our indictment complies with procedural rules and meets all legal requirements.

"First, let us answer this question: What is the role of a criminal trial? It guarantees every litigant the right to have recourse to an independent and impartial judge, ruling according to an adversarial procedure and within a reasonable timeframe. This judge is you, Your Honor, whom Haitian society has chosen to deliver justice. To live in poverty while the money that belongs to you has been stolen by defendants present here (the prosecution points its right index finger at the accused). What a great injustice you have endured!"

The prosecutor adjusts his glasses, looks back and forth between the audience and the defense bench, and continues:

— "Your Honor, the Haitian people have achieved their first victory. This victory comes with the national football team's qualification for the 2026 World Cup. This qualification is an honor for the Haitian nation, which has been tarnished by the dishonest actions of several high-ranking state officials. Beyond our qualification for the World Cup, this trial is another accomplishment of which the people can be proud."

—Magistrate, take a look outside and observe the enthusiasm of the people gathered in front of the courthouse to witness the verdict. They are demanding justice. Their slogan, "Kot kòb Petro Caribe a" (where the Petro Caribe money is), echoes throughout this courtroom. They are sending this message to those who are here to be judged.

A round of applause greeted the prosecutor's final sentence. An experienced magistrate, he knew perfectly well what this meant: when the courtroom applauds, it means that public opinion is inflamed.

He knows how to recognize that delicate moment when justice clashes with public emotion. These applauses, unusual in a courtroom, show that the trial is already transcending the strict bounds of the law. The courtroom is no longer just a place where judgment is rendered, but also a space where the public seeks a form of symbolic redress. By stirring the enthusiasm of the courtroom, the prosecutor is not simply fulfilling his role: he is giving official voice to a long-suppressed anger. Each clap releases a little of the frustration accumulated over the years. Emotion then enters the temple of law and blurs the line between dispensing justice and alleviating collective pain.

The prosecutor continues:

- "Your Honor, ladies and gentlemen, members of the audience, I ask for your indulgence and your full attention to understand the crimes committed by the accused.

- This "Petro Caribe" affair, we repeat, is difficult to explain, given the combined expertise of some and the experience and cunning of others, which were employed to perpetrate the largest administrative fraud ever committed in Haiti's history. The Court of Auditors' report establishes that, according to data received from the BMPAD (Bureau de Monetization des Programmes d'Aide au Développement), from March 5, 2008, the date of the first oil shipment's arrival, to April 14, 2018, the date of the last, 219 deliveries totaling 43.9 million barrels of fuel were made and sold in Haiti. To this must be added six shipments of asphalt and three shipments of fuel oil.

- The case is complex. The Court of Auditors has determined that approximately 4.2 billion US dollars have been embezzled. This embezzlement was carried out under the guise of sham projects, most of which never existed, or in rare cases were completed to less than 30%, while allocated funds were fully disbursed. As lawyers for the company, tasked with prosecuting these lawbreakers, we are taking the necessary time to analyze each contract and demonstrate the guilt of the accused. Honorable President, before elaborating on the charges, allow us to address these essential questions: What are the Petro Caribe funds? Where did these resources come from? What were they intended to be used for? Who squandered these funds? Who benefited? The answers to these pertinent questions will be provided during this special criminal session without a jury.

- First, we put the case into context, adds the public prosecutor. What is Petro Caribe?

- Signed by 18 countries, Petro Caribe is a Venezuelan government program sponsored by the late revolutionary leader Hugo Chávez. Haiti joined the program in May 2006. Following his inauguration for his second term, President René Préval, in the presence of Venezuelan Vice President José Vicente Rangel, signed Haiti's accession to the *Petro Caribe Cooperation Agreement*. The country received its first oil delivery in early 2008.

- A strict condition of the agreement stipulates that transactions must be channeled through a state agency. Thus, the Bureau for the Monetization of Development Assistance Programs (BMPAD) was created to manage the funds. The BMPAD, a public institution, is under the supervision of the Ministry of Economy and Finance (MEF). Its board of directors comprises seven members: the Minister of Economy and Finance (MEF); the Minister of Planning and External Cooperation (MPCE); the Minister of Trade and Industry (MCI); the Minister of Public Works, Transport and Communication (MTPTC); and the Minister of Foreign Affairs (MAF), the Governor of the Bank of the Republic (BRH) and the director general of BMPAD. The agency buys oil from Venezuela and resells it to local Haitian companies. These companies have 30 days to pay their invoices. BMPAD, for its part, has 90 days to pay 40% of the invoice to the Venezuelan government. The remaining 60% constitutes a long-term debt payable over 25 years with a two-year grace period and an annual interest rate of 1%. With each delivery of petroleum products to the country, PDVSA (Petróleos de Venezuela, SA) invoices the Bureau of Monetization, which, in turn, invoices the local oil companies. These payments are made by transferring funds to the Petro Caribe account held at the BNC (National Credit Bank). The main advantage given to the country in the agreement is the transformation of part of the invoice into a long-term debt at a preferential rate.

- Your Honor, from 2008 to 2018, Haiti accumulated approximately $2 trillion in profits generated by the Petro Caribe program. These profits were intended to finance social development projects. Where is this money? Reports from the Superior Court of Accounts and Administrative Disputes (CSCCA) indicate that the funds were squandered by the accused and their accomplices. Official investigations have implicated a large part of the Haitian political class in the scandal, including many high-ranking officials from the Préval and Martelly administrations. In November 2017, the Senate's Special Commission of Inquiry published a 656-page report identifying 15 former ministers and high-ranking officials. In this report, these leaders of the Haitian state are accused of corruption and embezzlement of public funds estimated at billions of dollars. The Martelly-Lamothe government spent approximately US$1.256 billion out of the US$1.7 billion (74% of all funds the Haitian government obtained from Petro Caribe funds over a decade) to finance projects that were not completed or never started.

- The involvement of senior state officials, particularly during Martelly's presidency, implicated managers at all levels, including those in supposedly autonomous agencies. A Senate resolution referred the matter to the Court of Auditors. The Court published an audit report in January 2019 showing that many state entities were delaying or refusing the cooperation it needed to carry out its work. Consequently, the Superior Court of Accounts and Administrative Disputes (CSCCA) were only able to investigate projects for which it had sufficient information.

- In May 2019, the Court of Auditors announced that its follow-up report had been further delayed due to insufficient resources. On the judicial front, in October 2018, a citizens' group from the civil society organization *Fondasyon Je Klere* filed a complaint with the investigating judge in charge of the case. According to a statement from the group dated March 26, 2019, the investigating judge ordered the freezing of bank accounts associated with certain individuals and companies implicated in the case, including former Prime Minister Laurent Lamothe and several former ministers. However, no official has ever been prosecuted for wrongdoing related to Petro Caribe.

- Civil society has long been mobilized to ensure that the Haitian justice system takes action against the accused. Public demonstrations took place throughout 2018 and continue to this day.

The prosecutor turns a blind eye for a moment. At that moment, his thoughts waver in time. He remembers. Long before this hearing, long before this trial, he had observed, like so many others, the slow decay of public affairs. Year after year, he had seen governments squander state resources with revolting nonchalance, confusing public goods with private interests.

He remembers the buried reports, the cases shelved without further action, the silences bought, the hollow justifications offered to a population lacking everything. This aversion to waste is not ideological; it stems from experience, from the repeated spectacle of a people sacrificed on the altar of impunity.

This deep repugnance towards the misappropriation of public money had led him to embrace the role of magistrate with the conviction that justice must not only punish offences, but restore a violated public morality.

The prosecutor pauses. He consults his notes before adding:

- "Magistrate, we beg the Court to allow us to present Table 1 detailing the resources generated by the Petro Caribe program from 2008 to 2016."

The president:

— "The Court authorizes you to do so."

The prosecutor opens the screen:

- **Table 1: Estimated resources generated by the Petro Caribe program from March 2008 to April 2016**

	PORTION OF FUNDING IN $	CASH PORTION IN $	TOTAL IN $
Fuel	$2,252,974,036.59	$1,969,071,812.30	$4,222,045,848.89
Asphalt	$1,951,056.74	$3,138,581.76	$5,089,638.50
Fuel oil	$3,871,590.23	$6,591,711.50	$10,463,301.73
Total resources generated from 2008 to 2016	$2,258,796,683.56	$1,978,802,105.56	$4,237,598,789.12

"It should also be mentioned that, following the 2010 earthquake, Venezuela officially cancelled US$395,000,000 of Haiti's debt. This debt relief should be considered an additional resource generated from Petro Caribe funds."

The prosecutor pauses again. It opens a file containing notes and continues:

"Your Honor, the defendants' behavior is criminal. In accordance with its contractual obligations, Haiti, like the 18 other signatory countries, was supposed to make the program a development tool aimed primarily at reducing hunger and poverty by stimulating the creation and circulation of wealth. The *Petro Caribe Agreement* clearly stipulates that the funds must enable member countries to finance worker cooperatives, as well as small and medium-sized enterprises engaged in projects aimed at food self-sufficiency. The benefits granted to Haiti in the agreement were put in place to allow the country to escape misery and poverty. However, corrupt leaders sabotaged this plan. Haiti has missed its opportunity for development once again. A rapacious elite allied with foreign mercenaries, has once again compromised the country's chances of progress. These Haitian leaders have squandered this tremendous development opportunity that was meant to give Haiti relative independence from international aid." These unscrupulous criminals, sitting in the dock, instead of using the program as an opportunity to lift Haitians out of poverty, have instead driven them deeper into extreme poverty through their criminal actions.

- The Haitian people suffer in silence, amid the complete indifference of those who are responsible for protecting their interests and guaranteeing their well-being.

The prosecutor glances around to gauge the effect of his words and continues:

- "Your Honor, the sixty-seven defendants present in court and their accomplices who are still at large represent a sample of spineless, corrupt, and audacious men who deserve exemplary punishment for the harm and damage inflicted upon the Haitian people. These incompetent criminals neglected a crucial clause in the agreement. Their failure to comply with this clause was the primary source of the ensuing chaos. These delinquents, now charged with embezzlement, breach of trust, fraud, and theft of public property, are well aware that the debt distribution (short-term, 40% and long-term, 60%) for the purchase of asphalt, fuel oil, diesel, gasoline, and kerosene would change drastically when the price of a barrel of oil fell below $40. They had a duty to know... They disregarded this clause." However, the contract signed with Venezuela clearly states that when the price falls below $40 a barrel, the interest rate rises to 2% and the term is reduced to 17 years. Furthermore, the proportion that must be paid within 90 days could reach up to 95%.

The prosecutor consults his notes and continues:

- "Your Honor, the Bureau for the Monetization of Development Assistance Programs (BMPAD) has a great responsibility in this matter. Created by a law passed in 2007 by the Haitian Parliament, and published in the official journal *Le Moniteur* on January 4, 2008, the government body serves as an intermediary between PDVSA (Petróleos de Venezuela, SA) and Haitian oil companies.

- The BMPAD has had three directors since the signing of the contract between the Haitian state and the Venezuelan government regarding the management of Petro Caribe funds. These were Mr. Michael Lecorps, who held the position from September 2008 to January 2015; Mr. Eustache Saint-Lot, who succeeded him from February 2015 to March 2016; and finally, Patrick Noramé, appointed by interim president Jocelerme Privert on April 16, 2016. Mr. Noramé was installed on April 20, 2016.

The prosecutor remains pensive. A headline published in *Le Nouvelliste* a year ago had caught its attention: "Thirst for Justice."

The article said:

- "While we are still waiting for the date of the Petro Caribe trial (the embezzlement dates back to 2008 and continued until 2018), grassroots organizations like Petro Challenger are demanding genuine, fair, and democratic justice. More mobilized than ever, they are putting pressure on the system…"

The prosecutor smiled shyly. The moment had arrived. Finally, the accused were facing justice. Without further ado, he consulted his notes again before adding:

- "Let's first look at the charges against Mr. Michael Lecorps."

At that precise moment, the courtroom held its breath. The general facts would now give way to individual responsibilities. The trial entered its most dreaded phase: the transition from conceptual debate to actual accountability.

Chapter 4

THE ACCUSED
MICHAEL LECORPS

Former commercial director of Public Law 480 (PL-480), Mr. Lecorps describes the BMPAD (Bureau for the Monetization of Development Assistance Programs) as functioning perfectly under his leadership. According to him, Haiti is an exemplary country with regard to settling the cash portion within 30 days to avoid the 2% interest that begins accruing on the 31st day after receipt of the petroleum product. He asserts that since his replacement in 2015, accounts payable management has not been what it used to be, because just a few weeks later, the government reported Venezuela's concerns about payment delays on Haiti's obligations.

The prosecutor continues:

- "Your Honor, during his hearing before the Senate Ethics and Anti-Corruption Commission and during his questioning by the investigating judge, Mr. Lecorps, former director of BMPAD (September 2008 – January 2015), stated that he does not disburse any payments without written instructions from the Ministry of Finance. He described BMPAD as a kind of cashier for said ministry. He stated that he is neither a supervisor nor a manager of the projects financed by Petro Caribe. He insists that he rigorously followed the transfer orders in accordance with the resolutions. And he affirms that he has nothing to reproach himself for."

— Mr. Lecorps disclaims responsibility for the disbursement decisions. His role, he says, is to execute transfer orders to the Public Treasury account.

The prosecutor glances towards the accused and declares:

- "Your Honor, how are we to understand the defendant's statement, which suggests that his role is merely to execute transfer orders to the Public Treasury account? The BMPAD, of which Mr. Lecorps was the Director General for 7 years, was created by the law promulgated on December 27, 2007, and published in the official gazette *Le Moniteur,* issue number 2, on January 4, 2008. The BMPAD thus replaced the PL 480/Title III Management Bureau, an autonomous financial body under the supervision of the Ministry of Planning and External Cooperation."

- This structure is responsible for contributing to the strengthening of the State within the regulatory framework for monitoring and evaluating development programs entrusted to the Monetization Office. It ensures the efficiency and timeliness of actions undertaken for the disbursement, control, and evaluation of counterpart funds in local currency.

- The Petro Caribe fund statements are prepared by the BMPAD's chief accountant, verified by the administrative and financial director, and approved by the director general. They are presented in two currencies: either the Haitian gourde or the US dollar.

- For the fiscal years ending September 30, 2008 and 2009, the accounts are presented in local currency. For the fiscal years ending September 30, 2010 through 2012, they are presented in US dollars.

- The reports for the 2008 and 2009 annual periods, intended to explain the institution's financial situation, have not been submitted. The financial statements for the periods 2010, 2011, 2012, 2014, 2015, and 2016 have not been balanced.

- The investigation also failed to uncover the existence of a debt amortization fund. This fund must be created and replenished with each delivery of petroleum products. The amount to be credited to this account will depend on the result of a calculation that will take into account the rate of return subject to the fund, the frequency of repayments, etc.

The prosecutor consults his notes before continuing:

- Purchase and sale transactions of petroleum products funding the Petro Caribe funds are conducted in US dollars. However, following an agreement between the Ministry of Economy and Finance (MEF) and the Bank of the Republic of Haiti (BRH) dated January 19, 2012, sales transactions are conducted 40% in US dollars and 60% in Haitian gourdes."

The prosecutor stares gravely at the ceiling before adding:

- "For its operations, BMPAD used the Haitian gourde and the US dollar, and also presented its financial statements using both currencies. However, as of September 30, 2016, the financial statements are presented in Haitian gourdes, but the US dollar transactions were not adjusted at the exchange rate of the Bank of the Republic of Haiti (BRH), as required by ISA 21 (International Standard on Auditing), which stipulates that " an entity that uses two currencies, a functional currency and a foreign currency, at the date of preparation and presentation of the financial statements, must convert, at the prevailing exchange rate, all components of its foreign currency into its functional currency." The effects of non-compliance with this standard are detailed in the investigating judge's order."

- The BMPAD did not use the BRH exchange rate to value these accounts in US currency, in accordance with the requirements of ISA 21 (International Standard on Auditing), as demonstrated by the table I am about to present.

Addressing the President of the Court, the prosecutor stated:

— "Your Honor, allow us to display on the screen a descriptive table in terms of liquidity for the four BMPAD accounts."

The president:

— "The Court accepts the request."

The defendants scrutinize the details displayed on the big screen with great attention.

LIQUIDITIES $

HTG Bank Account: BRH # 1112647111		3,727,592
HTG Bank Account: BNC # 1660-020244		1,260,199,087

Having local currency in local banks		1,263,926,679
US Bank Account: BNC # 1661-017504		2,878,004,959
US Bank Account: BNC # 1661-018590		10,835,366
Having US currency in local banks		$2,888,840,325
Total cash		$4,152,767

The prosecutor looks at the three former BMPAD executives and declares:

- "Your Honor, Mr. Lecorps, like the two other directors charged, failed in their duty to loyally represent the interests of the institution. They took no steps, during their time at the head of the BMPAD, to force the contracting companies to pay their debts."

- As of September 30, 2016, according to the BMPAD books, Sogener's accounts receivable show the sum of eleven billion four hundred two million three hundred ninety-seven thousand thirteen gourdes (11,402,397,013 HTG) for diesel deliveries from April 2012 to September 30, 2016.

- During his hearing, Mr. Jean Marie Vorbe stated that the delay was due to correspondence from the then Minister of Economy and Finance , addressed to the Governor of the Central Bank, requesting him to suspend all payments to Sogener. This constituted a disruption to the execution of the existing contract.

- Let's take the case of the debt of the State Electricity of Haiti (EDH) to the Petro Caribe program:

- owed by the EDH company to Petro Caribe funds amounts to $ 437,346,841, and its equivalent in gourdes is 28,662,312,449 HTG. It is broken down as follows:

Item Description	Amount ($)
1. Fuel and transport	$346,975,793
2. Lubricant and transport	$6,450,030
3. Equipment mobilization	$1,569,676
4. Operation and maintenance	$71,347,838
5. Tank rental	$3,988,255
6. Other expenses	$7,015,249
7. Total	$437,346,841

The public prosecutor's office continues:

- "This debt has three main components:

- The first represents unpaid fuel and lubricant costs from June 2009 to September 30, 2016, as well as unpaid transportation costs for these products from May 2008 to September 30, 2016. These two amounts total $353,425,823 or its equivalent in local currency of 23,162,397,477 HTG.

- The second relates to tank rentals and other expenses and extends from December 2009 to September 2016 and totals $11,003,504 or its equivalent in local currency worth 721,134,441 HTG.

- As for the last item, it concerns the mobilization of equipment and maintenance operations related to a contract signed on December 21, 2009, between the Director General of BMPAD, Mr. Michael Lecorps, and the foreign firm ESD ENGINEERING AND SERVICES SRL for the management and maintenance of the three power plants built by Venezuela. This contract lacks the approval of the Court of Auditors, the non-objection of the National Commission for Public Procurement (CNMP), and the signature of the Chairman of the Board of Directors of BMPAD. Therefore, this contract contains serious irregularities and was signed outside of any recognized standard. Its value as of September 30, 2016, totaled $72,917,514 or its equivalent in local currency, 4,778,780,531 HTG.

The prosecutor stares at the accused, Michael Lecorps, before declaring:

— "Your Honor, Mr. Lecorps concealed the truth. The investigation uncovered evidence that contradicts his statements. Under his administration, the BMPAD carried out, among other things, the purchase and installation of solar streetlights and the construction of a silo in Lafito to create a food reserve."

The prosecutor takes a break, looks at his notes, and continues:

- "How can a director who has disbursed over $1.5 billion for 10 resolutions and 275 projects tell us he has nothing to reproach himself for in such a scandalous affair? Mr. Lecorps is more deeply involved in this matter than he lets on. He is hiding the truth about the power plant project offered by Venezuela."

"Let's move on to other facts," said one of the deputy prosecutors, intervening in the debate:

— "ESD Engineering and Service SRL have a contract for the management and maintenance of three power plants built by Venezuela. This contract is between ESD Engineering and Service SRL and BMPAD for the management and maintenance of the plants (operations and upkeep). The investigation by the investigating magistrate confirmed that it is a Korean firm based in the Dominican Republic. It is not registered with the Santo Domingo Chamber of Commerce."

- This firm was awarded a contract worth over $800,000 per month, or approximately $10 million per year, paid from funds drawn from the Petro Caribe bank account without a bidding process. Mr. Lecorps stated that there was indeed a bidding process, but that it was initiated by Venezuela. The documents found indicate that this is not the case. Three months after his dismissal from the BMPAD, Mr. Lecorps was employed by this company as commercial director.

- His decision to take a job in 2015 with the same firm with which he had been under contract since 2009 for the operation and maintenance of three Venezuelan power plants, whose offices are based in the Dominican Republic, is highly questionable. He maintains that there is no conflict of interest because he accepted the position a few months after being replaced at the BMPAD (Bureau de Management et de Promotion de l'Aménagement et de Développement - Ministry of Planning and Development and Development), but the investigation is less certain, especially since the tendering process that led to the selection of this firm's services is being called into question.

- Mr. Lecorps officially served as the intermediary with Venezuela in setting up the Petro Caribe program structures. He states that the firm offered the best prices. He specifies that this firm's offer was more than 100% cheaper than those of the other bidders. The problem stems from the fact that the supposedly international tender was launched by Venezuela and awarded by Caracas.

- Mr. Lecorps added that the Cubans, responsible for maintenance for this firm, had to be replaced because they were incompetent due to mismanagement and had cost the power generation project significant sums. This is surprising, given that Mr. Lecorps acknowledged that the three plants were assembled by Cubans who, apparently, suddenly became incompetent after completing the assembly. The investigation confirmed that a Korean company based in the Dominican Republic with ties to Venezuela had been chosen to replace the Cuban firm in the contract for operating and maintaining the plants. The investigation did not confirm the existence of an actual call for tenders, although Mr. Lecorps claims that one was issued.

The prosecutor casts a brief glance at the accused and adds:

— "Your Honor, with regard to the projects implemented by the Bureau for the Monetization of Development Assistance Programs (BMPAD), the investigation proceeded to analyze two of them signed by the former director of the institution.

- It appears that these projects were not implemented rigorously and economically. Indeed, the investigation revealed several types of irregularities: harm caused to the project and the community, violations of the regulatory framework and best practices, as well as administrative shortcomings.

- The lack of documentation and relevant justification for the use of management fees related to the monitoring and evaluation of the "solar street lighting electrification" project are administrative irregularities that underlie the fraud and embezzlement of Petro Caribe funds. Indeed, the disbursement of an amount exceeding the actual value of the services provided under this contract caused damages estimated at 22,429,577.61 gourdes to the Haitian state.

The prosecutor consults his notes before continuing.

"Your Honor, the 'Ban'm Limyè Ban'm Lavi' (BLBL) solar street lighting electrification project is another example of irregularities within the BMPAD. Originally, the project owner was the Ministry of Public Works, Transport and Communications (MTPTC). Its implementation was subsequently entrusted to the BMPAD and the office of the Minister Delegate to the Prime Minister in charge of Energy Security (BMSE). The documentation obtained by the Court of Auditors did not allow it to understand the rationale for such a decision. The Court believes that such a practice is contrary to best practices, as it is recommended that a fund manager not be the project executor."

- In analyzing this case, the Court of Auditors found irregularities that prevented the efficient, effective, and economical implementation of this project. First, it noted the lack of a rigorous assessment of needs and costs. The BMPAD (Bureau de Management et de Développement Agricole et de Développement) used two resolutions to secure the $13,780,000 budget for the electrification program. The first resolution, passed on February 28, 2012, allocated $11,280,000, and the second, passed on December 11, 2013, allocated $2,500,000, for a total budget equivalent to 600,068,000 HTG.

- This funding was intended for the installation of streetlights across the country's 10 departments. The Court notes that instead of dividing the program into ten lots, the Bureau for the Monetization of Development Assistance Programs (BMPAD) awarded twenty contracts to the aforementioned firms. For the first phase, fourteen contracts were signed directly between the BMPAD and twelve pre-selected firms for a total amount of 133,946,580.50 HTG. The Court finds that this division of the contract violates Article 5.1 of the Public Procurement Law, as it allowed the BMPAD to circumvent the requirement for an open tender process.

- Furthermore, the Court of Auditors noted that, during the second phase of the project, the six remaining contracts were subject to open tenders, which resulted in the selection of a provisional awardee for lots 7 and 8 (South and Southeast respectively – SunTech Solar/BESUCO Consortium), and 5 (West – ELMECEN). It should be noted, however, that lots 10 (Grand'Anse – BUROCAD) and 4 (Artibonite and Centre respectively – GK Import-Export) were awarded based on the tender process, but the contracts were ultimately concluded following renegotiation with the firms to award them by mutual agreement. Lots 1 (North), 2 (Northeast), 6 (Nippes) and 9 (Northwest) were declared unsuccessful, and the BMPAD launched a restricted tender to award two lots to the firms SunTech Solar/BESUCO and ELMECEM and the other two lots were awarded by direct agreement which constitutes a violation of articles 34-1, 44-2 and 56 of the law of 10 June 2009 establishing the general rules relating to public contracts and public service works agreements.

- The CSCCA noted that the firm Enersa had a contract for the installation of 1,200 streetlights in the Northeast and Nippes departments. However, it was only able to install 60% of the ordered quantity (716), representing a value of 48,568,923.23 gourdes, while at the same time, it disbursed the equivalent of 87.2% of the contract amount, 70,998,500.84 gourdes, thus creating a loss of 22,429,577.61 gourdes to the project and the community.

- Similarly, the CSCCA notes that the office of the Minister Delegate to the Prime Minister in charge of Energy Security (BMSE) signed a so-called "Feedback Agreement" for the financing of the technical monitoring and evaluation of the BLBL project, with the aim of conducting the technical monitoring of the evaluation of the funded projects. From the review of these twenty contracts, it appears that six were awarded regularly, meaning that a formal tendering process was followed. For the other fourteen, the contracts were awarded directly between the BMPAD and twelve firms selected outside of the tendering procedures.

- According to the Superior Court of Auditors and Administrative Disputes (CSCCA), this constitutes a contract split that allowed the BMPAD (Bureau de Management et de Promotion de l'Aménagement et de Développement) to circumvent the requirement for an open tender for a project of this scale. The Court noted that the Besuco SA / Suntech Solar consortium had a contract for the installation of 1,200 streetlights; they installed 600, or 50%, while 100% of the funds had been disbursed.

- The BMPAD allocated 20,483,930 HTG to the BMSE (Office of the Minister Delegate to the Prime Minister in charge of Energy Security) for its management costs. The Court notes that this allocation was increased by two amendments at an additional cost of 9,079,150 HTG, thus bringing the total cost to 29,563,080 HTG. Furthermore, it deplores the lack of documented justification clearly demonstrating the relevance of these additions, which, moreover, resulted in an increase of approximately 44.32%

compared to the initial contract, thereby exceeding the 30% required by the provisions of the Law of June 10, 2009, establishing the General Rules Relating to Public Procurement and Public Service Concession Agreements.

The prosecutor consulted his notes for the umpteenth time before declaring:

- "Let us now examine the cases of Mr. Eustache Saint-Lot and Mr. Patrick Noramé."

Chapter 5

THE ACCUSED: ST-LOT/NORAMÉ

It is enlightening to hear the accused respond to the charges against them. It takes a singular talent to deny the obvious, reject the facts, and proclaim one's innocence when one knows perfectly well that one is not. Such behavior reveals a profound moral failing, to the point that one might wonder if this trial does not implicate, beyond the individuals involved, an entire social class.

The prosecution continues its closing arguments.

- "Your Honor, Mr. Saint-Lot, former director of the BMPAD (Bureau for the Monetization of Development Assistance Programs), Mr. Lecorps' successor, stated during the investigation that he found a structure already in place. He did not participate in setting up the operations that made the BMPAD the intermediary between PDVSA (Petróleos de Venezuela SA) and local oil companies."

- He explains the pricing structures applied by the BMPAD. Petroleum products are purchased according to the "Gulf Coast prices." This is a kind of index that constitutes a database of reference prices from which the present value of the product on the market in the area of operation is established. The products are then resold to local oil companies according to the "Platt Caribbean Posting," another reference price index for products in the Caribbean, as its name indicates. Between these two indices, there is generally a profit margin for the country. This margin is a profit collected by the Haitian state. Mr. Saint- Lot confirms that this profit from product sales is managed at the Ministry of Finance level. No Minister of Finance has provided the required details, neither before the Senate's Ethics and Anti-Corruption Commission, nor during the judicial investigation.

The prosecutor casts a glance at the accused Saint-Lot and declares:

- "Your Honor, this is how the edifice of lies is built: a pyramid of indices and technical references—'Gulf Coast prices,' 'Platt Caribbean posting'—designed to overwhelm the uninitiated. Financial jargon serves as an artificial fog. Behind these terms lies a simple, cruel, and recurring reality: a substantial profit margin, stemming from Venezuelan solidarity, disappears into the opaque labyrinth of the BMPAD and the Ministries of Finance and Planning. The Petro Caribe fund is not invested; it is absorbed. This is the first level of predation: capturing the financial oxygen before it even reaches the lungs of the country."

SHADOW POINTS

- The areas of uncertainty lie in the monthly deficit and subsidies to the energy sector. Mr. Saint-Lot and the successive Ministers of Finance have been unable to provide a satisfactory response to the investigation regarding energy sector subsidies. Given the size of EDH's (Electricité d'Haïti) debt to BMPAD and considering the fact that the State does not appear ready to pay its bills to the Sogener firm, which in turn cannot pay its debt to BMPAD, the investigating judge is wondering whether Petro Caribe funds are indeed covering hidden losses. The investigation reveals that while successive governments have chosen to subsidize electricity as a social policy, they must acknowledge that the Petro Caribe fund is financing the budget deficit and is not solely used for public investments.

- The investigation questions how the BMPAD, which is said to be managed with such rigor according to its two former directors, Lecorps and Saint-Lot, and which makes no disbursements without a published resolution, can continue to cover the operating expenses of the three power plants. On August 20, 2015, a memorandum of understanding was signed between EDH and the BMPAD, with the approval of the Ministry of Economy and Finance (MEF) and the Ministry of Public Works, Transport and Communications (MTPTC). This agreement defines the responsibilities of the parties within the framework of the operations of the power plants producing energy for EDH.

- During the hearings held at the Investigating Chamber, it was reported that the BMPAD must assume the following responsibilities:

- Portion generated per month: US$4,500,000.
- Monthly expenses for Sogener (credit sales): $1,500,000
- EDH's monthly expenses (across the three power plants): $4,000,000
- Fuel and transportation: $2,700/month
- Lubricant and transportation: $100,000/month
- Operation and Maintenance: $890,000/month
- Storage rental: $46,000/month
- Chemicals and other products: $264,000/month
- Monthly deficit to be covered for EDH activities: $1,000,000.

***

The monthly budget resembles a service bill for an invisible palace. Each line item —"lubricants and transportation," "chemicals"—is a conduit through which money leaks. The $890,000 monthly maintenance operation for power plants that are frequently shut down takes on the air of a pension for phantom machines. By reeling off these figures, the public prosecutor's office isn't detailing management practices, but rather dissecting a parasitic organism: Petro Caribe funds primarily serve to feed the bureaucracy that orchestrates its own squandering, a voracious entity that consumes the very resources it is supposed to produce.

The prosecutor consults his notes and continues:

- "Your Honor, the investigation has not identified the authority granted to EDH over the control or the orders of products delivered to the institution. The investigating judge, until the drafting of his order, remains awaiting contracts for streetlights worth over 40 million dollars charged to EDH's debtor account with BMPAD, while BMPAD managed this file and EDH allegedly only signed the contract, at least for part of this streetlight order."

- The delivery of products from BMPAD to power plants managed outside the EDH structure, but charged to its account, drew the investigating judge's attention to significant weaknesses in a bilateral agreement between Venezuela, Cuba, and Haiti.

The prosecutor, after a brief moment of reflection, added:

- "Mr. Saint-Lot asserts the effectiveness of his management as director of the BMPAD; however, the investigation noted that during his tenure, there were payment delays in Venezuela. This payment delay was apparently due to a shortage of foreign currency on the local market," the accused stated. "However, the investigation was unable to determine whether this was the case or if, concurrently, the BMPAD's reserves were used for other purposes. Furthermore, the investigating judge noted that commitments made from Petro Caribe funds did not take into account available cash. This resulted in significant payment delays or the need to reallocate funds previously earmarked for ongoing projects. This undisciplined management style forced the accused to scale back projects already underway or reduce payments allocated to ongoing work."

The prosecutor continues:

- "The investigation has revealed that the transfers, intended to repay the debt to Venezuela, remain partially in Haiti in an account at the National Credit Bank (BNC) controlled by Venezuelan authorities. The investigating judge did not understand why, given Venezuela's economic difficulties, the Venezuelan authorities would want to keep a portion of the funds in Haiti, albeit in dollars, in an account at the National Credit Bank. Faced with currency problems, the Venezuelan government is forced to resell the Dominican Republic's debt at a reduced price to replenish its public treasury; it becomes inexplicable that Venezuela is not repatriating even the smallest repayments made to it. Former director Saint-Lot indicated that these funds were being held at the BNC by Venezuelan officials who anticipated making them available for additional projects in Haiti, at their discretion."

This detail—the Venezuelan money held in Haiti—is a strange piece of the puzzle. It suggests collusion far beyond borders, an unhealthy familiarity between predators. Perhaps Caracas, mired in its own crises, chooses to turn a blind eye to the embezzlement, content to see regional allies maintain their grip on power through corruption. Or perhaps this money is a discreet reserve to finance other political operations, a bilateral slush fund. In either case, the Haitian people are doubly deceived: by their leaders and by foreign partners who pretend not to see the plundering of their aid.

The prosecutor briefly consults his notes again before adding:

- "Your Honor, new companies dedicated to distributing petroleum products have emerged on the Haitian corporate scene. These are Kimatzou and Diesel National Company (DNC), which have obtained access to Petro Caribe credit. As of March 31, 2016, DNC owed BMPAD US$976,889.76 and Kimatzou US$1,145,954.13. The investigation was unable to determine the terms of the agreements between these firms and BMPAD. A letter addressed to the new director of BMPAD seeking further information went unanswered. The investigation was also unable to ascertain the pricing structures or margins resulting from transactions with these new local petroleum *trading companies.*"

The prosecutor paused for a moment before continuing:

- "Let's take the case of Patrick Noramé now, the third director of the BMPAD, a protégé of Senator Nenel Cassy, who granted him over thirty-seven million gourdes from Petro Caribe funds in 2016. The Senate inquiry commission accused Noramé of having increased the BMPAD management fund to 437 million gourdes, whereas from 2008 to 2015 this fund never exceeded 131 million gourdes. "

- "I implicated Patrick Noramé, but the conclusion is incomplete given that we did not investigate from September 2016 to September 2017," stated Senator Évalière Beauplan. "However, the facts relating to the mismanagement of the BMPAD, under Mr. Noramé's administration, were established by the investigating judge's inquiry."

The prosecutor pauses. After catching his breath, he continues:

- "In a report submitted to the Haitian justice system, the Anti-Corruption Unit (ULCC) indicates that Mr. Noramé used his position as director of the BMPAD to embezzle funds from the Bureau of Monetization of Development Assistance Programs (BMPAD) for the benefit of Eveline Delima and Lunie Elsie Chery. These women used companies such as P-JIMEX, Research Center, and a store called DIFFÉRENCE to misappropriate funds."

- On March 27, 2023, investigating Judge Jean Wilner Morin issued an international arrest warrant against Noramé on charges of money laundering and embezzlement. He is targeted by this court order because he embezzled over 124 million gourdes related to a rice donation from Japan to Haiti, according to the findings of an investigation by the ULCC (Anti-Corruption Unit).

- To justify his decision, Judge Morin cites the law of September 28, 2016 on money laundering and the law of May 12, 2014, on the prevention and suppression of corruption.

The prosecutor pauses, stares at the accused Patrick Noramé, and declares:

- "Your Honor, Mr. Noramé embodies the final stage: the point at which the maneuvers to embezzle Petro Caribe funds become openly cynical and utterly shameless. After the technical directors Lecorps and St-Lot, comes the political director, Mr. Noramé, the protégé of a senator. Here, there is no more alibi jargon, no more feigned complexity; the embezzlement is direct, almost primitive: taking money from a Japanese rice donation and funneling it through shady dealers. This is corruption in broad daylight, no longer even hiding behind bogus projects. They steal food donated to Haiti and transform it into luxury items. If Lecorps and St-Lot emptied the coffers with sophisticated keys, Noramé is smashing them in with an axe."

The prosecutor looks at his notes and continues:

— "Another fact to highlight is this ambiguous relationship between the CSCCA and the BMPAD.

- At the time the 2008 emergency law was passed, the Court of Auditors did not intervene in the signing of contracts. It was only with the 2010 emergency law that it was required to approve the signing of projects between the Haitian government and contracting firms. In both cases, it judges the legality after the fact. The Court maintains an independent perspective; it ensures the technical compliance of the agreements signed by the government. Unfortunately, numerous inconsistencies have been observed in the documents from the Court..

- To begin with, the investigating judge was unable to confirm a standard procedure. Sometimes the signature of the CSCCA representative is affixed without identifying the signatory; sometimes it is affixed with identifying the signatory. Sometimes the signature is affixed without the seal of the Court of Auditors. Sometimes a member of the Court signs on behalf of another without the power of attorney being justified. Thus, during the same month, the Court of Auditors is represented by its president or by their deputy, without the Commission being able to determine what justified the deputy's substitution on one document and not on another that occurred in the same week.

- It should also be noted that when the Court signs, there is never a date, so for the investigation it is impossible to determine when the signature was affixed. In a context where many transactions are backdated, this is a key detail for determining the legality of certain documents examined. Furthermore, the investigation was unable to obtain the 2012 report on which former Premier Laurent Lamothe relies to allow the contracts denounced by former Premier minister Garry Conille to remain in effect. It also became clear that the CSCCA's delays in producing its reports do nothing to improve the effectiveness of public administration oversight.

The prosecutor continues:

"The Court of Auditors, supposed to be the ultimate safeguard, thus appears as a phantom guardian. Its representative validates documents lacking dates, seals, and sometimes even signs fanciful powers of attorney. This organized negligence is as culpable as active embezzlement. It means that the control system in place has been either corrupted or deliberately weakened, to the point of being nothing more than an administrative ritual devoid of any real impact. The irregular signature of an auditor then serves as a seal of impunity, reclassifying illegality as a mere 'administrative irregularity' and transforming a criminal act into a banal procedural anomaly. The control mechanism is thus neutralized: the perpetrators of the embezzlement act freely, while the body responsible for monitoring them no longer plays any effective role."

The prosecutor is perplexed. He is trying to grasp the reality. The more he thinks, the deeper he becomes trapped in a labyrinth. He shakes his head from side to side. "Haiti is a strange country," he says sadly. At the same time, he thinks about certain politically motivated crimes in the country. The assassination of Jean Léopold Dominique is the first case on the list. Who killed the journalist? So far, the investigation has not identified the perpetrators, either material or intellectual. Another crime has puzzled him for over thirty years: the murder of Father Jean-Marie Vincent. The priest was assassinated at the age of 48 on August 28, 1994, by armed men and soldiers in front of the Montfort Fathers' house on Baussan Street in Port-au-Prince. He takes stock: Yves Volel, Brignol Lindor, Mireille Durocher Bertin, Monferrier Dorval, Jovenel Moïse… The list of victims of political attacks grows every day.

Coups d'état, insurrections, political assassinations… From independence to the present day, Haiti has constantly faced the same political turmoil that pollutes the nation's political, economic and social environment.

The prosecutor fixes the audience with a grave expression before continuing:

— "The investigation has uncovered several irregularities in the management of Petro Caribe funds, which take different forms.

- First, the investigating judge noted that most of the documents that should have allowed him to assess the management of former minister Dorsainvil disappeared in the 2010 earthquake. Former Prime Minister Pierre-Louis, who could have helped the investigating magistrate to better appreciate the facts, chose not to appear at the investigating judge's office.

- The Ministry of Public Works holds a dominant position due to the substantial funding it receives. The purchase of equipment for the National Equipment Center (CNE), for example, does not comply with transparency standards regarding disbursements. The investigation failed to uncover an overpayment of $ 45,610,000 attributed to this transaction. This unjustified sum was identified through irregularities found within the $ 80,000,000 officially allocated for equipment purchases for the National Equipment Center (CNE) in the September 2008 resolution.

- According to the investigating judge's assessment, the $ 80,000,000 was not spent on the purchase in question, because the contracts found, thanks to the collaboration of the TPTC, indicate a sum of $ 57,053,511 invested for the purchase of equipment according to the following contracts:

DATE	**SUPPLIER**	**CONTRACT**	**AMOUNT $**	**TOTAL $**
October 9, 2008	COMPANY HAITIAN MOTORS	CONTRACT	$5,495,000	$5,495,000
October 9, 2008	SOGED	CONTRACT	$4,055,036	$9,550,036
October 9, 2008	AUTOMECA	CONTRACT	$10,622,000	$20,172,036
30, 2008	AUTOMECA	Amendment	$15,453,000 (A difference of $2,565,000 must be deducted from the total because 19 fewer trucks were delivered)	$35,625,036
December 30, 2008	AUTOPLAZA	CONTRACT	$4,010,000	$39,635,036

December 14	COMPANY HA Ï TIENNE DE MOTEURS	Amendment	$0	$39,635,036
December 30, 2008	COMPANY HA Ï TIENNE DE MOTEURS	Amendment	$0	$39,635,036
October 9, 2008	HAYTRAC		$9,816,300	$49,451,336
December 30 , 2008	HAYTRAC	Amendment	$10,167,175	$59,618,511
December 30 , 2008	AUTOMECA	81 trucks delivered instead of 100 ordered	$2,565,000	$57,053,511

With the picture presented on the big screen, the prosecution continued its closing argument.

— "Your Honor, it should be noted that these transactions have already raised concerns among parliamentarians, especially since these significant disbursements are taking place just before the launch of the 2010 electoral process. The Standing Committee of the Senate of the Republic of Haiti, Justice and Security, had already summoned the Minister of Public Works, Mr. Jacques Gabriel, and the head of the National Equipment Center (CNE) at the time, Mr. Jude Célestin, for this purpose on December 14, 2008.

—The Justice and Security Committee, seeking information regarding certain expenditures, had invited Mr. Jacques and Mr. Célestin. The speakers, namely the Minister of Public Works, Transport and Communications and the Director General of the

National Equipment Centre, confirmed the following to Parliament: the acquisition of heavy equipment was made through negotiated contracts. The final order for all heavy equipment was completed no later than December 12, 2008, and the final payment was made no later than December 31, 2008.

—This meeting did not allow us to detect the administrative loopholes in the case because this first Senate committee had limited access to the BMPAD accounts, but it still allowed us to obtain testimonies which today have the merit of completing the transactional panorama of interest for the investigation.

1- Under the heading "PURCHASE OF EQUIPMENT", a budget of $ 80,000,000 is planned and according to the testimony of the authorities before the Ethics and Anti-Corruption Commission, this purchase of equipment was paid in full no later than December 31, 2008.

2- As of December 31, 2008, an amount of $ 57,000,000 was disbursed and formally committed according to the BMPAD report from September 30 to December 31, 2008, and not $80,000,000 as provided for in the budget.

3- A balance of $22,800,000 is to be collected.

4- This sum is available in the BMPAD account and may be reallocated to other projects by amending resolution.

5- However, the BMPAD, in its successive reports, confirms that it only paid $57,000,000 of the $80,000,000 allocated for equipment purchases. The BMPAD reports that $22,800,000 was transferred to the Ministry of Finance to pay a 14th - month salary to civil servants for the start of the school year. However, a BMPAD memo indicates that the Ministry of Finance informed them that this sum was being used to complete the equipment purchase.

6- The investigation was unable to trace the transfer of this sum from the Ministry of Finance to the Ministry of Public Works which was to be carried out before December 31, 2008, according to what the BMPAD had declared.

7- From an account statement obtained from the Central Bank (BRH), the investigating judge was able to note that on May 26, 2009, the BMPAD transferred $22,800,000 to the TPTC account for the purchase of equipment.

8- It is important to clarify that, as of this date, the emergency law was no longer in effect. No new equipment purchase contracts had been signed. Any equipment purchase should have been subject to a formal tendering process. The investigating judge found no record of any tenders or contracts authorizing the use of these funds.

9- The investigation then deduces that the anomaly lies in the fact that the purchase of equipment did not only cost $57,000,000 as reflected in existing contracts, but $57,000,000 and more than $22,800,000, from another project.

10- The investigation was unable to assess the actual delivery of this equipment or even its continued existence. No comprehensive inventory of the CNE has yet been obtained by the investigating judge.

The prosecution remains perplexed. The amount of embezzled funds is beyond comprehension. Is it real that so much money was squandered at the expense of such a miserable and distressed people? They ponder this. This trial exposes a truth that goes beyond the guilt of the individuals named. Petro Caribe does not inherently impoverish Haiti; it reveals the difference between states that transform exceptional resources into sustainable public policies and those that abandon them to arbitrary decisions.

The crime is appalling. His voice filled with emotion, the prosecutor continued:

— "The case of the equipment purchase for the CNE is a microcosm of scandal. All the mechanisms are there: the inflated budget (80 million), the opaque negotiated contracts, and the advance payments, the transfers between obscure accounts, the changing justifications, and finally, the complete disappearance of the purchased item. Where is this 45 million US dollar worth of equipment? The investigation runs up against an administrative black hole. The money, however, has certainly vanished. It's the black magic of corruption: making not just a rabbit, but entire convoys of trucks and bulldozers disappear into the accounting limbo."

ITEM	SECTION	BUDGET $	PAYMENT $	BALANCE $
BUDGET	CNE Equipment	$80,000,000		
TRANSFER BMPAD	CNE Equipment		$57,000,000	$22,000,000
TRANSFER BMPAD	14th month (reassigned in favor of equipment purchase/CNE)		$22,000,000	---------------- -------
TRANSFER BMPAD	CNE Equipment		$22,000,000	$22,000,000
TRANSFER BMPAD	CNE Equipment		$22,000,000	$45,000,000

Once the figures were displayed, the prosecutor closes the screen and continued:

— "Your Honor, the review of all these inventories reveals a conflict of interest between the BMPAD's mission and its economic motivations regarding project execution. Indeed, the BMPAD was supposed to make the funds available to other institutions. Instead, it released funds for projects it had developed itself to serve its own institutional interests. To a very large extent, the BMPAD's management of Petro Caribe funds was conducted irregularly and fraudulently."

— The audit by the Court of Auditors has highlighted a significant economic relationship between the Haitian state and certain companies. It reveals a network of public-private actors operating outside of any standards or regulations. Indeed, in most projects, both local and international companies acted as contractors under the supervision of government ministries. However, this relationship is marred by legal and managerial irregularities.

—In the case of the Borgne/Petit Bourg de Borgne road rehabilitation project, the Ministry of Public Works, Transport and Communications (MTPTC) transferred funds to Agritrans S.A. and Betex, which turned out to be the same company (CSCCA, 2020). Following a site visit, the Court of Auditors concluded that there was a discrepancy between the sums spent and the actual work carried out (CSCCA, 2019, p. 159). According to Articles 8 and 9 of the decree of January 22, 2016, on public investment programs, projects should have received start-up funding to begin work, but subsequent funding should have been based on: 1) a statement of expenditures, accompanied by supporting documents; 2) a summary of financial transactions; and 3) the project's progress report. (Decree of January 22, 2016, Articles 8-9). However, in these cases, oversight was ineffective. The responsible ministers disbursed the funds without any regard for the relevant standards.

—For the Delmas-Nazon viaduct construction project, the Estrella company was awarded the contract through a negotiated procedure and without a certificate from the CNMP (National Commission for Public Procurement); the 2% tax due to the DGI (General Directorate of Taxes) was not collected (Senate of the Republic of Haiti, 2017). The initial funds were disbursed one month after the contract was signed, but work began five months after payment was received (CSCCA, 2019). In the second phase of the project, the entire advance payment was received. Supervision fees, however, represented 78% of the budget, and due to delays in the execution of the work, the supervision firm ceased operations, and the remaining work was completed without supervision (CSCCA, 2019).

- Thus, the picture is complete: from the signing of the contract to the abandonment of the construction site, the irregularities are numerous. Each step is an act of embezzlement: irregular awarding of contracts, advance payments made without any corresponding work, blatant overbilling for supervision, and finally, silence and incompleteness. The Delmas-Nazon viaduct, like so many other projects, is not a failure, but a success from the perspective of the fraudsters. A criminal success. It fulfilled what appears to have been its true objective: to serve as a front for transferring millions of dollars of public money to private interests. Its complete uselessness as infrastructure then becomes proof of its effectiveness as an instrument of embezzlement.

The prosecution pauses and, instead of continuing its presentation, requests a suspension of the hearing.

The president:

"The hearing is suspended and will resume tomorrow at 10 a.m."

Chapter 6

THE NUMBERS DON'T LIE

(The fourth day of the hearing)

Overcome by uncontrollable indignation, the prosecutor continued his presentation of the facts. Anger was etched on his face. Accustomed to prosecuting criminals, the corrupt, imposters, traitors, and outlaws, he was unable to comprehend the downfall of the Haitian elite whose corrupt members were grotesquely implicated in the squandering of Petro Caribe funds. He paused.

This pause is not accidental. It settles in the room like a suspension of time.

Before him, numbers cease to be mere arithmetic columns. They become unfinished roads, nonexistent hospitals, schools promised but never opened. In the silence of the courtroom, everyone understands that what follows is no longer a matter of political discourse, but of the implacable rigor of numbers. When numbers speak, they accuse more vehemently than words.

The prosecutor sighed. Without losing his train of thought, and with the same fervor that characterizes great prosecutors, he continued:

— "Your Honor, two presidents and five governments have been called upon to address the Petro Caribe issue as ratified by the Haitian Parliament on August 29, 2006.

— Under the presidency of René Préval (May 2006 to May 2011)

- Préval-Pierre-Louis government (September 2008 to October 2009)
- Préval-Bellerive government (November 2009 to May 2011)

The Préval -Pierre-Louis government signed only one resolution, dated September 10, 2008, for the amount of $197,500,000. This resolution concerns the initial use of revenues generated by the Petro Caribe agreement, and this sum is allocated under the heading of emergency relief. Under this heading, the Council of Ministers approved disbursements to enable the Haitian state to respond to the devastation caused by several hurricanes. In the space of a month, the country was struck by three hurricanes: Hanna, Gustav, and Fay.

In this context, the Haitian Parliament passed the first emergency law to provide relief to the affected populations. This law was passed on September 8, 2008, and published in the official gazette, Le *Moniteur,* on September 10 of the same year.

— Under the presidency of Joseph Michel Martelly (May 2011 to February 2016), three resolutions were passed:

- Martelly-Conille government (October 2011 to May 2012)
- Martelly-Lamothe government (May 2012 to December 2014)
- Martelly-Paul government (December 2014 to March 2016)

"None of these governments saw Petro Caribe as an opportunity to revitalize the Haitian economy and strengthen the regime from which it originated. The investigation by the investigating magistrate's office was unable to identify any real attempt to apply rigorously transparent management standards to these funds. All the prime ministers want to maintain control of the funds while demonstrating their indifference and nonchalance. They are indifferent to the need to establish a strong and coherent program that could have had a positive economic impact on the population."

The prosecutor consults his notes and adds:

- "Your Honor, the Haitian leaders who managed the Petro Caribe program are unscrupulous businessmen, driven by blind greed. They use their intelligence to steal and plunder. Otherwise, they would have rushed to propose measures to mitigate the financial risks associated with non-compliance with the agreement."

- Due to price instability on the international market, starting in September 2014, the price of a barrel of oil, after spending 40 months above $100, began a precipitous fall, bringing it to as low as $32.69 in February 2016. As stipulated in the agreement, with prices between $30 and $39.99 per barrel, BMPAD was required to pay 75% of its bills within 90 days. Therefore, it only had 25% left to invest in Petro Caribe funds.

- For example... When BMPAD purchased 20,000 units and the price of a barrel was $100, out of a $2 million bill, $1,200,000 went into the PetroCaribe funds. When the price fell to $32.69 per barrel, the bill for the same quantity was $653,832, and since the proportion to be allocated to the funds increased to 25%, the new inflow of cash was $163,458.

The prosecutor paused, his gaze sweeping the room. He was still thinking about the national team's qualification for the 2026 World

Cup. An entire country had risen up, united in jubilation. Yet successive Haitian governments had never fostered this unity around a development project. They had received a windfall, the equivalent of a golden goal at the last minute, and they had squandered it on useless passes, on selfish dribbling. The economic playing field remained barren. The prosecutor resumed his indictment, his voice more somber.

"Your Honor, representing society, the prosecution supports the case by highlighting a series of dysfunctions within national public and private institutions in Haiti. It considers this approach fundamental because these dysfunctions perpetuate a corruption that is eating away at the country and undermining its economic and social development. The weakness of state structures, the mismanagement of resources, and impunity weaken society, hinder development, undermine democratic values, and destroy respect for human rights and the rule of law. Given the cumulative effect of these conditions, it is no coincidence that Haiti is ranked as the poorest and most corrupt country in the Western Hemisphere."

"Your Honor, twenty years after the signing of the Petro Caribe contract, the Haitian people, betrayed by their leaders, suffer in silence, amidst the complete indifference of those who have the responsibility to protect their interests."

The prosecutor paused for a moment of reflection. At that instant, an image came to mind: that of the Haitian players celebrating their qualification for the World Cup. Placide and his teammates waved the national flag to the cheers of the Haitian crowd at the Ergilio Hato Stadium in Curaçao. There, Haiti played its final qualifying match against Nicaragua. This image of newfound pride served as the perfect counterpoint to the picture he painted: that of a predatory state, ranked first in corruption due to a self-serving and visionless elite. He continued to ask himself: how can a country produce, on the one hand, heroes who proudly uphold the national colors, and on the other, leaders who sully them with such contempt? The audience found the answer in the facts he presented.

The prosecutor shook his head gravely. Words seemed inadequate to express his disappointment. He stared intently at the presiding judge and declared:

- "Your Honor, let's briefly review a portion of Haiti's history, beginning with the political crisis that followed the lynching of President Vilbrun Guillaume Sam. From crisis to crisis, Haiti has lived in instability throughout its history, from 1806 to the present day. The reason is simple: the country is still led and administered by corrupt individuals, leaders without vision, and anti-nationalists, like these shameless criminals sitting in the dock. These scoundrels who squandered the Petro Caribe funds."

- The Americans occupied Haiti for 19 years, from 1915 to 1934. At the end of the occupation, political instability persisted, fueled by rivalry between high-ranking military officers, predominantly mulattoes, and Black populist movements vying for control of power. Provisional governments succeeded one another under Élie Lescot, Jean Dumarsais Estimé, Paul Eugène Magloire, Nemours Pierre-Louis, Franck Sylvain, and Daniel Fignolé. In 1957, François Duvalier seized power. In 1964, he became president for life of Haiti. Duvalier Sr. established a personal rule through denunciation and fostered terror with the help of his supporters, nicknamed Tonton Macoutes, veritable death squads. In 1971, before his death, Papa Doc designated his son, Jean-Claude Duvalier, as his heir. He then became the youngest president in the world and was nicknamed "Baby Doc". Jean-Claude Duvalier continued to rule in his father's footsteps before being forced, following a popular uprising, to relinquish power on February 7, 1986.

- A National Governing Council headed by the army's commander-in-chief, General Henri Namphy, and then took power. A new Constitution was adopted on March 29, 1987, and general elections were held on November 29, 1987. These elections were annulled after the massacre in Vaillant Alley, in which dozens of voters lost their lives. On January 17, 1988, following an election boycotted by the political class, Leslie Manigat, secretary general of the Rally of National and Progressive Democrats (RDNP) party, became president of Haiti.

- After five months in power, on June 17, 1988, Manigat was overthrown in a military coup. Henri Namphy took over. On September 17, 1988, Namphy was ousted by a coup led by General Prosper Avril. Accused of involvement in the Saint-Jean Bosco massacre of September 11, 1988, Avril left office after a year and a half. On March 13, 1990, a judge of the Court of Cassation, Ertha Pascal Trouillot, replaced him and organized the December 1990 elections in which Jean-Bertrand Aristide became President of Haiti.

- After six months in power, on September 29, 1991, Jean-Bertrand Aristide was overthrown in a coup led by General Raoul Cédras. For three years, the military and a paramilitary force, FRAPH, intimidated the population and assassinated several members of the resistance movement against the coup. These members, linked to the popular sector, advocated for Aristide's return. In 1994, Aristide was reinstated to power by the Clinton administration during Operation Restore Democracy.

- Aristide left power in 1996, and René Préval was elected president. Préval implemented the neoliberal plan, one of the conditions Aristide had negotiated with the Americans for his return. Préval completed his five-year term, and Aristide was re-elected in 2000. After several months of pressure from the international community, particularly France, "with the intervention of Régis Debray and Véronique de Villepin-Albanel," Aristide was arrested by the US Marshals and went into exile for a second time. The president of the Court of Cassation, Boniface Alexandre, served as interim president, and Gérard Latortue as prime minister. In February 2006, after an election marred by disputes over the vote count, René Préval won a second presidential term, supported by demonstrations in his favor. The only Haitian president to have completed both of his terms, Préval left power on March 14, 2011, in a country still reeling from the January 12, 2010 earthquake.

- On May 14, 2011, Michel Martelly was elected president of Haiti. Brought to power amid controversy and allegations of electoral fraud, Martelly left office in turmoil on February 7, 2016. The Haitian Parliament elected Jocelerme Privert as interim president. This appointment was a first in Haiti's modern history. It was the first time since 1946 that a Haitian head of state had been chosen through an indirect election. After a long period of electoral disputes, Jovenel Moïse became president of Haiti in 2017. During his term, political unrest and gang violence continued. The opposition demanded the president's resignation. "Long sleeve" or "*Peyi Lòk*" (Country Lockdown) protests were the slogan used by demonstrators in the streets of the capital. Jovenel Moïse was assassinated on July 7, 2021.

This succession of regimes and coups d'état created an unstable political environment, marked by impunity and weakened institutions. It is in this fragile context that the Petro Caribe scandal was able to take root. It is Haiti's history repeating itself, a tragic farce where the costumes change, but not the script. The accused are not accidents of history; they are its logical products, the heirs of a system where plunder is a tradition. Yet, in the midst of this infernal cycle, there is this glimmer of hope: the Grenadiers, who, on the football field, show that with clear rules, hard work, and passion, one can defy the odds. The court, today, is the arbiter of that same justice.

The prosecutor looks at the accused and, in a grave voice, declares:

- "Your Honor, just consider that some of the defendants present here have their hands in the assassination of President Jovenel Moïse...." Without dwelling on the subject, he continued:

"Your Honor, imagine the tragedy when accumulated Petro Caribe funds were squandered and embezzled by Haitian leaders in league with other mafia groups. The crime is heinous. Following the 2010 earthquake, Venezuela canceled Haiti's debt, which then amounted to $395 million. Three years later, the Haitian government found itself unable to honor its commitments to Venezuela. As of March 31, 2016, Haiti owed Venezuela $1.8 billion. The Petro Caribe accounts held a paltry $13.4 million. This minimal sum was insufficient to make debt payments. As a result, from July 2015 to January 2016, Haiti was unable to make a single payment on its long-term debt. The country resorted to buying on credit."

The prosecutor pauses for a moment. He casts a contemptuous glance at the defendants and continues:

- "Your Honor, while the country sinks into poverty, Petro Caribe funds are being used to fuel the greed of the accused. Moreover, they arrogantly flaunt their assets, as if they have lost all sense of morality. They have acquired property all over the world. Their assets amount to hundreds of millions of dollars, which they shelter in offshore companies and tax havens, so that they can better enjoy them and their close relatives."

The trial, for a time, ceases to be a mere legal procedure: it transcends the courtroom and enters the realm of collective memory. These governments are not simply chronological markers. They correspond to periods when these high-ranking officials still believed that urgency justified exceptional measures, that catastrophe authorized the relaxation of rules, and that the state could function without safeguards.

It is in these interstices – cyclones, earthquakes, crises – that the habit of circumvention takes root, transforming national emergencies into administrative methods. The prosecutor knows this: no emergency, however dramatic, justifies the permanent erasure of the traceability of public funds. It continues, determined.

- "Your Honor, the worst embezzlement occurred during the presidency of Mr. Michel Martelly, from 2011 to 2016, which coincided with the appointment of Mr. Laurent Lamothe as Minister of Planning and External Cooperation and Prime Minister, from 2012 to 2014. Mr. Lamothe, as the principal authorizing officer for the disbursement of funds, issued authorizations totaling $668.8 million for 149 projects. Official Haitian investigation reports concluded that, of the total $1,738,691,909 allocated to the projects, approximately 92% had been spent based on questionable authorizations and that virtually no projects had been completed." The country found itself unable to resolve its economic and social problems, and, moreover, from August 2023, it is spending $10 million a month on loan repayment.

- These malpractices committed by the accused doubly penalize the Haitian people. They penalize the impoverished father who cannot provide for his family, and they also penalize the farmer who lacks the means to cultivate his land. And here we find ourselves dealing with corrupt individuals whose accounts are overflowing with hundreds of millions of dollars.

The prosecutor paused to breathe before continuing:

— "The crime is horrific. Every time the Haitian population suffers the consequences of natural disasters, for the major governments in Haiti, it is an opportunity to steal. Every cyclone, every flood, every earthquake, provides a pretext for Haitian leaders to circumvent the legal rules for disbursement and facilitate the embezzlement of funds."

— Following the 2010 earthquake, the government, referring to the law of On September 9, 2008, a state of emergency was declared for a period of 15 days, from January 16, 2010, to January 30, 2010, renewed by decree on January 31, 2010, for another 15-day period. A bill was then submitted to the Chamber of Deputies and the Senate of the Republic amendment to the law of September 9, 2008, which was passed on April 15, 2010. Under the cover of this In accordance with the law, the executive branch issued a decree on April 21, 2010, declaring a state of emergency for a period of 18 months. This ended in October 2011.

- Subsequently, on August 9, 2012, a decree declaring a state of emergency throughout the territory was issued for a period of one month. During the same year, particularly in October, Haiti was struck by Hurricane Sandy, which caused enormous damage. Thus, on October 9, 2015, the government signed a decree declaring a state of emergency in the departments from the South, the Southeast, Grande-Anse, Nippes, the West and Artibonite for a period of one month.

- The main characteristic of invoking a state of emergency is that it allows the governments to bypass existing regulations. Among other things, the government can expedite the release of funds, make expenditures deemed necessary, reallocate budgetary appropriations to address

> the situation, and award contracts following procedures governed by public procurement regulations.

At this stage, the prosecutor requests the court authorization to display Table No. 2 concerning the use of Petro Caribe's financial resources, then Table No. 3 concerning the names of the various governments to which the disbursements were made, and finally Tables No. 4-1 and 4-2, concerning the budget authorized to finance the Delmas-Nazon viaduct construction project. The four tables are mentioned in the committal order of the investigating judge and in the indictment.

The president:

— "The Court accepts the request."

This request provoked a strong reaction in the dock. Attorney Antoine paid no attention to the commotion he had just stirred up among the defense. Very calmly, he continued:

– Table 2: Use of Petro Caribe's financial resources Amount in $

Funds allocated to financing development projects (2008 to 2016)	1,738,691,909.70
BMPAD budget funding (cumulative 2008 to 2016)	20,485,789.64
Power plant financing as of September 30, 2016	612,161,711.62

This amount is the sum of two components: EDH's debt ($425,447,805.13) and Sogener's debt ($186,713,906.49), situation as of September 30, 2016.

Table 3: Budgeted amount per resolution and per government

No	Resolutions	Presidency	Government signatory	Budget per resolution in $	Revised budget after allocation and deallocation $	Amounts transferred by the BMPAD
No. [1]	20/09/2008	PREVAL	Michèle Duvivier Pierre-Louis	$197,560,000	$197,560,000	$197,560,000
No. [2]	11/02/2010	PREVAL	Jean Max Bellerive	$163,287,848	$157,719,896.18	$157,719,896.18
No. [3]	24/08/2010	PREVAL	Jean Max Bellerive	$107,400,000	$94,597,097.69	$94,357,661.45
No. [4]	12/05/2011	PREVAL	Jean Max Bellerive	$108,799,883	$96,923,836.14	$96,923,836.14
No. [5]	28/02/2012	MARTELLY	Garry Conille	$234,956,000	$210,303,222.68	$210,303,222.68
No. [6]	18/07/2012	MARTELLY	Laurent Salvador Lamothe	$130,000,000	$96,195,625.80	$96,195,625.80
No. [7]	21/12/2012	MARTELLY	Laurent Salvador Lamothe	$374,800,000	$329,386,735.05	$329,386,735.05
No. [8]	11/12/2013	MARTELLY	Laurent Salvador Lamothe	$210,967,318	$164,517,228.97	$164,517,228.97
No. [9]	23/07/2014	MARTELLY	Laurent Salvador Lamothe	$141,778,568	$71,215,839.38	$71,215,839.38
No. [10]	10/09/2014	MARTELLY	Laurent Salvador Lamothe	$29,697,201	$7,000,000	$7,000,000
No. [11]	15/04/2015	MARTELLY	Evans Paul	$254,423,560	$47,525,624.19	$47,525,624.90
No. [12]	22/07/2015	MARTELLY	Evans Paul	$193,055,824.56	$174,308,966.07	$101,010,358.99
No. [13]	06/01/2016	MARTELLY	Evans Paul	$58,169,108.56	$58,169,108.56	16,204,383.67
No. [14]	09/28/2016	PRIVERT	Enex Jean-Charles	$3,268,729	$33,268,729	$15,984,874.63
TOTAL $2,238,164,040.74 $1,738,691,909.70 $1,605,905.87						

Table 4-1

Budget authorized to finance the Delmas-Nazon Viaduct construction project

Resolutions	Execution/ Supervision Firm	Initial Amount $	Assignment/ Reassignment $	Revised Amount $
December 21, 2012		$8,000,000	---------$	$8,000,000
December 11, 2013	Estrella/LGL SA	$4,000,000	$99,304.73	$3,900,695.27
September 10, 2014		$4,197,201.29	$4,197,201.29	------$
April 15, 2014		$10,709,660	$4,740,243.03	$5,969,416.97
July 22, 2015		$4,740,243	---------$	$4,740,243
January 6, 2016		------	$152,096.32	$152,096.32
September 28, 2016		$541,255	--------$	$541,255
	TOTAL			$23,303,706.56

Table 4-2

Budget authorized to finance the Delmas-Nazon viaduct construction project

Dates	Resolutions $	Cumulative $	Contract/ Amendment $	Contract/ Supervision $
2012-12-21	$8,000,000	$8,000,000		
2112-12-27			$16,588,378.51	
2013-01-03				$2,796,725
2013-12-11	$3,900,695.27	$11,900,695.27		
2015-02-26			$4,914,364.38	
2015-04-15	$5,969,416.97	$17,870,112.24		
2015-07-22	$4,740,243	$22,610,355.24		
2016-01-06	$152,096.32	$22,762,451.56		
2016-09-28	$23,303,706.56	$23,303,706.56		
			$21,502,742.89	$2,796,725
Real contracts			$21,069,462.80	$2,179,755

- "All these documents are available to the court," the prosecutor stated, before continuing:

— "Your Honor, this discrepancy between the figures shows that enormous sums have been embezzled. The investigation has uncovered various irregularities which demonstrate that the implementation of the Delmas-Nazon viaduct project by the MTPTC was not carried out efficiently, effectively, and economically, as embezzlement occurred (See the irregularities in the investigating judge's order)."

- The total amount of resolutions adopted to support the execution and supervision of the project is $23,303,706.56. However, the execution and supervision contracts awarded by the MTPTC total $16,588,378.51 and $2,796,725 respectively, for a total amount of $19,385,103.51.

The prosecutor continues:

- "Your Honor, these high-ranking state officials (the prosecutor points his index finger at the defendants) are implicated in all the financial scandals that are degrading the nation. In total, 8 companies and 229 individuals from Haiti were implicated in the 2016 Panama Papers financial scandal. These corrupt members of Haiti's economic and political elite had set up secret offshore companies to hide the money squandered at the expense of the masses. Misappropriating public resources has become a common practice among certain corrupt leaders and dishonest business executives who are proliferating in the country."

The prosecutor continues:

- "Corruption, a veritable scourge that erodes and weakens Haitian society, permeates every aspect of daily life. No sector is spared: business, commerce, health, education, diplomacy, or politics. *Transparency International's*

Corruption Perceptions Index report lists Haiti first among Caribbean countries most affected by this phenomenon. This endemic problem hinders the establishment of the rule of law."

- Indeed, the Haitian public administration is a veritable cash cow and, due to its recruitment methods, is riddled with incompetent and unscrupulous individuals. The financial irregularities, long denounced by national and international experts, have ultimately plunged the system into complete chaos, marked by arbitrariness. The phenomenon of corruption has become such a pervasive reality that it has reached such proportions that several international actors – including Canada, the United States, the Dominican Republic, the European Union, and the United Nations – have taken action against members of the Haitian political class and private sector accused of maintaining ties with armed gangs and participating in criminal activities.

- The scourge of corruption that plagues Haiti and its institutions is the greatest challenge to building a democratic society. The earthquake of January 12, 2010, sixteen years ago, offered a golden opportunity to criminals to transfer significant financial flows out of the country that could have been used to develop it. Public authorities were thus deprived of the direct and indirect tax revenue they needed to address the basic needs of the population. After the earthquake, there was an increase in calls for tenders, which were not the most competitive, but the most corrupt. There is certainly some truth to the fact that Haiti has always been a corrupt country since independence; however, it must be admitted that the level of corruption had never reached such a height. The misappropriation of Petro Caribe funds is a perfect example of dishonest acts committed by Haitian leaders.

A visible unease is etched on the faces of the accused. Some close their eyes while others lower their heads. They are all there, exposed before the world's cameras for the squandering of billions of dollars.

The prosecutor pays no attention to their humiliation, and with the same fervor, continues:

"Your Honor, what considerable sums have been embezzled under the guise of social programs while people live in squalor and misery. Corruption often takes the form of overbilling, especially in the construction sector. The natural disasters that have struck Haiti in recent years – hurricanes, floods, earthquakes – provide Haitian ministers and directors general with opportunities to embezzle ever-increasing amounts of money. Foreign NGOs have also contributed to corruption in the country, as demonstrated by a 2015 investigation by the American media outlet NPR (National Public Radio)."

"For decades, this state corruption has fueled a deep security and humanitarian crisis, characterized by impunity, violence, and a failing judicial system, placing Haiti among the most corrupt countries in the hemisphere."

Chapter 7

LET THE FACTS SPEAK FOR THEMSELVES

Forty years after February 7, 1986, the end of the Duvalier regime, Haiti has yet to find stability. Due to the actions of those implicated in corruption, the country has descended into profound chaos and is now under the control of armed gangs. The Petro Caribe affair has proven to be an unparalleled opportunity to raise awareness among Haitians of the perverse effects of corruption on all aspects of their social lives. This trial is the first sign of change. The rule of law, longed for by the Haitian people, appears to be a reality. Justice is being restored.

The prosecutor pauses. This pause is heavy. It is not for catching their breath, but to allow the weight of the facts to settle before they fall, one by one, like stones.

— "Your Honor," the prosecutor adds, "the second question we are answering is: how did the case come before the Haitian justice system?

— Pursuant to a resolution dated February 1, 2018· the Senate Assembly then headed by Senator Joseph Lambert requests the Court of Auditors to conduct a thorough audit of the management of funds Petro Caribe for the period from September 2008 to September 2016, in accordance to the constitutional and legal provisions relating to its mission.

— Following up on the correspondence of February 26, 2018 (Ref. SRH/JL/P/50/079) from the President of the Senate to the President of the CSCCA officially transferring to him the resolution of February 1, 2018, the Court declared itself competent to audit the management of PetroCaribe funds in accordance with the provisions of Articles 200 and 223, paragraph 2 of the Constitution of the Republic of Haiti of March 29, 1987, and Article 5 of the decree of November 23, 2005 establishing its organization and operation.

— The Republic of Haiti, through the Constitution of March 29, 1987, amended in May 2011, makes the Superior Court of Accounts and Administrative Disputes (CSCCA) a superior institution for the control of public finances (ISC), in harmony with the spirit of the Lima Declaration of October 1977 of the International Organization of Supreme Audit Institutions (INTOSAI), relating to the independent control of public finances with a view to the effective and credible realization of a thorough examination of the stewardship and use of public funds.

— In accordance with the provisions of Article 200 of the 1987 Constitution, the Court of Auditors is a financial, administrative, independent, and autonomous jurisdiction. It is responsible for administrative control and jurisdictional control of state revenues and expenditures, auditing of accounting State-owned enterprises as well as those belonging to local authorities. As for Article 223, Paragraph 2 of the constitution reads as follows: "Control of the execution of the law of Finance is ensured by parliament and the Superior Court of Accounts and Disputes administrative and all other institutions provided for by law.

—According to the provisions of paragraph 13 of Article 5 of this decree, the CSCCA's responsibilities include, in particular, "conducting all investigative, supervisory, advisory and consultative missions entrusted to it by the public authorities."

—So, as part of their investigative work, the CSCCA conducted audits to ensure the sound management of development programs and projects financed from Petro Caribe funds.

—As part of its investigative mission, the Court of Auditors structured its Methodological approach based on the following points: First, she set up several verification committees. Their mandate was to conduct interviews with managers and/or professionals from the audited institutions following a process of gathering information on each funded project starting from Petro Caribe funds, and this for the period from September 2008 to September 2016. Furthermore, the Court analyzed various documents as well as data originating from different information systems of institutions involved in the management of Petro Caribe funds.

The prosecution resumes its presentation, knowing it must now translate this map of failure into a narrative of guilt. It employs cold, clear, and incisive language to impose order. The subject of the investigation is a meticulously orchestrated analysis, based on an impeccable and methodically constructed methodology. Each "irregularity" noted by the Court of Auditors appears as the trace left by a predator. It's like analyzing, after a hurricane, not the visible damage, but the calculated trajectory of the wind. The figures from the CSCCA are not mere totals: they map out the coordinates of a shipwreck.

— "On January 31, 2019, the Court of Auditors submitted its first 291-page audit report on the management of projects financed by Petro Caribe funds. This is a partial report. Seven ministries, including the Ministry of Economy and Finance (MEF), the Ministry of Commerce and Industry (MCI), and the Ministry of Social Affairs and Labor (MAST), and nine public institutions (including the Prime Minister's Office) had either not submitted the required documents or had done so too late for review. Of the 409 projects identified, the CSCCA examined only a portion (less than a quarter). These projects were financed by Petro Caribe funds to the tune of just over $1.738 billion, of which 92% has been disbursed. Nearly two-thirds of the expenditures were decided by the Martelly administrations." And more than half of these projects were implemented by just two ministries: the Ministry of Public Works, Transport and Communications (MTPTC) and the Ministry of Planning and External Cooperation (MPCE).

—Based on this audit, the Court of Auditors made the following observation: the projects were not implemented efficiently, effectively, and economically. Irregularities of all kinds were identified. These included a lack of prior studies and analyses of needs, poor planning, numerous subterfuges to avoid calls for tenders, and even prior agreements. For example, for the project to acquire equipment for the MTPTC's Urban and Rural Equipment Maintenance Service (SEUR), the date of the invitation sent to suppliers to express their interest was the same (February 11, 2010) as the date the contract was signed.

The prosecutor pauses, consults his notes, and continues:

— "In the conclusion of their report, the judges of the Court of Auditors analyzed various documents as well as data from different information systems of the institutions involved in managing the funds. These include:

- Disbursement resolutions authorized by the board of directors of the Bureau for the Monetization of Development Assistance Programs (BMPAD);
- Transfers from Petro Caribe fund bank accounts held at the Bank of the Republic of Haiti (BRH) and the National Credit Bank (BNC);

- Development projects prepared by sectoral ministries and autonomous bodies, as well as contracts related to these projects;
- Disbursements authorized by the Ministry of Economy and Finance (MEF) to sectoral ministries and autonomous bodies to implement projects.

The commissions compared the project management practices of the audited institutions to recognized best practices in project management. The audit results are clear. Irregularities were found at all phases of the projects. These irregularities included cases of collusion, favoritism, and embezzlement. There were also instances of improperly received advance payments and work that began before the contract was finalized and signed. Funds were used for other purposes. In some cases, two firms were awarded contracts to perform the same work on the same section of road. Technical analysis files were often insufficiently documented. In addition, there were various administrative irregularities, as well as breaches of the regulatory framework and best management practices.

— According to data obtained from the BMPAD, from March 5, 2008, the date of receipt of the first oil shipment, to April 14, 2018, the date of receipt of the last, a total of 219 shipments totaling 43.9 million barrels of fuel were delivered and sold in Haiti. In addition, six shipments of asphalt and three shipments of fuel oil were received, resulting in an accumulation of available resources of $ 4,237,598,789.12, distributed as follows:

- portion of cash payable to Venezuela within ninety (90) days: $ 1,978,802,105.56 ;
- portion of financing available to the Haitian State and repayable over a period of between seventeen (17) and twenty-five (25) years: $ 2,258,796,683.56 .

— From September 2008 to September 2016, the CSCCA identified 409 projects originating from resolutions adopted in the Council of Ministers for a value of 2,238,164,040.74 billion US dollars. Following a series of reallocations and deallocations, the budget was revised to $ 1,738,691,909.70. According to BMPAD disbursement reports, $ 1,605,905,287.84 has been disbursed, representing 92.4% of project funding.

After consulting with the President of the Court, the Prosecutor displays on the screen the board no. 4 relating to the audited projects of the MTPTC financed by Petro Caribe funds.

Table 4: Audited MTPTC projects financed by Petro Caribe funds

No Projects Resolutions Budget $

1. Street rehabilitation in Cap-Haitian (phase I)	February 11, 2010 February 28, 2012	$7,390,216 $1,012,500
2. Street rehabilitation in Cap-Haitian (phase II)	December 21, 2012	$4,500,000
3. Street rehabilitation in Cap-Haitian and its surroundings	December 11, 2013	$2,500,000
4. Construction of the Cayes International Airport	December 21, 2012	$7,242,448.64
5. Construction of the Île-à-Vache International Airport	December 21, 2012	4,989,241.96
6. Rehabilitation of the Cayes-Jérémie road	April 15, 2015 July 22, 2015 September 28, 2016	$ 5,235,705.32 $8,764,294.68 $5,835,867
7. Repairs at the Port of Les Cayes	December 21, 2012	$1,677,021.87
8. Rehabilitation of Laboule Road 12 – Kenscoff	August 24, 2010 January 6, 2016	$6,548,429.22 $249,277.81
9. Maintenance of the Pétion-Ville – Laboule section 12	May 12, 2011 January 6, 2016	74,006.31
10. Additional works on the Laboule road 12 - Kenscoff	May 12, 2011 January 6, 2016	1,937,849.37 84,645.94

The prosecutor pauses again. He consults his notes before continuing:

"The Petro Caribe agreement has restrictions. Venezuela stipulates, for example, that 20% of the funds retained by Haiti can go to social programs, while 80% must be allocated to sustainable investment. This ratio is not respected in the resolutions. Less than 50% of the funds are spent on expenditures unrelated to sustainable investment. This lack of compliance with the agreement is not surprising, since the disbursement of Petro Caribe funds for social projects makes it easy to use the emergency law procedure and provides an opportunity to squander funds allocated to those projects."

The prosecutor continues:

— "Let's now examine the disbursements. The Petro Caribe funds were only integrated into the Republic's budget in 2012. Previous resolutions were executed by the BMPAD through transfers from the BMPAD account to the accounts of the various sectoral ministries, on the orders of the Ministry of Finance. Numerous invited witnesses, including former Prime Minister Conille, explained that the BMPAD is, to say the least, an inefficient structure in terms of good governance."

— Your Honor, the facts are there, the evidence is present. Dishonest officials have used their power, and defendants have used their affiliations to embezzle funds totaling billions of dollars.

—As for the indicators, the audit work of the Court of Auditors focused on project management, the contract award process, and the execution of work over the period from September 2008 to September 2016.

—Among the projects analyzed, we list: 1) the construction of the Marine Haïtienne viaduct; 2) the rehabilitation of the Borgne-Petit Bourg-de-Borgne road; 3) the rehabilitation of the Port-de-Paix – Port-Margot road section; 4) the construction of 15 bridges in the

Northwest; 5) the construction of the Delmas-Nazon viaduct; 6) the rehabilitation of the Carrefour Dufort-Jacmel road; 7) the dredging of the Bay of Port-au-Prince and the rehabilitation work on several streets in Pétion-Ville; 9) the Ti Manman Chéri program; 10) the Kore Etidyan Project; 11) the hospital rehabilitation and construction project; 13) the project for the construction of buildings housing the Parliament, the Court of Cassation, and the administrative complex; 14) the project for the construction of the Carrefour market; 15) The project to construct and renovate several sports centers. In total, approximately one hundred projects funded by Petro Caribe disbursements have been either not executed or poorly executed.

The prosecutor takes a moment to reflect:

- "A hundred promises that have never been kept. The public prosecutor imagines a map of Haiti. One could plant a hundred flags on it, not to mark victories, but to delineate the sites of a crime: here a hospital was supposed to be built, there a high school, further on a bridge. Today, the landscape is marked only by scars, voids that speak for themselves. Meanwhile, on screens, we see the ultramodern stadiums where the World Cup is taking place. This global tournament exposes two parallel realities: on the one hand, the spectacular capacity of certain countries to build themselves up, and on the other hand the equally spectacular capacity of nations like Haiti to destroy their own future."

The prosecutor resumed its presentation, its voice filled with bitterness:

- "This affair, Your Honor, constitutes a true crime not only against the Haitian people, but also a crime against humanity, when one considers the extent of the damage and the number of people victimized by the misuse of Petro Caribe funds and the embezzlement perpetrated

> by the accused. These funds were intended to carry out infrastructure projects: roads, bridges, among others; to build universities, vocational training centers, public schools, hospitals, ports and airports, sports centers, and to electrify the country. To divert and squander these public funds on fictitious projects, then use the stolen money to acquire luxury cars, build lavish residences, erect ranches, and pay lawyers to help them deposit the stolen money into offshore bank accounts, is a monstrous crime; a horrific and despicable act."

The prosecution paused for a moment, pensive. It couldn't believe the defendants could have embezzled billions without the complicity of foreign firms specializing in offshore banking transactions. The *Panama Papers scandal* came to mind. The investigation referred to a massive leak of 11.5 million confidential documents from the Panamanian law firm Mossack Fonseca. These documents, covering nearly 40 years of activity (from 1977 to 2015), detailed how wealthy individuals, including world leaders, politicians, and celebrities, used shell companies and offshore accounts to conceal wealth, evade taxes, or launder money. The documents were obtained by an anonymous source ("John Doe") and shared with German journalists Bastian Obermayer and Frederik Obermaier of the *Süddeutsche Zeitung newspaper* , who published several articles and detailed analyses.

Several defendants in the Petro Caribe case are implicated in the Panama Papers scandal. To date, no prosecutions have been recorded against those who have been denounced. In Haiti, the yearning for justice remains unchanged. Those at the top, the wealthy, dictate the law. There are no prisons for the privileged. The Petro Caribe trial demonstrates, for once, that in Haiti, justice does not belong to the most powerful. The force of justice within this courtroom is not limited to the respect of the law. It is embodied in a vibrant, humane action, focused on defending the most vulnerable and aiming to punish the defendants present here who have shamefully squandered Petro Caribe funds.

Setting the stage for the hearing, the public prosecutor declared furiously: "The Petro Caribe affair... The crime transcends Haiti's borders. It is transnational."

This statement resonates in the courtroom (Transnational). The word suddenly conjures up the invisible accomplices: the tax lawyers of Miami, the bankers of Panama, the intermediaries of Santo Domingo, the businesspeople in Venezuela, the American lobbyists in Washington. Petro Caribe is no longer simply a Haitian trial; it is an act of resistance against a global system of predation, a system where certain powerful countries exploit weaker countries as if they were their colonies. On the football field, Haiti faces nations with strong institutions. Here, in court, it confronts the demons of an international system that facilitated its plundering. Thus, it is waging war on two fronts.

As he repeated these words, the public prosecutor saw the shadow of Jovenel Moïse pass before him. He pondered for a moment and declared to himself:

- "Some of the defendants present are indeed complicit in the assassination of the former president."

The prosecutor takes a moment to carefully wipe his glasses before continuing:

— "Petro Caribe funds were squandered through shameful and fraudulent practices, such as overbilling, influence peddling, money laundering, fraud, theft, bribery, etc. Contracts awarded without competitive bidding and through restricted tenders were signed with hastily assembled firms. Some unfinished projects were paid for in full; for others, disbursements were made without any record of completion. The 656 pages of the report by the Special Senate Commission of Inquiry (CSSE), known as the "Beauplan Report," illustrate the mismanagement and corruption of some fifteen former ministers, several former heads of government, and about fifteen Haitian, Dominican, and other companies."

A piercing cry abruptly interrupts the proceedings. A young man stands up and loudly proclaims (pointing his index finger at the defendants): "Gade volè yo" ("Look at the thieves!"). The prosecutor's gaze immediately falls on a group of students sitting in a visible corner of the courtroom. They are wearing the same blue and red shirts with the inscription "kot kòb Petro Caribe a" (where is the Petro Caribe money) on the back. They are there, waiting silently, observing everything said during the hearing.

After quickly assessing the tension in the audience, composed mainly of lawyers, journalists, former civil servants, and other aides, the prosecution's gaze fell upon one of the defendants, Mr. Laleau. He no longer dared even look at them. He now understood the consequences of his actions. The Petro Caribe affair was becoming a suffocating trap, and he had no chance of escape.

Chapter 8

THE ACCUSED LALEAU/ LAMOTHE/BELLERIVE

Is it the weight of the accusation, is it fear, or is it a conscience awakening? The accused look dejected. Their dull, vacant gaze bears the mark of profound anxiety, as if they were already searching for a way to escape the moment that holds them captive. Better to die than to live with this shame and humiliation, some tell themselves in the secrecy of their thoughts. Are they losing hope of getting out of this mess? Because yes, this time the people will not stand idly by. They will not let them escape condemnation. Carried away by the weight of the injustice these criminals have heaped upon them, the Haitian nation, with all its might, wants justice. Thus, in this courtroom, in the streets, in the homes, the trial is increasingly taking on the character of a political demonstration where the nation reclaims its rights.

The prosecutor's gaze falls upon his notes. This trial does not yet repair. It does not rebuild. But it names, documents, and exposes. And in a country like Haiti, where forgetting has long served as public policy, speaking the facts aloud already becomes an act of rupture.

The prosecutor continues:

- "Your Honor, we now consider the case of Mr. Wilson Laleau, former Minister of Economy and Finance under the Martelly-Lamothe government, and former Chief of Staff to President Jovenel Moïse. Mr. Laleau's name is mentioned twenty times in the report of the Special Senate Commission of Inquiry into Petro Caribe funds covering the period from September 2008 to September 2016."

- Speaking of a company called Société d'Investissement Simon Bolivar (SAM), the report mentions and quotes (page 20):

— "Besides its existence, two (2) particular points have attracted our attention:

- In this company, designated SAM, the Haitian State is a stakeholder and therefore a shareholder. However, the distribution of share capital is not mentioned anywhere;

- In accordance with the provisions of the law governing public limited companies: every entity is required, upon its creation, to open a bank account at the BNC (National Credit Bank) in which one-quarter (1/4) of the share capital is deposited. The opening of this account is confirmed by the issuance of a certificate by the financial institution for this purpose.

— The certificate issued by the BNC is for twenty-five thousand gourdes (25,000 HTG), which constitutes an anomaly in the formation of this company with regard to the legislation in force.

- The notice authorizing the company to operate, signed by the Minister of Commerce Wilson Laleau, bears the date of May 29, 2012, and the related documents are published in the Official Journal of the Republic of Haiti, *the Monitor* # 84 of Wednesday, May 30, 2012.

- Wilson Laleau, under the Martelly/Lamothe government, signed the resolution of February 28, 2012 (page 212). As Minister of Economy and Finance (MEF), Laleau held important positions in public finance management and the coordination of international aid. He approved budgets for specific projects and implemented fiscal measures.

- Among the ministers in the Martelly-Conille and Martelly-Lamothe administrations, Wilson Laleau's name appears in six resolutions adopted by the Council of Ministers. In the resolution of December 21, 2012, signed by all the ministers of the Lamothe government, Wilson Laleau's name is listed twice (page 263). The same is true for the resolution of December 11, 2013, where Wilson Laleau's name appears twice (page 276). The same is true for the resolution of July 23, 2014, the fourth of the Martelly-Lamothe administration (page 400). Laleau's name is also listed among the ministers who signed the resolution of September 10, 2014 (page 413). On pages 450 and 470 of the report, Laleau's name is mentioned among the ministers of the Martelly-Paul administration who adopted the resolution of July 22, 2015.

  —The report further indicates that the firm IBT Group Haiti, which had a large contract with the Haitian State, was registered in the country in March 2013 with the authorization of Wilson Laleau as Minister of Commerce and Industry (page 444).

— In its conclusion, the Senate Ethics and Anti-Corruption Commission recommends that legal action be initiated against Wilson Laleau, former Minister of Finance, for embezzlement or misappropriation of public funds (page 528).

The signatures line up like fingerprints. The prosecution isn't looking for isolated errors, but repetition. A single signature can be a mistake. Multiple signatures become a mode of governance.

In the courtroom, each cited page serves as a reminder that governing means leaving written traces that time always catches up with.

The prosecutor consults his notes and declares:

— "Your Honor, taking the opposite view to criticisms suggesting that Petro Caribe funds were misused or misappropriated, Mr. Laleau wrote the following on page 33 of his book, *Haiti, Petrocaribe and its Misconceptions :*

— "... *For anyone who takes the time to seriously analyze the Petro Caribe case in relation to the scandal its management caused, and considering what has been said above, it is reasonable to think that there is a great deal of exaggeration in the accusations levelled against most of those implicated. It must be said that the measures to strengthen the management of funds in the implementation of the PetroCaribe agreement, launched in Haiti in August 2007, had to be put in place gradually. For example, it wasn't until 2012 that the projects and related financing from this fund were integrated into the national budget and that disbursements were subjected to the procedures stipulated in the Law on the Preparation and Execution of Finance Laws (LEELF). Every change of government is accompanied by scandals that tarnish the image of those who, directly or indirectly, were involved in the decision-making process." However, improvements to the public finance management system have gradually allowed for the implementation of new legal procedures and reduced the role of authorizing officers, particularly those in the Ministry of Economy and Finance, in final decisions regarding Petro Caribe fund disbursements ...* »

The contrast is striking. On one hand, a book that argues, nuances, and puts things into perspective. On the other hand, reports, audits, and sworn testimonies. The prosecution doesn't get sidetracked by opinions; it focuses on the facts. It confronts a personal narrative with the rigid structure of the facts.

The prosecutor continues:

— "Your Honor, Mr. Laleau has once again failed to tell the truth. There has never been any improvement in the public finance management system related to the Petro Caribe funds. To corroborate the facts, the investigating judge referred in her committal order to several entities and institutions to help clarify ambiguities in the case. Some of the information she considered in formulating her conclusions came from reports by the Superior Court of Accounts and Administrative Disputes (CSCCA), reports by the Bureau for the Monetization of Development Assistance Programs (BMPAD), and various contracts obtained from officials in different ministries as well as from individuals who had access to relevant documents. The investigating judge took into account the Senate hearing concerning the former prime ministers who administered PetroCaribe between 2008 and 2016; ministers, directors general, and other senior officials who may be able to shed light on the management of the funds.

- Garry Conille, former prime minister;
- Evans Paul, former prime minister;
- Laurent Salvador Lamothe, former prime minister;
- Jean Max Bellerive, former prime minister;
- Ronald Baudin, former Minister of Finance
- Georges Lemercier, former Minister of Finance;
- Wilson Laleau, former Minister of Finance;
- Marie Carmelle Jean Marie, former Minister of Finance;
- Eustache St-Lot, former director of the BMPAD;
- Yves Germain Joseph, former Minister of Planning;
- Michael Lecorps, former director of BMPAD;
- Jacques Rousseau, former Minister of Public Works;
- Florence D. Guillaume, former Minister of Public Health.
- The companies interviewed are as follows:
- HADOM, ROFI, DOCE and affiliates;

- E-Power;
- BEGES;
- ESTRELLA;
- SOGENER;
- TECINA;
- VORBE & SONS.

The prosecutor casts a cold gaze upon the accused, scrutinizing him as one might a criminal. He was not merely that of a state official examining a defendant; it was the fixed gaze of a nation forced to swallow its dreams.

He continues:

"Your Honor, Mr. Laleau is not the only one who lied: Mr. Lamothe also deceived us by saying he had no involvement in the misappropriation of Petro Caribe funds. Three months after the resignation of Prime Minister Garry Conille, the Haitian Parliament ratified the government of Prime Minister Laurent Salvador Lamothe. His government took office in May 2012 and led the country until December 2014. He signed six resolutions during his time in office."

— The investigation reveals that the Martelly-Lamothe government managed the largest public investment budget Haiti has ever had at its disposal. In addition to the 668, 315, 429, 20 dollars, it is necessary to add the amounts of subsidies granted through the BMPAD to Électricité d'Haïti. The majority of the funds allocated to Venezuelan and other power plants were disbursed under the Martelly-Lamothe government, amounting to approximately US$400,000,000.

—The investigating judge noted that the $ 400,000,000 allocated to subsidies for the energy sector (electricity production) was paid from Petro Caribe funds, off-budget, since no resolution was passed to authorize the allocation of funds for this purpose – and without a resolution, no provision is entered in the budget.

—The investigating judge also noted that the BMPAD's accounts receivable are mostly accounting entries that disguise energy subsidies as receivables. Mr. Michael Lecorps, in his testimony, explained that it was the public auditors who told him to record the value of the oil delivered to Sogener in the EDH account as if it were an account receivable. The judge received confirmation that these were indeed fraudulent entries.

The investigation by the investigating judge revealed that not only are these funds unproductive, but their disbursement was not authorized by any resolution. Contrary to the testimonies of successive finance ministers, and particularly that of Minister Marie-Carmelle Jean-Marie, there are expenditures covered by the BMPAD even if they are not yet budgeted.

"The investigating judge discovered that under the Martelly-Lamothe administration, many projects, despite significant initial advances and even deposits into accounts, were never completed. These include, among others: the Île à Vache airport, the Cayes airport, the Carrefour viaduct, the Fontamara hospital, the Fontamara market, the Martissant hospital, and many others."

The name "Martelly" echoes once again in the courtroom. Simply uttering it is enough to conjure up a past laden with tension and bitter memories. Before donning the presidential sash, there was Sweet Micky: the flamboyant artist, king of kompa, electrifying and bawdy, whose songs resonated throughout the Champ de Mars during the carnival parade. It had been promised that he would bring the energy of carnival to the presidency. Now, in the dock, the true cost of that promise is revealed: a charade of development where the masks are contracts and the music, the silent hiss of billions vanishing into thin air. The promised stadiums were supposed to be his ultimate stage. His legacy, in reality, is this inventory of "fictitious stadiums," and the profound betrayal of the very youth who still dance to his old rhythms. His son, Olivier, a corrupt businessman, enjoys a privilege that his father's administration denied to thousands.

The prosecutor glances at the accused and continues:

— "Under the Martelly-Lamothe government, the firm Sotec benefited from special provisions in the January 2014 resolution allocating US$9,000,000 to settle outstanding invoices. This firm was responsible for executing contracts such as the port of Jérémie and the Jérémie wharf in Cité Soleil. These projects involved sums exceeding US$45,000,000. As with other fraudulent contracts, negotiated contracts appear to be the norm, and the contracts are backdated. The investigation No studies justifying the choice of such an investment could be found. Furthermore, these ports have not been used since their completion. In fact, public investment specialists confirm that this investment does not meet the priority level it was given and does not justify the level of investment allocated to it.

— Furthermore, the investigating judge noted that the firm Sotec benefited from negotiated contracts, unrelated to any urgency and without competitive bidding, while many firms, of the same or greater capacity, did not have the opportunity to participate in even a restricted tender which could have benefited the State and revitalized the national construction sector.

— Under the Martelly-Lamothe administration, the firm Hadom signed a contract for the construction of the Ministry of Commerce building. The construction cost is estimated at $17.5 million (funded by Petro Caribe and the Public Treasury). This construction was included in the Martelly-Lamothe government's resolution of July 18, 2012, for an amount of $ 10,000,000, which has been fully disbursed.

— Hadom, after receiving more than 80% of the funds allocated for construction, was unable to proceed with the work. It had to cede its rights to OECC, which ultimately completed the project, but at the cost of additional expenses for the Haitian state.

— For the construction of the Île-à-Vache airport, the Estrella firm signed a contract worth $19,525,143. The project, entitled "Île-à-Vache Tourist Destination," includes major construction projects, including the building of a standardized international airport with a 2.6-kilometer runway.

— The firm Estrella received 25% of the contract amount ($ 4,989,241.96) according to the resolution of December 21, 2012, while the degree of completion of the work did not exceed 10%.

The prosecutor consults his notes before continuing:

"Your Honor, in a press release issued on November 17, 2017, Mr. Lamothe's private office stated that the three main charges relayed in the Beauplan report against the former prime minister were not subjected to any rigorous verification, thus proving the negligence, if not the bad faith, of the document's authors. All of this leads the former head of government to question the true motivations behind this exercise, which, according to him, constitutes yet another fallacious pretext to corner citizens who served their country in the difficult context of the 2010 earthquake, by attempting to tarnish their image and obscure their achievements. During a press conference held on Tuesday, November 28, 2017, former Prime Minister Lamothe denounced the irregularities that riddle the Beauplan report. 'The Beauplan report is the biggest lie of the century,' Lamothe asserted."

"There again, Mr. Lamothe lied. His government ratified certain fraudulent contracts from the Préval-Bellerive government. These contracts were renewed despite the irregularities, and some have not been executed or completed."

The prosecutor looks at the two defendants, Martelly and Lamothe, seated side by side in the dock, and declares:

— "Your Honor, here is a summary of the management of Petro Caribe funds by the Martelly-Lamothe government.

Following Garry Conille's resignation, Laurent Lamothe was appointed Prime Minister by President Martelly on March 1, 2012· His appointment was ultimately approved by the Senate on April 10, 2012, by a vote of 19 to 3. He was officially sworn in on May 16, 2012.

— During this term, the objective of his government is to rebuild the country following the 2010 earthquakes. In September 2013, the Lamothe government put in place a participatory democracy program, the " *gouvenman lakay* " or (government at home), in which members of the government take turns traveling to the different departments of the country and commit to concrete actions after public exchanges .

— The Martelly - Lamothe government inherited several resolutions taken by the Bellerive and Conille governments under the aegis of the presidential decrees of January and April 2010 declaring a state of emergency over the entire extent of the national territory until October 2011.

Most of the work planned under the resolutions passed by the Conille and Bellerive governments was carried out by Lamothe, who issued a decree declaring a state of emergency following Hurricane Sandy. While Haiti is still struggling to recover from the damage caused by the January 12, 2010 earthquake and Tropical Storm Isaac in August 2012, Hurricane Sandy also left a heavy toll. Sandy struck Haiti on the night of October 24, 2012, causing enormous damage. One hundred and twenty million dollars in agricultural losses: the flooding destroyed 70% of the crops and caused heavy livestock losses.

"Once again, the government will dip into Petro Caribe's accounts to repair the damage. Lamothe declared a state of emergency on October 30, 2012, across the entire national territory. During this emergency period, the government signed several contracts."

In the air-conditioned, elegant offices of the Prime Minister's office, the storm is not a tragedy, but an opportunity offered to the accused to unlock millions. This is the cynical mechanics of the disaster economy: human suffering is transformed, on paper, into logistical pretexts, then into contracts, and finally into silent deposits in distant accounts. The storm's victims, doubly victimized –first by nature, then by their protectors– now become invisible spectators in this room. Their silent testimony carries more weight than a financial audit.

The prosecutor continues:

— The Martelly-Lamothe government signed five resolutions for a total of US $891.9 million (188 projects). However, after the reallocation of US $223.1 million and thirty-nine projects, the revised total is US $668.8 million for 149 projects.

— The main objective of these solutions is the reconstruction of infrastructure affected by the January 12, 2010 earthquake and Hurricane Sandy.

— These are the following solutions:

	Projects	$	Amount $	$	Disbursement $	
Date	Remaining	Initial	Disaff.	Revised		%
July 18, 2012	26	$130,000,000	$33,304,347.20	$96,695,625.80	$96,195,125.80	99%
December 21, 2012	63	$379,500,000	$50,113,264.96	$329,386,735.04	$329,386,735.04	100%
December 11, 2013	45	$210,967,319.33	$46,450,090.46	$164,517,228.87	$164,517,228.87	100%
July 23 , 2014	14	$141,778,568	$70,562,728.62	$71,215,839.39	$71,215,839.39	100%
September 10, 2014	1	$29,697,201.29	$22,697,201.29	$7,000,000	$7,000,000	100%
Total	149	$891,943,088.62	$223,127,659.53	$668,815,429	$668,315,429.19	100%

After a short pause, the prosecutor continues:

— "The Lamothe government is monitoring the contracts signed by the Préval-Bellerive government. However, it should be noted that it was during the Martelly-Lamothe administration that the work related to the reconstruction of Haiti after the 2010 earthquake truly began. The disbursement rate for the projects under these six resolutions is 100%."

One hundred percent disbursement; the figure represents a masterpiece of bureaucratic horror. In the perverse logic of this plunder, efficiency is measured not by completed projects, but by the speed at which public wealth is converted into private gain. The complete "success" of the disbursement is the absolute failure of the state. In a parallel universe, this same 100% could have been the percentage of children vaccinated, of homes electrified. The tragedy lies in the precision of the figure, which documents not an error, but a perfect crime.

The prosecutor declares:

— "Your Honor, the majority of contracts signed by the State using Petro Caribe funds under the Préval-Bellerive and Martelly-Lamothe governments were overpriced: the Cerca-Carvajal road, the rehabilitation of the Lafito road, the Fontamara market, etc. According to the investigating judge's inquiry, there was overbilling in the construction of the Lafito road. The cost per kilometer of road in the contract is estimated at $ 1,995,153, while for the same month, the cost per kilometer of road by another firm operating in the same sector (Petite Rivière-Petit Trou), with similar project specifications, was estimated at $ 1,484,454. This represents a positive difference of $ 510,699 per kilometer. Another problem arose with the Cerca-Carvajal road. The road's length is less than that specified in the contract. It actually measures 10.5 kilometers, while the Ministry of Planning paid for 17 kilometers.

The prosecutor shakes his head. After a brief glance towards the dock, he continues:

— "Let's talk about the socio-community infrastructure construction contract:

— Awarded by mutual agreement and approved by the Court of Auditors, this contract was signed on November 20, 2012, for an amount of $ 18,411,135 , to which was added an amendment of $ 5,517,257.42 , bringing the total amount of the contract related to the project to $23,928,392 . This contract did not receive a no-objection opinion from the CNMP.

The 2 % advance payments from the DGI were not collected, the guarantee was not noted during the analysis of the contract, and the eligibility documents were not provided .

— The signatories are:

- Laurent Salvador Lamothe, Minister of the MPCE;
- Frank Romain Junior, Sotech Operations Director;
- Nonie Mathieu, president of the CSCCA.

This latest revelation literally takes the audience's breath away. Without wasting any time, the prosecution consults its notes and continues:

— "Never two without three. Mr. Bellerive also concealed the truth. Prime Minister Jean-Max Bellerive is the third prime minister to take office after René Préval's election as President of Haiti for his second term. He follows Prime Ministers Jacques Édouard Alexis and Michèle Duvivier Pierre-Louis, whose terms ended on September 5, 2008, and October 30, 2009, respectively."

— Jean-Max Bellerive, the 14th Prime Minister of Haiti, was confirmed by the Haitian Parliament on November 11, 2009. His government (November 2009 to October 2011) signed three resolutions totaling $ 348,240,830.01. These resolutions were as follows:

— The resolution of February 10, 2010 for $ 157,719,896.18;

— The resolution of August 23, 2010 for $ 94,597,097.69;

— The resolution of May 11, 2011 for $ 95,923,836.14.

— In the three resolutions, 41 contracts were personally signed by former Prime Minister Jean-Max Bellerive, in his capacity as Minister of Planning and External Cooperation. Mr. Bellerive signed these 41 contracts as part of the funding from the Petro Caribe agreement.

— The investigating judge's order verified the assertions in the Conille Report, according to which, of the forty-one contracts signed, thirty-five were awarded without competitive bidding. Of these thirty-five contracts, sixteen, for a total amount of $ 28,256,194.81, were signed on May 12, 2011, by former Prime Minister Bellerive, 24 hours before his resignation was submitted to President René Préval on May 13, 2011; five contracts, for a total amount of $ 11,243,023, were signed by the accused between October 7 and 12, 2011, while the order appointing his successor had already been published (*Moniteur* – Supplement #140 of October 7, 2011). The remaining fourteen contracts were awarded to the general partnership Milfort Augustin & Co., formed by Jocelin Milfort and Jackson Augustin, known as J&J Construction. These contracts were signed between January 2011 and August 2011.

— The negotiated contracts signed by Jean-Max Bellerive were awarded to the following entities:

COMPANIES	AMOUNT
BECA ENGINEERING	$ 6,142,109.76
Consortium Tropic Build World Wide holding llc. / JRD construction SA	$ 2,995,400
CONSTRUCTORA ADOM	$ 5,000,000
SECOSA (Supervision, Evaluation and Construction SA)	$ 33,594,304.17
IBI GROUP – DAA	$ 7,517,550

MILFORD AUGUSTIN COMPANY	$ 5,735,698.69
SADA CONSTRUCTION	$ 7,168,000
CONSORTIO MMC RENTER	$ 2,360,000
GI CONSULTANT	$ 3,500,000
GTC (Works and Construction Group)	$ 1,025,000
GILBERT CHENET	$ 250,000
GRUPO SITA (SRL)	$ 3,575,000
RHT PLAZA SA	$ 4,360,000
TURBO CONSULTING	$ 129,000

The six other contracts awarded through restricted tenders were signed with the firms Hadom SA, Rofi SA, and Construcciones y Diseños RMNSA. The investigation revealed that these six contracts were not the first agreements signed between the Haitian government and firms affiliated with companies whose majority shareholder is Félix Bautista. In fact, firms affiliated with Bautista had previously benefited from debris and waste removal contracts. These were two contracts, worth ten million and five million dollars respectively, signed in February 2010.

— Regarding the six contracts signed following restricted tenders, they are:

— Legislative Palace/contract signed with the firm Constructora Hadom SA for $33,765,366.08;

— Bowenfield residential development (Phase I and II)/contracts signed with the firm Construcciones Y Diseños RMNSA for a total of $ 135,309,218.65;

— Fort National residential development (Phase I, II, and III)/3 contracts signed with the firm Rofi SA for a total of $ 178,951,296.90, according to the statement of account of the Dominican journalist Nuria Piera, this amount would be $ 174,308,996.90.

— Among the contracts awarded by the Préval-Bellerive government, two groups can be identified. The first group consists of thirty-five negotiated contracts, and the second group comprises six contracts awarded through restricted tenders. Among the negotiated contracts are those in response to the emergency and those concerning projects affecting regions unaffected by the earthquake.

"The absence of the CNMP (National Commission for Public Procurement) from all these cases constitutes a serious failure in terms of oversight, because the CNMP is the body that declares the urgency and, based on that, decides which contracts to award. Jean-Max Bellerive has violated the rules. He distributes contracts to whomever he pleases, without even obtaining a certificate of no objection from the highest authority responsible for strengthening public procurement standards."

Mr. Bellerive's actions embody the old unwritten law that has governed Haiti for generations: proximity to power prevails over any established procedure. The certificate of no objection is not a mere administrative formality; it constitutes the thin line that still separates the republic from a return to the feudal system. By ignoring it, he is not only circumventing a process, he is asserting that the state is not a system of laws, but an extension of his own will. It is a gesture that reaches back in time, beyond Duvalier, beyond the occupation, to the very origins of the post-independence state, where authority was personal, not institutional. The courtroom, with its rituals and codes, is embarking on an attempt to build another kind of country in real time, using the rubble left by Bellerive and others as both evidence and foundation.

The prosecutor continues:

— "Your Honor, former Premier and former Minister of Planning, the accused failed to consider that even in an emergency, the government must obtain a "no-objection" certificate from the CNMP. This is a mandatory formality. Despite former Premier Bellerive's efforts to justify various infrastructure projects, the investigation concluded that many contracts signed under the emergency circumstances did not have the characteristics of such contracts.

— The firm GTC signed a contract for eighteen kilometers of road under the Bellerive administration. The firm received $21,000,000 out of a total of $22,000,000 but completed only 40% of the work for which it was contracted, namely 8 kilometers of road out of the 18 kilometers stipulated in the contract. Disbursements for this work were made from 2010 to 2014. However, the investigating judge's inquiry was unable to understand the disbursements made from September 2010 to September 2014 because the payments did not correspond to the percentage of work completed. During his hearing before Parliament, Mr. Yves Joseph Germain (former Director General of the National Equipment Centre (CNE)) confirmed the Latortue Commission's suspicions regarding the firm GTC. Thanks to Minister Germain's statements, the Ethics and Anti-Corruption Commission was able to identify recurring weaknesses under the administration of Premier Laurent Lamothe, who renewed most of the contracts denounced and signed under the Préval-Bellerive administration.

The prosecutor wipes his face, and then consults his notes, before continuing:

— "The Hadom firm received $10 million as an advance payment for the construction of the Ministry of Foreign Affairs, representing 50% of the total budget. After months, work never began. The same firm received $10 million as an advance payment for the construction of the Haitian Parliament building, representing 30% of the budget. Although the funds were disbursed, after months, work still did not start. CONSTRUCTURA HADOM SA, the company awarded the contract for the construction of the Legislative Palace for $ 33,765,660.08, was created on July 28, 2010 (Ref: *Official Gazette* of September 13, 2010). At the time the contract was signed by former Prime Minister Jean-Max Bellerive on November 8, 2010, it was only three months old." Therefore, it does not meet the criterion of five years of experience. For the awarding of this contract, the Bid Evaluation Committee consisted of: Hervé Day, Michel Content and Lionel Grand'Pierre.

— The Haitian state paid more than 80% of the amounts to the firm Hadom for the construction of the Ministries of the Interior and Commerce, this firm was unable to advance the work and was forced to cede its rights to the firm OECC which completed the work with additional disbursements drawn from PetroCaribe funds.

Analyzing the shareholder profiles makes it easy to detect the intent to defraud. Hadom and Rofi have the same shareholders. DISENOS MRN SA is affiliated with both companies. This invalidates the claim that these contracts resulted from restricted tenders; they are, in fact, negotiated contracts. The maneuver is blatant and the favoritism obvious. Including three related firms in a single tender confirms suspicions of collusion and corruption in the awarding of contracts.

"These firms, like the majority of those that have signed contracts with the Haitian state, do not meet the criteria for seniority or experience. Former Prime Minister Jean-Max Bellerive acknowledged that in some cases, he was the one who asked Dominican contractors to form a local company to meet the prerequisites."

The prosecutor shakes his head. After a brief glance at the accused Bellerive, he continues:

- " The awarding of twenty-two negotiated contracts The awarding of a total of thirty-five contracts to the firms Secosa and J&J Construction represents preferential treatment and smacks of cronyism. The following irregularities are found in this category of contract:
- Contracts not accompanied by an estimated quote;

- Unidentified place of execution (contract signed with Secosa for the development of sports infrastructure in 10 municipalities: $ 4,450,000) ;
- Nullity of the contracts signed with J&J Construction (company dissolved at the time the contracts were signed);
- Overbilling of certain supervision contracts with J&J Construction (ex: supervision contract for the construction of the Cerca Carvajal High School: 14.1% when the industry standard is 10%);
- Signing of an amendment of 55 million gourdes (99% of the initial contract) for the construction of the Pignon High School, far exceeding the ceiling set at 30% of the initial contract in violation of article 21 of the decree of October 26 , 2009 specifying the terms of application of the law of June 10, 2009 ;
- Signing of around forty contracts on behalf of the various sectoral ministries.

— This is not within the purview of the Minister of Planning.

- The absence in certain contracts of a clause guaranteeing the interests of the State in the event of work stoppage or contract cancellation constitutes a violation of article 88-2 of the law of June 10, 2009.

— For all these repeated violations of the law of June 10, 2009 on public procurement, Mr. Jean Max Bellerive has been charged with:

1) Abuse of office (Article 5.5)

2) Overbilling (Article 5.8)

3) Influence peddling. (Article 5.9)

4) Nepotism (Article 5.10)

5) Illegal awarding of public contracts (Article 5.12)

— In accordance with the law of March 12, 2014, concerning the prevention and suppression of corruption, specifically articles 5.5, 5.8, 5.9, 5.10, and 5.12; the law of February 1, 2017 , on the preparation and execution of finance laws, specifically article 98, which defines the criminal liability of authorizing officers who have committed management errors; the decree of May 17, 2005, concerning the revision of the general civil service statute, specifically articles 178 and 181, regarding management errors committed by a civil servant; and finally, the order of February 16 , 2005 , concerning the general accounting regulations , specifically article 21 , regarding the liability of authorizing officers .

Bellerive puts his hands to his head, as if crushed by the weight of what is unfolding. Tears, discreet but irrepressible, begin to mist his eyes. The prosecution, impassive in the face of this raw distress, nevertheless continues its closing argument with the same fervor and declares:

- "Your Honor, beyond the fraudulent maneuvers tainting the bidding processes, there are also legal violations related to the very status of the signatories: suspicions of corruption and bribery. In several resolutions, former Prime Minister Bellerive signed the contracts in his capacity as Minister of Planning and External Cooperation, while the sectoral ministries were excluded from the process, even though they are the only ones authorized to negotiate projects and contracts within the framework of the Petro Caribe resolutions. The investigation is astonished to note that the Ministry of Planning was the only one to negotiate and sign all these contracts, without exception, while various sectoral ministries such as Public Works, National Education, and Social Affairs, although involved, were sidelined."

The prosecutor consults his notes and continues:

- "The consortium Tropic Build Worldwide Holding and JRD Construction SA signed a contract with the Haitian government for the acquisition and installation of prefabricated houses and community centers. The total contract amount was $2,995,400. $2,600,000 had been disbursed, and the remaining balance was $395,380. On July 21, 2011, an initial disbursement of $1,797,240 was made by the government led by former Prime Minister Jean-Max Bellerive. The firm did not perform any of the work stipulated in the contract. The Minister of Planning, Ms. Joséfa Raymond Gauthier, ordered a second disbursement of $802,780 to this firm on June 6, 2012."

- According to reports, the construction firm Tropic Build, represented by Enrico Propescu (passport number #217797841) with a registered office in the United States, and a second address A/S Architectura group, 1920 Hallandale Beach Blvd, Suite 908, Florida, 33009, USA, has not executed anything despite these two disbursements.

- This firm is associated with a Haitian firm called JRD Construction (trading as Denis & Co), whose legal representative is Mr. Jean Renel Denis (005-014-588-3), an engineer at the CNE, and whose registered address is Delmas #376, Haiti. The firm is a new general partnership located in Pétion-Ville, Route de Frères, Rue Saint-Louis Jeanty #34. Mr. Jean Renel Denis and Ms. Jeanne Asmine Louissaint Denis (001-146-857-8), Vice-President, registered JRD Construction with the Ministry of Commerce and Industry under No. [0] F005, Folio 288, Register XI, on January 8, 2015.

The prosecutor turns his gaze towards the accused for a moment and declares:

- "Former Prime Minister Jean-Max Bellerive received financial contributions in kind and in cash (bribes) from the firms Hadom, Rofi, and Doce, the investigation reveals."

The prosecutor shakes his head gravely and continues:

- "Regarding hospital construction and rehabilitation projects, the construction of the Simbi Continental Hospital in Martissant benefits from an amount of $ 6,500,101.08. Article 1 of the contract states that the work will be carried out at Simbi Continental Martissant 25 #53, across from Palmera Plaza. This contract was evaluated by a team of engineers who noted that the work was 69% complete. The total amount disbursed is $ 5,190,349, representing 86.4% of the total cost of the work.

- $ 6,000,404 for the construction of the Wireless Hospital. Disbursements related to this contract have not been identified, as the documents have not been sent to either the Senate Committee or the Investigating Chamber.

The signatories are:

- Florence Duperval Guillaume, Minister of MSPP, and GianFranco Florenza, Director General of IBT."

The prosecutor, his voice choked with anger and indignation, continues:

— "Regarding the rehabilitation and maintenance work on the Baie de L'Acul / Carrefour RN3 (Barrière Battant) road , a contract was signed between the Haitian State, represented by Mr. Jacques Gabriel, Minister of Public Works, Transport and Communications, Mr. Ronald Baudin, Minister of Economy and Finance, and the CEO of V&F Construction SA , Jean Marie Vorbe. The amount is $ 32,721,688 (contract + addendum). "

- Serious irregularities were observed. The project was awarded through a negotiated procedure without the approval of the CSCCA (Superior Court of Accounts and Administrative Disputes) and without obtaining a certificate of no objection from the CNMP (National Commission for Public Procurement). No document relating to the 2% advance payment deductions by the DGI (General Directorate of Taxes) was submitted.

The prosecutor reviews his notes again before adding:

— "Now let's take the case of Garry Conille.

— Born on February 26, 1966 in Port-au-Prince, Haiti, Mr. Conille is a Haitian politician and senior civil servant, a physician, and a development expert. He served as Prime Minister of Haiti twice: from 2011 to 2012, under President Michel Martelly, and then from June to November 2024, under the Presidential Transitional Council.

During the Martelly /Conille administration, only one resolution was adopted by the Council of Ministers, on February 28, 2012. This resolution was signed by the Minister of Agriculture, Natural Resources, and Rural Development, Mr. Hébert Docteur. It was motivated by various reasons, such as the need to build public markets and bridges, strengthen the country's sports infrastructure, rehabilitate certain wharves, and construct airstrips and roads throughout the country. A sum of $ 230,139,272 from Petro Caribe funds was disbursed for the implementation of these projects.

- Your Honor, the analysis of the contracts signed by the Ministry of Agriculture and Rural Development involving PetroCaribe funds reveals numerous irregularities.

- Rehabilitation of the Cul de Sac plain irrigation system:

- This project was authorized by two resolutions, one dated February 28, 2012, and the other June 22, 2015, for a total of $ 8,497,775.86, or 382,399,913.70 HTG. The investigation examined the management of the contract. It appears that the project was not implemented efficiently or economically. Several irregularities were found in its development and implementation.

- The investigation revealed that the Ministry of Agriculture, Natural Resources and Rural Development (MARNDR) committed irregularities that caused harm to the community. The judge noted that the departmental director of agriculture for the west had requested a loan of 18,675,750.09 HTG from Minister Thomas Jacques to carry out activities unrelated to the project. The investigating judge's inquiry was unable to determine whether this loan had been repaid in a timely manner to avoid delays in the execution of the contract.

- The judge was greatly surprised to discover that a check for 5,000,000 HTG had been made to Ms. Linda Thomas as a loan for activities related to the fair organized by the Ministry of Agriculture, Natural Resources and Rural Development (MARNDR). Ms. Linda Thomas had no business relationship with the Western Departmental Directorate of Agriculture (DDAO) to warrant such a sum of money. The judge believes that this irregularity also caused harm to the project and the community.

Furthermore, the investigation also uncovered breaches of the regulatory framework and best management practices. The investigating judge noted that a project sheet had been prepared by the Directorate of Agricultural Infrastructure (DIA) and the Western Departmental Directorate of Agriculture (DDAO). The provisional budget established in the technical sheet was 328,000,000 HTG, and the planned execution period was five months, from May 5,

2012, to October 5, 2012. This deadline was never met; the work was carried out over a period of more than three years, from August 2012 to September 2015. The failure to meet the deadlines had consequences not only on the cost of the project but also on the final quality of the irrigation system. According to the investigating judge, such irregularities in management practices are unacceptable for projects of this scale.

The investigation found that the Ministry of Agriculture, Natural Resources and Rural Development (MARNDR) awarded ten contracts for this project. Of these ten contracts, two were awarded through restricted tendering processes, signed with the firms ANAPAAAH, represented by Jerry Mourra, and Seca, headed by Nazaire Israël. The other eight contracts were awarded by private agreement. The investigation concluded that this approach was not optimal, as it involved splitting contracts that could have been awarded either through public or restricted tendering processes.

- The judge also noted that projects were being carried out both internally and by private firms. This practice is not economically viable. For a project valued at 382,399,913.70 HTG, this constitutes an irregularity that could have an impact on the community.

- Furthermore, the investigation estimates that an amount of 54,406,743.93 HTG remained in excess of the funds disbursed for the project. According to the report prepared in December 2014 by the DIA, the total project expenditures amounted to 327,993,169.77 HTG. However, the documentation provided to the investigating judge was unable to determine how the MARNDR used this sum of money.

The prosecutor could feel the weariness setting in, not in his voice, but in the courtroom. Too many elements, too many figures, too much evidence for a single session. The audience, too, needed a moment to catch its breath in the face of all this shady dealing.

At this stage, the prosecutor addresses the Court:

— "Your Honor, given the late hour, we request a recess."

The president glances at his watch and declares:

— "The hearing is suspended and will resume tomorrow at 10 a.m."

Chapter 9

WHERE ARE THE TWENTY-FIVE STADIUMS?

(The fifth day of the hearing)

The prosecution sets the maximum sentence. For a moment, it forgets the trial. It doesn't even see the defendants. In its mind, it has a vision of what Haiti could have been if the Petro Caribe funds had been properly managed. In a completely renovated Sylvio Cator Stadium, Haitians would have witnessed the national team's victory and, at the same time, the Grenadiers' qualification for the World Cup. From then on, this sacrificed generation would have found its identity and pride not in exile, but in a home triumph. The dream is still so tangible, so attainable. It has been traded, by corrupt leaders, for private jets, luxury properties in Florida, and offshore bank accounts. The Grenadiers' qualification for the 2026 World Cup sparked a fragile national joy; this testimony reveals that it is a joy obtained at the expense of the leaders. It is the resilience of the Haitian people in the face of their state's plundering. This people, a specific sample of whom gather around the Palace of Justice, with ropes in their hands and brandishing signs with the inscription : "kot kòb PetroKaribe a, (Where is the Petro Caribe money)," thus expressing their quest for truth and accountability.

The prosecutor is returning to reality.

For nearly four days, the Port-au-Prince courthouse has been the rallying point for people from all walks of life in the country. That morning, the atmosphere at the courthouse was tense. The Petro Caribe trial was still the main event in the news. There was also talk of the World Cup matches, primarily the games of the Haitian national football team against Scotland, Morocco, and Brazil. Many political figures, journalists, young people, and other prominent individuals were present, just as they had been in the early days, to follow the proceedings.

Early Thursday morning, June 11, 2026, the courthouse was stormed by a crowd eager to learn the truth about the misappropriation of billions of dollars from the Petro Caribe funds. The major revelations made by the press during the first days of the trial, the relevance of certain pieces of evidence presented, and the socio-political standing of the main defendants quickly established this case as one of the biggest trials ever held in Haiti.

In the audience, the only topic of conversation was the handcuffed defendants who were now paying the price for their actions.

The Court enters. The room rises as the president and members of the public prosecutor's office take their seats.

The president:

— "The hearing is open."

The prosecutor has the floor:

- "Your Honor, we request the floor to continue the presentation of the facts."

The president:

- "The Court authorizes you to do so."

The prosecutor pays no attention to the commotion he has just caused in the room. "Where are the twenty-five stadiums?" he repeats, looking towards former Prime Minister Laurent Lamothe and Olivier Martelly, the son of the former president.

The issue goes beyond a simple sports project. It reflects a societal choice. In other countries benefiting from the Petro Caribe program, notably the Dominican Republic, concessional funds are used to stabilize the energy sector, invest in sustainable infrastructure, and reduce the state's budgetary burden. In neighboring Dominican Republic, roads, power plants, and public facilities are yielding concrete and visible results. In Haiti, Petro Caribe funds are being squandered.

The question remains unanswered, even more oppressive than the hushed silence of the courtroom. "Where are the twenty-five stadiums?" This question is more than a request for an audit: it sounds like an indictment of a stolen future. At that moment, the ghost of the Sylvio Cator Stadium, that aging relic of Port-au-Prince, seems to materialize in the room. Its cracked concrete and neglected lawn bear witness to the Haitian leaders' contempt for public property. The twenty-five promised modern stadiums are not merely unfulfilled projects; they symbolize unrealized potential, the unrequited aspirations of millions of Haitians. Their absence casts the image of a physical void in the landscape, a black hole in the national treasury. While the Petro Caribe trial unfolds at the Palace of Justice in North America, in ultramodern stadiums, the Haitian national football team, the Grenadiers, prepares to play in the 2026 World Cup. The irony is stark: Haiti plays its qualifying matches abroad, in stadiums that were actually built. Its own stadiums, never constructed, despite being paid for with blood and oil, exist only in falsified accounting records.

Very calmly, the public prosecutor continued:

- "Your Honor, on July 12, 1952, the country commemorated the inauguration of the Paul Eugène Magloire Stadium, hereafter known as the Sylvio Cator Stadium. No sports facility of such magnitude had ever been built in the country before. Between 2010 and 2015, the prospect of new stadiums was met with great hope. Funds from the PetroCaribe program were disbursed for the construction of twenty-five stadiums. This project was part of a program within the Ministry of Sports, under the responsibility of Olivier Martelly."

- When questioned about this, former Premier Lamothe stated that he did not sign any contracts related to the stadium construction. In a video posted on social media, Lamothe maintains that at the time the contracts were signed, he held no ministerial position related to foreign affairs, planning, or even the role of premier, which, according to him, absolves him of any responsibility in this matter. He asserts that the administrative commitments related to these projects were signed by Garry Conille, who was premier at the time.

- The supervision of the sports parks fell under the *Foutbòl pou chanjman program* , headed by Olivier Martelly, Lamothe states. Technical supervision of the work was provided by the company J&J Construction, while an advisor from the National Palace was involved in the process. The relevant ministries, he clarifies, played primarily an administrative role.

- Lamothe states that he has nothing to do with this matter. He asserts that all the contracts were initialed either before his arrival at the Prime Minister's office in August 2012 or after his resignation. He then details the chronology of the contractual commitments.

- The first contract was signed on May 12, 2011, by Jean-Max Bellerive, then Minister of Planning, for the construction of ten sports parks for a total of US $4,450,000, or US $445,000 per park. Another contract was signed on the same date for US $1.6 million. On September 6, 2011, a third contract for eight sports parks was signed for a total of over US $10 million, or over US $1 million per park. A fourth contract was signed on July 9, 2012, by Joséfa Raymond Gauthier, then Minister of Planning and External Cooperation, for the construction of five sports complexes. On July 5, 2015, another contract was signed for the installation of synthetic turf for 385 million gourdes.

This line of defense is not new. Laurent Lamothe, former Minister of Foreign Affairs and former Prime Minister, presents himself as an administrator rather than a decision-maker, citing the technicalities of the procedures and the chronology of signatures. But in Haiti, power is not limited to signed contracts; it is also exercised through direction, continuity, and silence. The absence of a signature is not always an alibi to erase the crime.

The prosecutor continues:

- Your Honor, Laurent Lamothe lied. The report from the Ethics and Anti-Corruption Commission reveals the exact opposite. Some resolutions signed under his government are problematic.

- Three months after the resignation of Prime Minister Garry Conille, the Haitian Parliament ratified the appointment of Laurent Salvador Lamothe as Prime Minister. His government took office in May 2012 and led the country until December 2014. During its term, it signed five resolutions:

- July 18, 2012, a first resolution for an amount of $96,195,625.80;
- December 21, 2012 a second resolution for a total of $329,386,735.05;
- December 11, 2013 a third resolution for a value of $184,517,228.97;
- July 23, 2014 a fourth resolution for an estimate of $71,215,839.30;
- September 10, 2014 a fifth resolution for a figure of $7,000,000.

As the figures add up, another accounting method emerges: that of unrealized projects. In the Dominican Republic, Petro Caribe funds are financing roads, power plants, and visible infrastructure. In Haiti, the amounts mentioned point to sham projects and grotesque schemes. The accounting speaks for itself, but the construction sites remain buried.

The prosecutor continues:

— The total amount of resolutions passed under Mr. Lamothe's government was $668,315,429.20. Resolutions passed under Garry Conille's government were incorporated into the budgets managed by the Lamothe administration. The Commission therefore considers that the Martelly-Lamothe government exercised its decision-making power over the $668,315,429.20 voted by its cabinet, and over the $210,303,222.68 previously budgeted under the Martelly-Conille government.

- Furthermore, the Martelly-Lamothe government monitored disbursements on contracts entered into by the Préval-Bellerive and Martelly-Bellerive administrations. It also dealt with some residual files from the Préval-Pierre-Louis administration, though to a lesser extent.

- The Commission noted that the Martelly-Lamothe government managed the largest public investment budget Haiti had ever had at its disposal. In addition to the $878,618,651.88, the amounts of subsidies granted through the BMPAD to Électricité d'Haïti must be added. The majority of the funds allocated to Venezuelan power plants and other projects were disbursed under the Martelly-Lamothe government, amounting to approximately $400,000,000.

- The Commission noted that the amounts (approximately $400,000,000) allocated to subsidies for the energy sector (electricity production) were paid from PetroCaribe funds, off-budget. Since no resolution authorized this use, no corresponding provision had been included in the budget.

- The Commission also noted that the BMPAD's accounts receivable are mostly accounting entries that disguise energy subsidies as receivables. Mr. Michael Lecorps, former director of the BMPAD, stated that it was the public auditors who instructed him to record the value of the oil delivered to Sogener on behalf of EDH as if it were an account receivable. The Commission received confirmation that this was indeed a case of accounting manipulation.

- The Commission realized that not only are these amounts unproductive, but their disbursement was not authorized by any resolution. Contrary to the testimonies of successive Finance Ministers, and particularly that of the former Minister, Marie-Carmelle Jean-Marie, there are expenditures covered by the BMPAD even if they are not yet budgeted.

The prosecutor continues:

- "Your Honor, it is important to highlight the lack of serious oversight of projects and contracts initiated by the Lamothe government. Indeed, in the majority of cases, contracts signed between the Haitian government and contractors under former Prime Minister Lamothe received an advance payment immediately upon signing. These amounts represent a significant but variable percentage, sometimes reaching up to 50% of the contract value, suggesting that they were subject to arbitrary decisions. Accounting summaries show that the Martelly-Lamothe government continued disbursements until certain stipulated amounts were settled, without any attempt to coordinate payments with project execution."

— The Martelly-Lamothe government was obligated, before signing the resolutions, to take into account the report of Premier Garry Conille. This was not done. The Latortue Commission discovered that a large majority of contracts under Lamothe were renewed before any serious investigations. Certain funds, including those allocated to Fort National and Bowenfield, were diverted and reallocated to Senator Bautista's firms for other projects, such as the Morne à Cabri project.

- Instead of terminating the contracts signed under former Premier Conille and issuing new ones to reflect the changes, the Martelly-Lamothe government kept them and added amendments. This reprehensible practice, according to Planning Minister Joséfa Gauthier, is a continuation of a system established by former Minister Bellerive, who drafted the first amendments on May 16, 2011.

The prosecutor pauses and then continues:

— "Let's now turn to the case of Olivier Martelly. Under his father's regime, Olivier Martelly became one of the most visible figures in national sports policy. In the public eye, the line between biological lineage and delegation of power blurs long before it reaches the benches of this court. The former president's son calls the statements of the Minister of Sports, Max Attys, who accuses him of wasting and embezzling funds intended for the construction of sports infrastructure from the Petro Caribe program, lies."

In a letter published on July 15, 2020, in the newspaper *Le Nouvelliste*, Olivier Martelly recalls that he served as President Martelly's advisor on youth and sports matters during his term. Appointed by presidential decree in June 2012 as Coordinator of the Commission for Supporting Sports Infrastructure and Accompanying Haitian Youth (CACUSAJH), he explains that his work consisted of "promoting sports activities for young people and monitoring the implementation of infrastructure projects decided upon by the government, which could contribute to the development of youth in the field of sports." He emphasizes that these interventions were part of the "Foutbòl pou chanjman" (Football for Change) program.

—Olivier Martelly protests in the most vehement and categorical manner, against the statements of the former Minister of Youth and Sports. He affirms that, as an advisor, he was never authorized to commit the Haitian State. He was also never accountable for public funds and never managed public funds on behalf of or with the State.

The prosecutor pauses again and, in a firm voice, gives his opinion on the matter.

— "Your Honor, Olivier Martelly is completely contradicting himself. He claims to have had no authority to commit the Haitian state. This is false. In September 2018, he submitted a request for discharge to the Court of Auditors for his management of the Presidential

Commission, which he headed under his father's administration. This request was rejected by the CSCCA."

The damning indictment, delivered in a terse tone by the prosecution, had the effect of a dagger thrust into the defendant's heart. He buried his face in his hands and began to cry.

The prosecutor, without taking the time to express sympathy for the accused's sentence, adds:

— "Your Honor, as the discussion turns to the qualification of the Haitian national football team, the question arises: where are the new stadiums? History adds a cruel irony here. While the Haitian team qualifies for the World Cup, the country remains unable to provide its players with a field that meets international standards. The Dominican Republic, despite not participating in the World Cup, has sports infrastructure financed in part by Petro Caribe funds; Haiti has nothing, or rather, Haiti has the players and its Dominican neighbor has the stadiums."

The president shook his head. The prosecutor smiled inwardly; "as soon as a magistrate shakes his head, it means he's made up his mind."

Without leaving anyone to guess his thoughts, he continued:

— "Your Honor, we don't even have a decent football pitch in Haiti. State money that was meant to build sports centers has been embezzled. 'Nèg yo kraze lajan an…' (These gentlemen stole the money), declared the Minister of Sports, Max Attys, during a press conference."

A profound weariness pervades the courtroom. Outside, the country is momentarily united by the Grenadiers' qualification for the World Cup, a rare moment of collective pride. Inside, they are dissecting the corpse of a parallel universe where this pride could have been domestic, every day. The unbuilt stadiums become the ultimate symbol of the corruption of Haitian leaders who have crippled an entire nation. The defendants did not simply take the money; they knowingly chose to deprive the people of their shared dream spaces. The crime thus transcends mere fraud and stems from a profoundly anti-social evil.

The prosecutor continues:

— "From the outset of its investigation, the Ethics and Anti-Corruption Commission received documents attesting to expenditures of over $100,000,000 for sports center facilities. In its investigation, the Commission found that this amount was inaccurate. It was only able to locate two contracts, signed respectively by the Bellerive and Lamothe administrations with the firm Secosa. These contracts concerned the construction of sports centers and the installation of artificial turf for games. The initial documents proved to be forgeries."

The prosecutor casts a contemptuous glance at the accused and continued:

"Your Honor, the crime is heinous and the accused are lawless criminals. In the Borgne/Petit Bourg-de-Borgne road rehabilitation project, two firms were awarded contracts to perform the same work on the same section of road. Furthermore, both companies have the same tax registration number, the same accreditation number, and the same business license number. In the "Vincent Gymnasium Rehabilitation" project on Romain Street, a start-up advance of $163,457.43, representing 35% of the initial contract amount, was paid. Article 83 of the implementing decree of October 26, 2009, sets the start-up advance at 25%." As part of the "Rehabilitation of 7 kilometers of road in Lafito" (mill road, 4 lanes), the investigation found that the entire 2% provisional advance payment required in accordance with regulatory provisions, totaling $197,563.28, was not deducted from the invoices submitted by the firm HL Construction SA.

So far, Sophia Martelly has remained silent. A former first lady and central figure in several social programs implemented under the Martelly administration, she embodies, in the public eye, the humanitarian face of the government: that of mothers receiving assistance, children attending school, and so-called vulnerable families. In the collective imagination, her name is associated with compassion and social action. But before the Court, this symbolic capital constitutes neither proof nor protection. The trial does not judge stated intentions; it examines financial flows, management mechanisms, and the actual destination of public funds.

The prosecutor stares at Sophia Martelly, seated with her head bowed in the dock reserved for the accused, and declares:

- "Your Honor, in light of the irregularities uncovered during the investigation, it is fair to say that the ' *EDE PÈP* ' program was a massive waste of public funds. The investigation by the investigating magistrate's office revealed consistent evidence of financial malfeasance. Funds allocated to beneficiaries of the cash transfer component, particularly the *Ti Manman Cheri*, *Kore Etidyan*, *Bon Dijans / Bon de solidarité,* and *Kore Moun Andikape projects*, were misappropriated."

- In relation to the projects implemented by the Bureau for the Monetization of Development Assistance Programs (BMPAD), the Court proceeded to analyze the two BMPAD projects.

- It appears that these projects were not implemented efficiently, effectively, and economically. Indeed, several irregularities were observed: some caused harm to the project and the community, others contravened the regulatory framework and best practices, and still others related to administrative management.

Examples of irregularities that caused harm to the project and the community:

- The disbursement of an amount exceeding the actual value of the services provided in the case of a contract, caused damage estimated at 22,429,577.61 gourdes in the context of the solar street lighting electrification project.

- The lack of documentation and relevant justification for the use of management fees related to the monitoring and evaluation of the solar street lighting electrification project.

Examples of irregularities in the regulatory framework for management:

— The lack of rigorous needs and cost estimates demonstrates poor project planning. This is the case, for example, with the solar street lighting electrification project, as well as the project for the construction of food security storage silos.

Examples of administrative irregularities:

- Failure to comply with the provisions of the law of 10 June 2009 establishing the general rules relating to public procurement and public service works agreements was observed in the case of the solar street lighting electrification project, and the project on the "construction of storage silos for food security."

- Regarding the projects implemented by the Ministry of Public Works, Transportation and Communications (MTPTC), the Court of Auditors analyzed twenty out of 142 projects, representing a value of $ 218,129,224.98, or more than 31% of the revised budgets of the fourteen resolutions. It appears that these projects were not implemented efficiently, effectively, and economically.

Indeed, several irregularities were observed, including those that caused harm to the project and the community, those that contravened the regulatory framework and best practices, and finally, those presenting irregularities of an administrative nature.

The prosecutor continues:

- "Your Honor, in its report on the Petro Caribe affair, the Court of Auditors not only examined the projects carried out, but also studied the process by which they were selected. The corruption appears blatant when one sees how one project is chosen over another, often without a prior feasibility study. The investigation into the misappropriation of funds shed particular light on the arbitrariness that reigns in this area. For example, Petro Caribe funds, earmarked for a social housing project in Port-au-Prince, were misappropriated to purchase and renovate a hotel in Jacmel. The investigation confirmed that there is not the slightest trace of hotel renovation, and moreover, the funds have disappeared. An amount of $ 1,181,246.56 was allocated by the resolution of April 15, 2015, for the project to build a bridge over the Haut du Cap River. This sum was misappropriated and allocated to another project." However, according to the Court of Auditors' investigation, the funds have disappeared.

The prosecutor declares:

"Your Honor, stabilizing the country to attract investment must be the objective of a progressive government. The national sectoral general assemblies and the *Core Group* share this position. Yet, the various Haitian governments that have come to power, particularly those that administered the Petro Caribe program, have squandered funds by committing the following offenses: influence peddling, nepotism, illegal awarding of public contracts, overbilling, forgery, misuse of corporate assets, abuse of office, and several other acts classified as crimes under the law."

At this stage, the prosecutor closes his case, and addressing the president of the court, he declares:

— "Your Honor, given the importance of this trial, I believe it is necessary to request a postponement to allow me to communicate with my fellow deputy prosecutors."

The president:

— "This reprieve is granted. The hearing is suspended. It will resume at 10 a.m. tomorrow."

Chapter 10

THE AUDIT

(The sixth day of the hearing)

Standing by a window on the first floor of the courthouse, Me. Antoine can see everything from where he is. He eagerly awaits the dean's call to begin the session. It is the sixth day of the trial. Outside, he watches the angry crowd: "Kot kòb Petro Caribe a" (Where is the Petro Caribe money?), they shout. He silently contemplates the rooftops of the Dessalines barracks and the National Palace. Both buildings hold their place in the country's history.

Built in 1918, according to the plans of architect Georges Baussan, a former student of the École des Beaux-Arts in Paris, the National Palace is considered the most beautiful palace in the Caribbean. Like the Palace of Justice and the Port-au-Prince City Hall, the building draws its style from French Renaissance architecture and closely resembles buildings erected in France during the late 19th century.

Painted entirely white, the 20,000-square-meter building has three stories, and its entrance pavilion features a portico with four Ionic columns. The roof has three domes and numerous dormer windows. The first palace built on this site was destroyed during a revolt in 1869 that overthrew President Sylvain Salnave. The second palace was destroyed in 1912 when a powder magazine exploded in the basement. The explosion killed the then-president, Cincinnatus Leconte, one year and one day after his inauguration, as well as several hundred soldiers.

In the streets, the cries of the protesters grew louder and louder. Thousands of people gathered to demand justice and protest against their difficult living conditions – poverty, unemployment, unsanitary housing and brutal insecurity – while corruption was rampant.

The prosecutor shakes his head gravely. He thinks to himself:

"How could these high-ranking state officials, accused of theft and dragged before this Assize Court, have the audacity to embezzle all these billions while the Haitian people are starving? What is happening in Haiti is unacceptable. Inequality exists everywhere in the world. In Haiti, it is glaring. The people are starving, mistreated, and despised. It is therefore necessary to break this chain of disparity in order to build the nation. The solution must be revolutionary. The system must be dismantled to change Haiti. Punishing those responsible for the squandering of Petro Caribe funds is the beginning of the work."

Me. Antoine is deep in thought, his eyes half-closed. His eyelids are heavy. He has barely slept for almost a week. He has spent hours studying his notes and preparing his case, knowing that the prosecution he is leading faces a strong defense jointly led by seasoned lawyers.

The prosecutor returns to reality with the voice of the bailiff who tells him:

— "General Prosecutor, it is time to take your seat."

He looks at his watch. Ten o'clock! The time has come to do justice to a nation too often robbed, too often deprived of clear accounts and courageous decisions. The prosecutor is aware of this.

- "Okay, I'll be there right away," he replied to the bailiff.

The court enters. The room rises to its feet as the president and the prosecutors take their seats. As soon as the president steps onto the stage, the air crackles with the tension of the unfolding drama. The courtroom is bathed in light filtering through the large windows. This light casts rays upon the polished woodwork and the files stacked on the desks. The oppressive morning heat is palpable, intensified by the presence of the tightly packed crowd of spectators. Judges, lawyers, journalists, and ordinary citizens occupy every available seat. Their gazes are serious, sometimes strained, and aware of the significance of the moment. In the background, a few murmurs quickly fade away, as if everyone is weighing the weight of what is unfolding. The rustling of papers and the discreet creaking of the benches punctuate the waiting. Some adjust their jackets, others lean forward to whisper comments, while journalists silently move their cameras. Every movement seems amplified by the absolute silence that reigns in the room.

The prosecutor intervenes:

— "Your Honor, the prosecution requests the floor."

— "The Court grants you the floor, dear sir," replied the president.

The prosecutor continues:

— "I request the Court's permission to continue elaborating on the facts."

— "You have it, the president declared.

As the company's lawyer, the public prosecutor knows that the figures he is about to share are not abstract numbers. They correspond to enormous sums, dubious disbursements, forged signatures, and sham contracts signed, while the country descends into lawlessness.

In the room, everyone guesses that this time, it won't be fine phrases that make up the speech, but the figures themselves.

The prosecutor cast a look of disgust at the defendants. Staring at Martelly, Bellerive, Lamothe, Laleau, and their associates, he thought of those corrupt Haitian politicians who had squandered the state coffers, from Cambronne to Duvalier, including Chanoine, Lafontant, and others. He shook his head. Haiti has written the most glorious page of history in the world. It inflicted a humiliating defeat on the most powerful army of the time, forcing Napoleon Bonaparte to abandon his plan to occupy America and sell Louisiana to the Americans. Haiti helped Miranda and Bolívar liberate a group of countries on the South American continent from the yoke of slavery. It contributed to the independence of Greece. How can this country, after so many achievements, be on the list of the poorest countries in the world? The answer is simple: high-ranking officials, placed at the head of the state, like these defendants prosecuted for the squandering of Petro Caribe funds, have led the nation to bankruptcy.

Impunity has become the norm. Despite these blatant crimes and billions stolen, the accused went about their business for years without being held accountable. A weak and hesitant justice system, often riddled with corruption, offered them a safe haven. The courts struggle to reach a verdict, judges, paralyzed by fear, turn a blind eye to the crimes; and the laws, though written to protect the people, remain unenforceable. These Haitian leaders have thrived in the vacuum left by the state, a vacuum that has benefited the most cunning.

The prosecutor, with their eyes fixed on Martelly, wonders how so much evidence can coexist with so much impunity, and why the institutions meant to deliver justice are so powerless to protect the nation.

At this thought, a veil of sadness covered his face. He consulted his notes before continuing:

- "Your Honor, on February 1, 2018, the Senate Assembly requests the Court of Auditors to conduct a management audit of the authorizing officers of the Petro Caribe funds from September 2008 to September 2016, in accordance with Article 200 of the Constitution and the decree of November 23, 2005 amending that of November 4, 1983. The CSCCA has conducted audit work in order to ensure the sound management of the development programs and projects financed by the Petro Caribe funds."

- THE On January 31, 2019, the Court submitted an initial 291-page report on the management of projects financed by the funds. A second 612-page report, submitted in May 2019, analyzed the management of the funds. The third and final report was submitted to the President of the Senate, Pierre François Sildor, on August 18, 2020. It revealed irregularities that had caused harm to the community. This 1,067-page report covers 36.3% of the amounts voted on in the various resolutions. The audit work focused on four main areas: project design, the contract awarding process, the execution of the work, and project closure.

The prosecutor glances towards the dock and declares:

- "Your Honor, allow the prosecution to detail the irregularities and misappropriations of funds observed in the CSCCA audit:"

- Three reports from the Court of Auditors have uncovered numerous instances of fraud and embezzlement in the management of funds. The period covered by the reports spans eight years, from September 2008 to September 2016, and covers three presidencies: that of René Préval (May 2006 to May 2011), that of Michel Martelly (May 2011 to February 2016), and that of Jocelerme Privert (February 2016 to February 2017). The total resources generated by PetroCaribe from 2008 to 2018 amount to more than $4.237 billion.

- According to data received from the BMPAD (Bureau de Monetization des Programmes d'Aide au Développement), from March 5, 2008, the date of the first oil shipment's arrival, to April 14, 2018, the date of the last shipment's arrival, 219 deliveries totaling 43.9 million barrels of fuel were made and sold in Haiti. In addition, there were six shipments of asphalt and three shipments of fuel oil. All of these delivered and sold products generated cumulative revenue of approximately $4,237,598,789.12, distributed as follows:

    - $1,978,802,105.56: Portion paid in cash or within a period not exceeding ninety (90) days;
    - $2,258,796,683.56: portion financing or long-term loan repayable over a period of 17 to 25 years.

Resource usage as of September 30, 2016	Amount in $
Funds allocated to financing development projects (2008 to 2016)	$1,738,691,909.70
BMPAD Budget Funding (cumulative 2008 to 2016)	$20,485,789.64
Power plant financing as of September 30, 2016	$612,161,711.62
Long-term debt repayment as of September 30, 2016	$21,882,502.87
Total usage from 2008 to 2016	$2,393,221,913.83

Source: Data compiled from financial statements obtained from the BMPAD (2008 to 2016)
Table from the CSCCA report

Each figure displayed in the table is more than just a dollar amount. This is proof of the staggering scale of the embezzlement. More than $4 billion allocated to the country's development was redistributed, transferred, and never used for the public good. Every line of the report tells a story of promised funds and broken promises, a cold accounting that opens the debate on the mismanagement of Petro Caribe funds. An oil program, whose profits should have been used to build roads, schools, hospitals, and complete many other projects; yet, the billions were squandered…

The prosecutor continues:

- "The revenue from the sale of petroleum products from Venezuela," the Court's final report states, "constituted a significant financial lever for successive governments between 2008 and 2016 and even beyond. But, at the same time, it contributed to increasing the country's level of debt." (page 26)

- From September 2008 to September 2016, the CSCCA identified 409 projects stemming from 14 resolutions adopted by the Council of Ministers, totaling US$2,238,164,040.74. Following a series of reallocations and adjustments, the budget was revised to US$1,738,691,909.70. According to BMPAD disbursement reports, US$1,605,905,287.84 (92.4%) was disbursed for project financing. The breakdown of resolutions adopted by the Council of Ministers under the administrations of the three presidents is as follows: under the presidency of René Garcia Préval, four resolutions were signed, totaling US$546.6 million; Under Michel Joseph Martelly, nine resolutions were passed for a total of approximately $1.04 billion; finally, under Jocelerme Privert, only one resolution was passed for $16 million.

Enormous funds were allocated, and bureaucratic efficiency was almost perfect, but entirely reversed. In a football match, such a percentage would mean the ball was in play for almost the entire game. Here, it means the money has almost entirely left the state coffers, disappearing into the black hole of corruption. These men and women (the prosecution points its finger at the accused) were remarkably efficient at emptying the state coffers, but utterly incapable of producing the slightest public good. The contrast is striking: an administration capable of disbursing billions with lightning speed, yet incapable of effectively executing a project.

The prosecutor looks up at the accused, his silence amounting to an accusation.

— "All these documents are in the file," the prosecutor added, before continuing:

— "Your Honor, that we display on the screen the amount budgeted by resolutions and by government."

— "The Court authorizes you to do so, Prosecutor," the president replied.

The prosecutor then opens the large screen and displays the data.

	Resolutions	Presidency	signatory government	Budget by resolution $	Revised budget after allocations $	Amounts transferred by BMPAD $
1	20/09/2008	Preval	Michèle Duvivier Pierre-Louis	$197,560,000	$197,560,000	$197,560,000
2	11/02/2010	Preval	Jean Max Bellerive	$163,287,848	$157,719,896	$157,719,896.18
3	24/08/2010	Preval	Jean Max Bellerive	$107,400,000	$94,597,097.69	$94,357,661.45
4	12/05/2011	Preval	Jean Max Bellerive	$108,799,883	$96,923,836.14	$96,923,836.14
5	28/02/2012	Martelly	Garry Conille	$234,956,000	$210,303,227.68	$210,303,222.68
6	18/07/2012	Martelly	Laurent Lamothe	$130,000,000	$96,195,625.80	96,195,625.80

7	21/12/2012	Martelly	Laurent Lamothe	$374,800,000	$329,386,735.04	$329,386,735.05
8	11/12/2013	Martelly	Laurent Lamothe	$210,967,318.33	$164,517,228.97	$164,517,228.97
9	23/07/2014	Martelly	Laurent Lamothe	$141,778,568	$71,215,839.38	$71,215,839.38
10	10/09/2014	Martelly	Laurent Lamothe	$29,697,201.29	$7,000,000	$7,000,000
11	15/04/2015	Martelly	Evans Paul	$254,423,560	$47,525,624.19	$47,525,624.90
12	22/07/2015	Martelly	Evans Paul	$193,055,824.56	$174,308,966.07	$101,010,358.99
13	06/01/2016	Martelly	Evans Paul	$58,169,108.56	$58,169,108.56	$16,204,383.67
14	28/09/2016	Privert	Enex J. Charles	$33,268,729	$33,268,729	$15,984,874.63
				$2,238,164,040.74	$1,738,691,909.70	$1,605,905,287.84

The prosecutor closes the screen and declares:

- "An analysis of the 41 contracts signed in 2010 by the Haitian government revealed that six were awarded following the competitive bidding process. The others were signed with individuals close to the government. The firm awarded the public works contract for the Legislative Palace, for $33 million, was created on July 28, 2010 (*Le Moniteur,* September 13, 2010). At the time of signing the contract, on November 8, 2010, it was therefore only three months old, while the law requires five years of existence and experience. A newly founded Dominican company was awarded a contract for the construction of eight kilometers of road, already laid out, for $33 million. The international average at that time was around one million dollars per kilometer of road." Another Dominican firm obtained a contract worth $133 million in November 2010. This firm was founded in May 2006. A third firm, owned by Dominican Senator Félix Bautista, obtained several contracts for a total value of $178 million.

- As for the negotiated contracts, totaling US$83 million, a single firm secured nine of them in six months, worth US$33 million; another obtained sixteen for US$6 million. Of these 35 negotiated contracts, sixteen were signed in a single day, May 12, 2010. In addition to these contracts signed with Dominican firms for over US$380 million, the lease of two helicopters for US$1.5 million per year is a clear example of corruption within the state and the country's poor governance.

- In light of the results obtained and the irregularities observed, it is fair to say that the *EDE PÈP program* was a massive waste of public funds, the Court of Auditors writes in its second report. Hundreds of thousands of beneficiaries without phone numbers. All this waste, according to the Court, was orchestrated in the name of fighting poverty and social exclusion, to the detriment of the most vulnerable populations who were supposed to be the beneficiaries of the programs.

The prosecutor thinks for a moment. He pauses and then said:

- *EDE PÈP* program was supposed to support the most vulnerable Haitians by providing them with financial assistance, school supplies, and social support. In reality, hundreds of thousands of beneficiaries didn't even have phone numbers, making any follow-up impossible. The funds, instead of being distributed to the people, were misappropriated at various stages: overestimation of amounts, fictitious suppliers, and falsified reports. According to the Court, this waste was orchestrated in the name of fighting poverty, but deprived the most vulnerable populations of the promised aid."

- By comparison, the Dominican Republic, with a smaller social budget, has implemented similar programs like "*Progresando con Solidaridad*" *(Progressing with Solidarity)* , which closely monitor beneficiaries using reliable databases, verified phone numbers, and regular field visits. Every *peso* spent is tracked and evaluated, allowing for a real impact on the lives of poor families. In Haiti, the money from the *EDE PÈP program*, which could have transformed lives, was squandered, demonstrating not only inefficiency but also the degree of corruption among those in charge. Where the Dominican Republic invests in transparency and monitoring, Haiti invests in waste and fraud.

— The Court of Auditors revealed in the final report that it had detected consistent indications of financial malfeasance in part of the funds intended to be allocated to the beneficiaries of the money transfer component, and in particular the projects: *Ti Manman Cheri* , *Kore Etidyan* , *Bon Dijans* / *Solidarity Bond* and *Kore Moun Andikape.*

- *Ti Manman Cheri*: The Court discovered that 20,850 "fictitious" beneficiaries were paid and never had a phone number. Regarding the mobile canteen, the government ordered the disbursement of $13 million, and the CSCCA obtained no evidence of how this money was used. Concerning the *Kore Etidyan* project, the figures for the number of enrolled students are erroneous, having been inflated and not reflecting reality. The investigation into the *Solidarity Bond / Dijans Bond projects* revealed that a total of 60,757 fictitious beneficiaries were paid. The FAES artificially inflated the amounts advanced as direct transfers to the beneficiaries, either in cash or in kind.

The prosecutor adds:

- "*Ti Manman Cheri!* The very name is a stab in the collective conscience. These men and women stole under the guise of supposed concern for mothers. They embezzled money intended for students, the poor, and the disabled. This perversion of humanitarian discourse is perhaps the most heinous crime. Today, the country resonates with its *Grenadiers*, a nickname that exudes strength and honor. Two narratives clash: the noble one, chosen by the people and associated with sport, and the ignoble one, imposed upon them by their leaders through the mismanagement of public affairs."

The prosecutor continues:

- "The investigation further revealed that the alleged payment amounts do not correspond to reality. An advance of over one million dollars was transferred to Chal Construction for the rehabilitation of the Carrefour road section in Trois-Rivières-Trois-Anse-à-Foleur. The Court of Auditors' report shows, with supporting images, that no work was carried out to repair this section of road. Moreover, the project execution reports were not available in the documentation provided to the Court by the Ministry of Public Works, Transport and Communications (MTPTC). The equivalent of 80,662,176.45 HTG, drawn from the budget allocated to the Port-de-Paix/Port-Margot road section rehabilitation project, was used for other purposes. The Ennery/Cap-Haïtien road improvement project, costing approximately six million dollars, was negligently managed, according to the Court."

The prosecutor pauses. He takes a moment to catch his breath, and then continues:

- "Amidst all these shady dealings, the name of one financial institution has been clearly mentioned. It is the FAES (Economic and Social Assistance Fund), a government agency in Haiti that aims to reduce poverty and support vulnerable populations through programs such as food aid, infrastructure improvements (roads), and job creation. The FAES often works with the IDB and the WFP to finance social security and post-crisis recovery projects. A key player in social and economic development efforts in Haiti, managing funds and projects aimed at improving citizens' living conditions, the FAES is deeply implicated in the major scandal related to the misappropriation of Petro Caribe funds. Billions of dollars, intended for social development, were embezzled by unscrupulous Haitian and foreign politicians and businesspeople."

- Regarding the FAES, it's worth remembering that this is the organization that made $67 million disappear. This fund was intended to help the poor, women, and students through the eight *EDE PÈP social programs*. However, the program turned out to be an extraordinary scam, with a total of 81,607 fictitious beneficiaries.

- As an example, the investigation indicates that the total amount injected and received directly from TMC beneficiaries between 2012 and 2016 amounted to 579,986,600 HTG. This figure does not correspond to reality. Indeed, according to data compiled by the investigation based on invoices and transfer orders obtained from FAES, the amount paid to mothers is actually 211,791,800 HTG. There is therefore a discrepancy of approximately 368,194,800 HTG, which confirms that the figures for payments to beneficiaries are misleading and do not reflect reality. Furthermore, no payments were made for the subsequent fiscal years 2014-2015 and 2015-2016.

Chapter 11

THE EMBEZZLEMENTS ARE ENORMOUS

Reviewing his notes, the public prosecutor continues:

— "Your Honor, the majority of contracts signed between the Haitian State and suppliers are tainted by irregularities. These irregularities include the misappropriation of funds allocated to the implementation of certain projects, the payment of unjustified invoices, the falsification of payroll slips, and a number of projects undertaken without a needs assessment and cost estimate."

Installation of a Computer Laboratory in the Commune of Les Cayes

— The investigation audited the project to install a Computer Laboratory in the commune of Les Cayes. Several actions taken by the Ministry of Tourism and Creative Industries (MTIC) did not meet good management criteria.

— The contract, valued at 3,125,000 HTG, was awarded without competitive bidding on August 21, 2015, without any documented justification. The method used to award this contract is inappropriate. Indeed, the amount is less than eight million gourdes, and the

Ministry of Information and Communication Technologies (MTIC) has not demonstrated that it awarded the contract based solely on a memorandum of understanding or invoice, while adhering to the principles of equal treatment of candidates, competition, transparency, ethics, efficiency of public spending, and public accounting rules (Article 27-1 of the Law of June 10, 2009, on Public Procurement and Article 6, second paragraph, of the Decree of May 25, 2012, on Thresholds).

However, the project was delivered more than 45 days late compared to the delivery date stipulated in the contract.

Construction of the Fontamara Public Market

The Court of Auditors reviewed the project financed by the Petro Caribe fund and implemented by the Ministry of Planning and External Cooperation (MPCE). The Court noted that the fourth clause of this contract refers to the decree of December 5, 2012, extending the state of emergency for one month, while the contract was signed in November 2012. Therefore, it is unusual for a contract signed in November 2012 to refer to a decree issued later. Furthermore, the first resolution concerning the financing of this project was adopted on December 21, 2012; nearly a month after the contract was signed.

— The review and analysis of the documents submitted to the Court established that the amounts stipulated in the contract were not fully paid to the contractor and that the project was not completed. It was simply abandoned. However, disbursements totaling $6,164,385.12 were made, representing 39.4% of the contract amount.

— The visit carried out by the CSCCA technical team revealed that a large part of the work still remains to be completed. The beams remain without formwork, the metal-framed halls have not been erected, the main and secondary road improvements have not been carried out, and the parking areas and unloading platforms for the different types of vehicles have not been completed.

INSTITUTION AUDITED
MINISTRY OF PLANNING AND
EXTERNAL COOPERATION

Project Name	Construction Public Market Fontamara
Resolutions	• December 21, 2012: \$6,500,000 • July 22, 2015: \$4,974,035.29 • January 6, 2016: \$300,000
Funding	PetroCaribe Fund
Firm	IBT, LLC
Contract awarding process	• By agreement • Contract Value : \$15,647,900 • The contract received a favorable opinion from the CSCCA • Absence of a no-objection opinion from the CNMP • The date of signing the contract is unclear (November 2012) • The contract straddles two emergency decrees
Responsibilities	Minister • Laurent Salvador Lamothe (MPCE) • Yves Germain Joseph (MPCE) • Michel Présumé (Secretary of State MPCE) • Wilson Laleau (MEF) Contractor • Execution Firm: Gianfranco Florenza (IBT, LLC) • Natacha Brea (CSA Central, Inc.) • Gino Charles (CSA Central, Inc.)

The presentation of facts at this particular stage of the proceedings is not simply a list of unexecuted or abandoned projects; it is an implacable narrative construction, moving from the macroeconomic context (millions of dollars disbursed) to micro-level evidence (contracts signed without any description of the work). Every figure is an incredible distortion.

In the same vein, the public prosecutor's office continues:

Urban Renovation in Hinche (phases I & II)

20, 2012, a contract was signed between the Haitian State, represented by the Minister of Planning and External Cooperation, Mr. Laurent Salvador Lamothe, and the firm Secosa, represented by Jean-Émile Laferrière, for the urban renewal of the city of Hinche (phases I & II), including drainage and paving. The Court examined the project and noted several irregularities.

— The contract contains no description of the work and no timetable. The Court is of the opinion that the absence of such fundamental parameters constitutes a risk that public funds will not be allocated to the relevant work, that budgets will be exceeded and objectives will not be met, thereby causing harm to the project and the community.

— The interests of the State are not protected. The Court notes that the contracting parties have not taken into account the provisions of Article 76 of the Decree of 29 September 2005 (*Moniteur* of 5 October 2005, Special No. 10) on income tax.

— The Court's technical team conducted a site visit. The technical documents (plans and topographic surveys) provided by the MPCE do not allow for a clear distinction between the work that should be carried out for each phase (I & II). The site visit revealed that the drainage work on Véronique 1 to Véronique 6 streets, all perpendicular to the street (Maguana Hotel area), has not been completed. Furthermore, streets 10A and B1 to B6 have not been identified by the Court.

Road Renovation/Noailles Croix des Bouquets Artistic Village

— On October 7, 2011, a contract was signed between the Haitian State, represented by the Minister of Planning, Mr. Jean Max Bellerive, and the contracting firm ECCO SA, represented by

Franck Richard Cave. This contract, awarded without competitive bidding, was signed without a notice of objection from the National Commission for Public Procurement (CNMP).

- resolution of July 18, 2012 for an amount of $2,000,000
- resolution of December 21, 2012 for an amount of $1,500,000
- resolution of December 11, 2013 for an amount of $1,000,000
- Total: $4,500,000

— The Court found irregularities in the regulatory framework. The file submitted by the service provider ECCO SA did not contain the basic elements required for it to submit a bid. These include, in particular:

- the articles of association for the company ECCO SA
- the resolution on the appointment of leaders
- the certificate of completion of the tax clearance, the last payment of which is dated May 12, 2009. It cannot be ensured that the company is up to date or active at the time of the contractual signing on October 7, 2011.

— Regarding irregularities, the Court noted that the disbursement granted for the amount of the advance to the firm ECCO SA was not respected and amounts to 57%, more than double what was initially provided for in the contract.

— Moreover, Article 7 states that an amount representing 40% will be paid to the contractor upon signing the contract, namely $890,000. In contrast, the advance payment was $1,278,804, a difference of $388,804.

— The Court noted that important clauses designed to protect the interests of the Haitian State were not included in the contract, in particular:

- the 2% withholding tax;
- The amount of $10,172.66 as advance repayments on the provisional deposit was not deducted from the contract.

Construction of the Bus Station and Public Market in Miragoâne

— On October 20, 2011, a contract was signed by the Ministry of Planning and External Cooperation (MPCE), represented by Mr. Jude Hervey Day, and the firm INGENIERIA ESTRELLA, represented by J. Alejandro Adames B. The Court noted that no duration, no description of the work and no schedule were specified in the contract.

— The Court noted the following irregularities:

- the 2% withholding tax is not recorded in the contract;
- The method of repayment of advances is not stipulated.

—The Court also noted irregularities in the regulations. The 25% advance payment initially stipulated in the contract for the firm INGENIERIA ESTRELLA was not respected. 30% was disbursed instead of 25%, amounting to $984,000 instead of $820,000.

- The Court noted discrepancies in compliance with the regulatory framework regarding the solicitation process related to cost estimation. The initial projected cost for the project was $7,735,135, equivalent to 331,598,275.83 gourdes. This contract should have been subject to an open tender (reference Article 2 of the Order of May 25, 2012), which sets the threshold for public procurement of works at 40,000,000 gourdes. Furthermore, the CNMP's no-objection notice was not obtained, which constitutes a violation of Article 106 of the Order of October 26, 2009, specifying the implementing procedures for the law establishing the general rules relating to public procurement and concession agreements for public works.

- Regarding the physical progress of the work, the planned duration is 24 months. The initial payment was made on April 22, 2013. Following problems related to the land expropriation, work finally began in September 2014. However, the Court's technical team visited the site and observed that the contractor had completed the landscaping, earthworks, retaining wall, drainage, and roadwork. Nevertheless, some foundations for the market have been prepared, while others remain at the foundation stage. The final payment was made in February 2016. During this period, the work reached a completion rate of 35.27%, according to the comparative assessment by Groupe Trame, the supervising firm.

- Ultimately, the Court finds that construction work on the public market and bus station in Miragoâne has been abandoned. Officials from the Ministry of Planning and External Cooperation (MPCE) did not specify the reasons for this failure.

Project Summary

- According to the information gathered, the amount of $8,600,000 adopted by the resolution of April 15, 2015 has been partially disbursed. The contract' s estimated cost of $7,735,135 does not correspond to the resolution authorizing the project. The amount paid for completed work represents 46%, or $3,550,801.66. However, 20% of this 46% was disbursed on April 22, 2013, as a start-up advance to account number 121252214 at the BNC (National Credit Bank), entitled "MPCE Public Investment Program," even though the project had not yet been identified by the BMPAD Board of Directors. In fact, 26% of the amount was disbursed under the resolution adopted on April 15, 2015. Herntz St Marc, the UTE's deputy coordinator, noted that due to the expropriation issue, work began in September 2014, seventeen months late from the date of the first payment.

- The financial management analysis shows that there was no prior planning for the project. Those in charge only took advantage of the emergency law to evade the obligation to use competitive bidding.

Responsibilities

First level	1. Laurent Salvador Lamothe, Chief Authorizing Officer of Expenditure 2. Yves Germain Joseph, Chief Authorizing Officer of Expenditure 3. Giovanni Dorélien, Deputy General Manager 4. Sabine C. Dalice, Deputy Administrative Director.
Second level Managers of the supervision firm	1. Elizabeth Coicou, General Manager (TRAME Group) 2. Nathalie Abraham, Administrative Director (TRAME Group)
Third level Head of execution firms	1. Patrice Milfort, Managing Director

Overbilling, embezzlement, fraud, theft, abuse of power, influence peddling, forgery, criminal conspiracy… The account of the facts continues:

Construction of the Fermathe-Frères road section via Duplan, Soisson, Meyotte, Girardeau

— "A contract has been signed between the Ministry of Planning, represented by Minister Jean-Max Bellerive, and the managers of the firm Groupe de Travaux de Construction, represented by engineer

Yves Coles, for the construction of the section of the Fermathe-Frères road via Duplan, Soisson, Meyotte, Girardeau.

- The contract stipulated 18.2 kilometers. However, the Court's assessment determined that only 9 kilometers had actually been completed, representing 49.45% of the total work. 9.02 kilometers of road remained to be built. Yet, 92.86% of the contract amount, or $21,075,724.64, had been disbursed.

- The Court noted several irregularities. The amount allocated to the contract did not correspond to the amount stipulated in the resolution authorizing the project. The initial payment, a partial advance, was disbursed for a contract signed on February 11, 2010. This contract was replaced by another signed on December 15, 2010, following a decision by officials to reduce the project's cost.

Responsibilities

<u>First level</u> Names, surnames and titles of central administration officials	1. Jean Max Bellerive (MPCE) principal authorizing officer of expenditures 2. Laurent Salvador Lamothe (MPCE), principal authorizing officer of expenditures 3. Yves Robert Jean, Director General (MPCE) 4. Wilner Valcin, Deputy Director General (MPCE) 5. Giovanni Dorélien, Deputy Director General (MPCE) 6. Sabine C. Dalice, Deputy Administrative Director (MPCE)

Second level The managers of the supervisory firm	1. Bernard Chancy, Managing Director 2. Philippe Larouche, head of mission
Third level The managers of the construction works group	1. Eng. Yves Coles, General Manager 2. Engineer Mrs. Marie Jose Joseph

Construction of the Arcahaie Public Market

—A contract was signed between the Ministry of Planning, represented by Jean Max Bellerive, and the firm GTC, represented by Mr. Yves Coles, for the construction of the Arcahaie public market. The Court noted several irregularities in the execution of the project.

— The two resolutions for a total of $4,000,000 were adopted in May 2011 and February 2012. The contract has been signed since May 10, 2010.

Administrative Disputes (CSCCA) notes that the project was already underway when the two resolutions were passed and had received funding from the Public Treasury through the Public Investment Program (PIP). The amount disbursed for the project before the resolutions were passed was $2,163,500. In addition to this amount, the Court found that an unjustified additional $100,000 was paid to an individual named Gilbert Chenet. In total, $4,100,000 was disbursed from PetroCaribe funds for this project, representing an overpayment of $100,000.

Responsibilities

First level Names, surnames, titles of central administration officials	1. Jean Max Bellerive, Chief Authorizing Officer (MPCE) 2. Jude Hervey Day (MPCE) 3. Joséfa R. Gauthier (MPCE) 4. Laurent Salvador Lamothe (MPCE) 5. Ronald Beaudin (MEF) 6. Marie Carmelle Jean Marie (MEF) 7. Wilner Valcin, Deputy Director General (MPCE)
Second level	
Third level	Yves Coles, Managing Director, GTC

Urban Renewal of Limbe (Partial Funding)

—A contract was concluded between the Ministry of Planning, represented by Jean-Max Bellerive, and the firm J&J Construction, represented by Hérode Thélusma.

—The Court's review of the contract revealed that not all contractual provisions were being met in its execution. An open tender process should have been launched to select the contractor. The information contained in the Terms of Reference (TORs) does not allow for anticipating events that could negatively impact the objectives pursued, and, more importantly, for making the best decisions to mitigate the likelihood of such events recurring.

— The document supporting the award of this contract was not issued based on a prior and documented needs assessment, in violation of the justification and traceability requirements imposed by public procurement procedures. No invoice was submitted and no progress report is identified for validating the level of completion.

— The firms responsible for supervision are designated and identified in the documents for a contract amount of 18,000,000 gourdes. No provisional or final acceptance documents were provided in the file.

— The lack of documentation did not allow the Court to confirm whether the guidelines provided for in the regulatory and contractual frameworks were respected, in particular with regard to the withholdings provided for, such as retention of guarantee (5%), good performance (5%) and taxes (2%).

Audited Institution: Ministry of Planning and External Cooperation (MPCE)	
Resolutions	1. May 12, 2011: $3,500,000 2. July 18, 2012: $2,000,000 3. December 21, 2012: $2,000,000 Total: $7,500,000 (Petro Caribe Fund)
Responsibilities	
First level Names, surnames and titles of the heads of the Central Administration	1. Jean Max Bellerive, Chief Authorizing Officer (MPCE) 2. Jude Hervey Day (MPCE) 3. Aviol Fleurant (MPCE) 4. Ronald Beaudin (MPCE) 5. Marie Carmelle Jean Marie (MPCE) 6. Wilson Laleau (MEF) 7. André Lemercier Georges (MEF)

Second level	1. Herod Thelusma (J&J Construction)
Third level	1. Paul-Erick Bruno, Executive Director (BECA Engineering)

The reports are damning. Official documents reveal serious misconduct, major breaches of duty, and incriminating evidence, cornering the defendants named in the indictment. The prosecution pays no attention to the effect its presentation has on the court. It continues to publicly disclose the projects: contracts negotiated clandestinely, inflated prices, misappropriated funds, and never executed. In short, sham projects…

Reconstruction of the Toussaint Louverture High School (including supervision)

—"The main findings related to this project are as follows:

- The contract amount of $8,029,900 or 341,400,031.39 gourdes exceeds the public procurement threshold requiring an open tender, as stipulated in Article 2 of the Decree of May 25, 2012, which sets the Public Procurement Thresholds and the Intervention Thresholds of the National Public Procurement Commission for works contracts up to 40,000,000 gourdes. The project benefited from the emergency law period.
- In the course of executing the contract, the Court noted the existence of two firms through the files of the Market in question:

1) The firm International Business and Trade LLC (ref: firm's registration file). This firm was selected when the contract was signed.

2) IBT HAITI S.A. This firm was used to receive the funds.

— However, the Court was unable to locate the following legal documents:

- The issue of the official journal of Haiti (Le Moniteur) publishing the existence of the firm "IBT HAITI SA" or the right to operate "IBT, LLC" in Haiti;
- The firm's notarized status and the list of its shareholders;
- The certificate of incorporation of its share capital issued by the National Credit Bank (BNC) representing 25% of the share capital.

— As for the foreign firm IBT LLC, the Court noted that the signature of the Consul of Haiti in Miami was not authenticated by the Ministry of Foreign Affairs in Haiti during the registration of the files of said firm as required by the law on public limited companies.

— The amount disbursed represents $6,654,069.24.

The Court noted that the first phase had been completed. However, more than 80% of the contract amount had been spent, so a new contract was required to complete the remaining work. However, the Ministry of Planning and External Cooperation (MPCE) failed to provide any information to the student community or users regarding the interruption of the second phase of the project.

— The project is not completed due to lack of funds, which reflects poor planning.

Project Summary

— The project is not completed due to a lack of funds, which reflects poor planning.

— As for the files of the firm IBT, LLC & or IBT HAITI SA, no publication of their existence in the official journal "*Le Moniteur*" has been traced as required by law;

— Finally, the amount of the provisional advance payment of $146,588.74 was not collected on behalf of the Directorate General of Taxes (DGI).

Ministry of Planning and External Cooperation (MPCE)	
Project name	Reconstruction of the Toussaint Louverture High School
Resolutions	December 12, 2013: $2,000,000 April 15, 2015: $5,544,708 July 22, 2015: $1,816,427.65 July 6, 2016: $2,843,391.25
Total Financing	$12,204,526.90 (PetroCaribe Fund)

Responsibilities	
First Level	1. Laurent Salvador Lamothe, Chief Authorizing Officer (MPCE) 2. Yves Germain Joseph, Principal Authorizing Officer (MPCE) 3. Michel Présumé, Secretary of State for Planning 4. Giovanni Dorélien (Deputy Director of the MPCE) 5. Sabine C. Dalice, Assistant Director MPCE 6. Marie Carmelle Jean-Marie (MEF) 7. Wilson Laleau (MEF) 8. Ghammald Francillon (UTE/PRU coordinator of the MPCE)
<u>Second level</u> Those responsible for the supervision firm: CSA Central Inc.	
<u>Third level</u> The managers of the firm IBT Haiti SA	

Rehabilitation of the Borgne Road/Petit Bourg de Borgne section

— The Borgne Road / Petit Bourg de Borgne rehabilitation project was financed through two resolutions taken in the Council of Ministers for a final value of $633,199.52.

Resolution History

Resolutions	Initial amount	Assignment/ Reassignment	Revised amount
July 18, 2012	$1,000,000		$633,199.52
April 15, 2015		$366,800.48	
Total	$1,000,000		$633,199.52

— The CSCCA examined this project and noted that the actors involved in its management managed it without concern for efficiency, effectiveness and economy and not in compliance with the applicable legal and regulatory framework.

— The Court's review of expenditures related to the use of the project start-up advance leads it to conclude that the advance was misused. A portion (66%) of the start-up advance (19,000,000 HTG) was disbursed and used nearly two months before the contract was signed. The Court finds that this decision by the Ministry of Public Works, Transport and Communications (MTPTC) caused irreparable harm to the project and the community.

The Court of Auditors noted that the Ministry of Public Works, Transport and Communications (MTPTC) had transferred 14,000,000 HTG, representing 48.5% of the funds, to the Northern Departmental Directorate (DDN) of the MTPTC. In the absence of supporting documentation for this transaction, the Court is unable to determine the legality of the use of these funds.

The Court makes a troubling observation regarding the second transaction related to this advance. Indeed, on August 26, 2014, well before even being solicited, submitting a technical and financial offer, or signing any contract, the company AGRITRANS received 5,000,000 HTG (check #123564). The transaction description states that this sum is intended for the purchase of fuel for the rehabilitation of the Borgne-Anse à Foleur section of road, a separate project from the rehabilitation project for the Borgne-Petit Bourg de Borgne road section.

— This transfer of 5,000,000 HTG was made to the company AGRITRANS for the purchase of fuel for work related to another project, "the rehabilitation of the Borgne/Anse à Foleur section." The CSCCA considers this decision by the MTPTC illegal and serious. It constitutes an act of misappropriation of public funds that has caused harm to the project and the community.

26 August, 2014, the president of AGRITRANS, Mr. Jovenel Moïse, sent a letter to Minister Jacques Rousseau (MTPTC) along with an invoice requesting an advance of 6,000,000 HTG for the purchase of materials (cement, planks, and aggregates) for the hydraulic concrete paving of the road. The Court was unable to verify that this advance was actually repaid.

The Court noted that, on May 20, 2015, 15,378,893 HTG was withdrawn from the funds of the "Rehabilitation of the Port-de-Paix/Port-Margot section" project and paid to AGRITRANS SA for the execution of the Borgne/Petit Bourg de Borgne road rehabilitation project. A total of 33,818,893 HTG, representing 84.6% of the contract cost, was allocated to AGRITRANS to carry out this project.

— Taking funds dedicated to a specific project and allocating them to another goes against good project management practices and, above all, such a way of doing things causes harm to that project and to the Port-de-Paix/Port-Margot community.

— In its audit work, the Court of Auditors made a disturbing discovery. It noted that, on December 12, 2014, for the same project, the MTPTC awarded another contract to a second firm, namely BETEX, for the execution of works on the same section of the Borgne/Petit Bourg de Borgne road.

- The contract signed between the Ministry of Public Works, Transport and Communications (MTPTC) and BETEX is worth 34,998,785.50 HTG, and this project comes two months after the first contract. Therefore, the MTPTC has signed two contracts for the same project: one with AGRITRANS SA for 39,990,399 HTG and the other with BETEX for 34,998,785.50 HTG.

- During the audit, the CSCCA noted another surprising detail. The contract was signed for the rehabilitation project of the Borgne and Petit Bourg de Borgne section, while the quote associated with this contract relates to a different project, namely the rehabilitation project of the Anse à Foleur/Côte de Fer section.

- A comparative analysis of the two contracts reveals that, for the same project, both companies have the same tax registration number, the same accreditation number, and the same business license number. Furthermore, they share the same technical staff and, most importantly, have the same track record of achievements. Even worse, this analysis shows that the two companies carried out the exact same projects on the same dates, in terms of their specific areas of expertise.

- The Court held that awarding a second contract for the same project, combined with the fact that the submitted estimate actually corresponds to a different project, is nothing more than a scheme to embezzle funds perpetrated by officials at the Ministry of Public Works, Transport and Communications (MTPTC). Such irregularities not only harm the project and the community, but also violate regulations and sound management practices.

In this regard, concerning responsibilities, the Court recalls the following provisions, in particular Article 37 of the Decree of May

17, 2005, concerning the organization of the central government administration. This article stipulates that: "The Minister is personally responsible for the acts he signs or countersigns." The Court also wishes to recall that Article 21 of the Order of February 16, 2005, concerning public accounting, stipulates that "the authorizing officer is solely responsible for commitments he has entered into in violation of the laws and regulations in force or beyond the limits of the allocated appropriations."

Responsibilities	• Jacques Rousseau, Minister of Public Works, Transport and Communications • Jovenel Moïse, President of AGRITRANS SA • Martel Webert Pierre, President of BETEXS • Fritz Saint-Paul, signatory for the CSCCA

Consternation is widespread. Each side has its own specific reactions. On the defense side, there's panic. How can they defend a case with all this evidence of fraud and embezzlement? The facts of the misappropriation are so compelling that no further proof is needed to know the truth. The reality is there. No doubt, no uncertainty. The accused have shamelessly plundered the state.

On the side of the plaintiffs, there was surprise. The young members of the Petro Challenger collective knew full well, before the trial, that billions had been embezzled. They were unaware that the methods used were so despicable and unethical.

The prosecutor, focused on its role of presenting the facts of the case, continues:

Rehabilitation/development of public squares (Saint-Anne – Geffrard - Occide Jeanty - Airport and Canapé-Vert)

- "The contracts relating to these five public squares were signed by mutual agreement in November 2012 under the aegis of the decree of November 5, 2012 declaring a state of emergency over the entire national territory for a period of one month, in accordance with the law of April 15, 2010.

Accounts Receipts and Disbursements by Execution Firms

Firms	Projects	Amount of disbursements $/HTG
SOGECOMAT	Construction of Places Saint-Anne and Geffrard	$736,586.99 / 44,423,206.74
CEEPCO HAITI SA	Construction Place Occide Jeanty	$2,789,450.02 / 142,877,798.37
TECINA	Construction Place Canapé-Vert	$340,416.10 / $14,659,148.39
GENERAL CONSTRUCTION AND DISTRIBUTION SA	Airport Square Construction	$1,925,517.72 / 90,475,281.22
Total		$5,791,970.83 / 292,435,434.7

Public Square Rehabilitation/Construction and Development Project

Resolutions	July 18, 2012: \$5,000,000 or 209,718,500 HTG December 21, 2012: \$3,000,000 or 127,824,900 HTG April 15, 2015: \$3,085,072.65 or 145,836,320.28 HTG April 15, 2015: \$3,994,216 or 188,812,981.10 HTG Total PetroCaribe financing: \$8,909,143.35 or 380,520,060.82 HTG

Responsibilities	<u>First Level</u> : Laurent Salvador Lamothe, Minister of Planning Yves Germain Joseph, Minister of Planning Michel Présumé, Secretary of State for Planning <u>Second level</u> Renald Pascal, CEO of SOGECOMAT Harold R. Charles, CEO CEEPCO HAITI SA Gérald Émile Brun, Vice-President of TECINA SA

Project Summary

- According to available information, the project, totaling 292,435,434.72 HTG, was approved through three resolutions totaling \$8,909,143.35 or 380,520,060.82 HTG. No documentation was provided to justify the funding. The project's execution appears to violate both sound public fund management and good project management practices.

- The contracts were signed by the three contracting parties: the project owner, the contractor, and the CSCCA. The significant lack of documentation justifying expenditures and the delivery of the planned quantities indicates a serious deficiency in control mechanisms. The MPCE did not comply with regulations concerning project accounting, as all the accounting documents necessary for auditing the project were not available. This project should have maintained general accounting for all operations, in accordance with the general rules and principles of public accounting. (Article 17 of the decree establishing the implementing procedures for the decree of October 4, 1984, concerning Public Investment funds).

Construction of 5 km of sidewalks in the city of Port-de-Paix

- A contract has been signed between UCLBP and the firm BDFK for the construction of 5 kilometers of sidewalks in the city of Port-de-Paix.

- Upon reviewing the file, the CSCCA noted the following irregularities:

- The contract amount of 18,000,000 HTG is below the 40,000,000 HTG threshold established by Article 2, paragraph 1 of the decree of May 25, 2012, which sets the threshold for awarding public works contracts. UCLBP contracted a single firm to execute the project. Furthermore, the contract was awarded without consulting suppliers or engaging in competitive bidding.

- The 60% start-up advance exceeds the 30% threshold and is not guaranteed according to articles 83 and 83-1 of the law of June 12, 2009.

- The 2% advance payment for the amount of 108,000 HTG was collected, but not paid to the DGI.

- The technical specifications, including plans and clearance, have been paid by UCLBP for 88.20% of the funds, amounting to 15,876,000 HTG. The remaining 10%, amounting to 1,800,000 HTG, has not yet been paid.

Responsibilities	First Level
	Mr. Harry Adam, Executive Director
	Mr. Ervé Pierre Louis, Director of Buildings and Head of Social Projects
	Ms. Micheline D. Rampy, Administrator
	Mr. Lenord Louis Dorcely, Chief Accountant
	Second level
	Jorice Dorsainvil, Director of the firm BDFK

Construction of the Anse-à-Galets public square

- A contract worth 1,500,000 HTG was signed between UCLBP (Housing and Public Buildings Construction Unit) and the firm PG CONSTRUCTION for the construction of the public square in Anse-à-Galets.

- Upon reviewing the file, the CSCCA identified several irregularities. The contract amount falls below the threshold of 40,000,000 HTG established by Article 2, paragraph 1 of the decree of May 25, 2012, which sets the threshold for awarding public contracts for works. UCLBP contracted only one firm to carry out the work. Furthermore, the project was awarded without consulting suppliers or holding a competitive bidding process.

- The 60% advance payment exceeds the 30% threshold and is not guaranteed according to Articles 83 and 83-1 of the Law of June 12, 2009. There are no progress reports (statements of account) on the work completed. The 2% advance payment of 27,000 HTG was collected but not paid to the DGI (General Directorate of Taxes). No certificate of completion or conformity has been issued by UCLBP (Urban Planning and Construction Project Management Unit), even though all funds, amounting to 1,470,000 HTG, have been paid to the firm.

Responsibilities	First level
	Mr. Harry Adam, Executive Director Mr. Ervé Pierre Louis, Director of Buildings and Head of Social Projects Ms. Micheline D. Rampy, Administrator Mr. Lenord Louis Dorcely, Chief Accountant Second level Pierre Gagnol, Director of PG CONSTRUCTION

Construction of the Duvivier Sub-Commission in Cité Soleil

A contract worth 10,315,638.43 HTG was signed between UCLBP (Unité de Construction de Logements et de Bâtiments Publics) and the firm FICONES for the construction of the Duvivier Sub-Commissariat in Cité Soleil.

Upon reviewing the case, the Court of Auditors noted the following irregularities:

The amount disbursed is below the threshold of 40,000,000 HTG established by Article 2, paragraph 1 of the decree of May 25, 2012, which sets the threshold for awarding public contracts for works. Only one firm was contracted to carry out the work. Furthermore, the contract was awarded without consulting suppliers or putting the project out to tender.

The 60% start-up advance exceeds the 30% threshold and is not guaranteed according to articles 83 and 83-1 of the law of June 12, 2009.

Analysis of the contract reveals the absence of a progress report. The 2% advance payment of 82,525.11 HTG has not been paid to the DGI (General Directorate of Taxes). The project completion deadline has not been met, as evidenced by the certificate of completion and conformity issued by engineer Charles Maxi, the project manager at UCLBP (Housing and Public Buildings Construction Unit), which attests to the complete completion of the work on January 20, 2015. 60% of the funds were paid by the Ministry of Planning and 40% by UCLBP.

Responsibilities	<u>First level</u> Mr. Harry Adam, Executive Director Mr. Hervé Pierre Louis, Director of Buildings and Head of Social Projects Ms. Micheline D. Rampy, Administrator Mr. Lenord Louis Dorceley, Chief Accountant <u>Second level</u> Mr. Jean David Dorcius, Director of the firm FICONES

After reviewing a series of projects, the prosecution paused for a moment of silence in the courtroom. The sheer amount of funds committed, the hundreds of millions of dollars embezzled, the contracts signed without any serious follow-up—it was all staggering.

Each project, instead of improving the lives of Haitian citizens, became an opportunity for the defendants to enrich themselves. The lack of supporting documentation, the absence or falsification of accounting records, and the ignorance of basic public accounting principles revealed a systemic failure in the management system. The Petro Caribe funds, which were meant to be used to build schools, roads, and hospitals, with the goal of providing basic services to the population, were squandered and misappropriated.

The prosecutor pauses. He closes the screen before adding:

— "Your Honor, may the court adjourn the hearing and allow us to present the remainder of the audit at a later session."

The president:

— "This reprieve is granted. The hearing is adjourned. It will resume tomorrow at 10 a.m."

In the silence preceding the adjournment of the hearing, one certainty takes hold: this trial is not merely judging individuals; it questions the very relationship between the Haitian state and society. It also raises the issue of the complicity of non-governmental organizations in the misappropriation of PetroCaribe funds.

The prosecutor is appalling. The question remains: what are all these NGOs doing in Haiti? What are the results of their actions? Millions of dollars are allocated each year to help Haiti; yet, instead of progressing, the country is becoming poorer every day. Haiti ranks last in the Western Hemisphere in terms of the Human Development Index. From underdevelopment to entrapment, the socio-economic situation is worsening. Living conditions are increasingly alarming. Millions of Haitians are being driven from their neighborhoods by armed gangs. The majority of skilled professionals are leaving the country and going into exile abroad.

The prosecution remains confident despite everything. The Petro Caribe trial represents, more than ever, a true trial of hope. It opens a path that reminds us that justice is an essential pillar of social cohesion, guaranteeing peace, equality before the law, and the protection of rights. This respected and sometimes feared power is indispensable for building Haiti.

Chapter 12

THE CSCCA QUANTIFIES THE EMBEZZLEMENT

(The seventh day of the hearing)

A man of robes and silence, the dean is an austere figure in the courtroom. His face, etched by years of judicial practice, bears the marks of countless hearings, weighty decisions, and dilemmas resolved in the name of the law. His voice is measured, devoid of emphasis, but each word he utters carries the quiet authority of experience. He knows that, in this trial, it is not only the law that is at stake. It is under the watchful eye of history that the verdict is being decided.

The night before the trial, as night fell on Port-au-Prince, the senior judge struggled to sleep. In the quiet of his office, he pondered at length the significance of the Assize Court hearing. He considered the weight of public expectations, the fragility of the institutions, and the fine line a judge must walk between the rigor of the law and the visible or invisible pressures of the moment. He knew that the Petro Caribe trial was not to be treated like any other: it engaged his conscience as much as his office. As a neutral party in the proceedings, he could not help but be astonished, in his silence, by the size of the contracts and the irregularities marring their execution. The acts of embezzlement were evident…

With palpable gravity, the dean opens the seventh day of the hearing.

— "Prosecutor, you have the floor to continue your presentation of the facts."

Me. Saint-Juste, one of the deputy prosecutors, stood up and declared:

— "Your Honor, allow the prosecution to continue by emphasizing the audit, which allows for the analysis of contracts and the highlighting of irregularities."

With authorization granted, the prosecutor opens the screen:

"Support for the Mechanization of Agriculture"

Six contracts totaling 167,520,245.50 HTG were signed between the Minister of Agriculture, Natural Resources, and Rural Development, represented by Minister Thomas Jacques, and representatives of the various firms. Four of these contracts were signed on January 4, 2013; one on January 25, 2013; and the last on August 26, 2015. The Court of Auditors notes that these contracts only partially reflect the conditions stipulated in the technical specifications (duration, schedule, description of work). Furthermore, none of the six awarded contracts specify a completion timeframe, which is contrary to best practices.

- The Court notes that in implementing the first contract, the Ministry of Agriculture, Natural Resources and Rural Development (MARNDR) paid 19,755,598.99 HTG more than the amounts stipulated in the two resolutions. The Court considers this a misuse of public funds. The MARNDR spent more money than the amount specified in the resolution, namely 247,726,795.99 HTG.

- The Ministry of Agriculture, Natural Resources and Rural Development (MARNDR) spent 14,324,259.99

HTG more than the disbursements received from the Ministry of Economy and Finance (MEF). This decision violates regulations and best practices. The Court noted that the MARNDR took out a non-repayable loan of 31,303,375.54 HTG to complete the project. This sum was drawn from the account of the Rouyone/Léogâne drainage infrastructure rehabilitation project. This irregularity had a negative impact on the project's implementation and on the community.

- The Court found that the Ministry of Agriculture, Natural Resources and Rural Development (MARNDR) transferred $1,239,000 to a Cuban trust account in Havana to purchase spare parts for the Artibonite Valley Development Organization (ODVA). According to the summary table of spare parts, only $987,092.91 was used for these parts. However, the Court was unable to trace the requisitions. The Court also found that this Cuban trust had benefited from an exemption from all customs duties and import taxes.

- The Court also noted that the various payments did not correspond to the pace of progress of the work or delivery of services. For example:
- Haytrac: an initial advance payment of 50% of the contract amount was made upon signing. The remaining 50% was not mentioned in the contract, and the firm refuses to pay the 2% deposit.
- Automeca: an initial advance payment of 50% of the contract amount was made to this company upon signing the contract. The second installment was paid upon delivery of the agricultural machinery. Automeca paid the 2% advance but requested a receipt for its accounting purposes.
- The firm Grades: an initial advance of 50% of the contract amount was paid upon signing the contract.

- Transsagri firm: an initial advance of 50% of the contract amount was paid upon signing the contract.
- By paying half of the total amount upon signing, the MARNDR violates articles 83 and 83-1 of the law of June 12, 2009 which stipulates a maximum of 30% will be paid at the time of signing the contract.

Responsibilities	
First category Names, surnames and titles of administration officials central	1. Thomas Jacques, Minister, Principal Authorizing Officer of the MARNDR 2. Fresner Dorcin, Principal Authorizing Officer of the MARNDR 3. Pierre Guy Lafontant, General Manager 4. Phito Blemur, coordinator (UEP) 5. Martine Tanis Eugène, public accountant 6. Jean Francis Pierre, public accountant 7. Senat Antoine Amerlin, Chief Accountant 8. James Noël , financial controller
Second category Infrastructure Department agricultural	1. Montes Charles, Managing Engineer DIA 2. Ms. Emilie R. Delinois, DIA Administrator 3. Arnoux Gourdet SAE/ DIA

The prosecutor pauses, his gaze sweeping the courtroom before settling on the presiding judge. He inwardly hopes that the court grasps the importance of the trial and that the presentation of the facts demonstrates the scale of the crime in light of the billions of US dollars embezzled. These 50% advances are not mere management details. Article 83 of the law is unequivocal: a maximum of 30% will be paid upon signing the contract. By paying half the total amount upon signing, the State deprived itself of a crucial means of oversight. It transformed public funds into a gift without any obligation in return. Worse still, by failing to stipulate the payment of the balance or by tolerating the refusal to pay the DGI (General Directorate of Taxes) the 2% provisional advance – this minimum tax contribution – the drafters of the contract deliberately created a legal and financial vacuum. This is no longer negligence; it is a scheme of embezzlement. The massive advance payment frees the contractor from any pressure to complete the work, while the refusal to pay the deposit deprives the State of a basic tax proof.

Reading the 656 pages of the Court of Auditors' latest report, the irregularities are blatant. Yet, upon closer examination, beyond the shortcomings in project execution, an entire architecture of corruption in Haiti emerges, leaving no doubt those officials from both the public and private sectors have benefited in one way or another from the misappropriation of Petro Caribe funds. Corruption is widespread. To quote Frédéric Thomas in his analysis, " *Anti-Corruption Movements: Issues and Ambivalences* ," "the entire project implementation chain, from planning to supervision and final handover, has not so much been flawed as simply circumvented and diverted." Thus, what is striking is perhaps less that the rules and conditions were not respected, but rather the fact, as highlighted by *Ensemble contre la corruption* (Ecc), that all the control mechanisms and bodies, all the checks and balances, and, first and foremost, the Court of Auditors itself (but also Parliament and the judiciary) failed… »

Throughout the prosecution's case, the public prosecutor presented a series of identical examples to demonstrate a recurring pattern, a normalization of illegality. He hoped to show the court, through this repetition, proof of passive or active collusion: the State not only violated its own rules, but also orchestrated the conditions for the embezzlement. Each contract thus arranged was not a market transaction, but a disguised transfer of funds. The Criminal Court therefore understood that behind each "administrative irregularity" has laid illicit enrichment, resulting in the impoverishment of the community, which was deprived of the resources these projects were intended to generate.

The prosecutor's office continues to list the projects audited by the CSCCA:

Ministry of Tourism and Creative Industries (MTIC)

—"From September 2008 to September 2016, the MTIC was responsible for the design and implementation of territorial development projects called the Special Plan for Les Cayes. This program includes nine projects financed by PetroCaribe funds through five resolutions, 22/12/2012; 23/07/2014; 15/04/2015; 22/07/2015; 6/01/2016, for a total amount of $49,649,394.81.

- The Court proceeded to analyze the nine projects:
- Projects comprising the Cayes Special Plan

Projects	Enforcement firm	Project values $
Construction of a bus station	GB DESIGN & CONSTRUCTION ITS	$33,424,875
Construction of the Cayes Tourist Port	MAN CONSTRUCTION	$14,101,362.50

BBQ work - Sports Centre - Market Thursday	PERIMETER	$34,174,593.75
Storage Park (Container Market)	SDECO S. A.	$27,045,480
Construction of Débouchette Elementary School	CYRUS	$25,575,870.37
Soil preparation in Vernet: Southern department	MAN CONSTRUCTION	$5,999,334
Installation of 20 streetlights	GK IMPORT-EXPORT	$2,000,000
Development of the Vernet Tourist Market (Cayes)	GB DESIGN & CONSTRUCTION SA	$7,498,513
	ATALOU MICRO SYSTEM	$3,125,000

The figures rain down like a deluge of stones. There are Thirty-four millions, thirty-three millions, and twenty-seven millions. The raw numbers pile up like a mountain on the screen. The sums allocated to projects that are often never carried out revolt the conscience of Haitians and even foreigners closely following the proceedings. On November 8, 2010, three companies belonging to Dominican Senator Félix Bautista signed eight contracts with the Préval/Bellerive government in 24 hours, for a total of US$385 million. These three companies are: Hadom, Construcciones y Diseños, and Rofi, for the construction of, among other things, the Legislative Palace of Haiti (seat of Parliament), social housing in Bowen Field, and the National Fort in Port-au-Prince. The Martelly/Conille government signed twenty negotiated contracts with the Dominican firm Estrella to carry out work between September 2011 and July 2015.

Contracts here and contracts there, it's no longer a list of projects, but an inventory of plunder. On a bench in the middle of the courtroom, one of the leaders of "Petro Challenger" stares at the figure for the bus station: $33,424,875; he nods, his gaze fixed on the ceiling. A woman near him widens her eyes at the cost of the computer lab: $3,125,000. Thinking of her children's school, where subsidies never arrive, she clenches her teeth. The anger, initially silent, rises a notch with each line item, each firm or company cited as a government contractor, each sum that defies comprehension. It becomes a dull, palpable hum. And then, it explodes.

From the back of the courtroom, a hoarse voice, amplified by anger and fury, thundered through the audience: "Ban n vòlè!" (You gang of thieves!), shouted a student, who is a member of the Petro Challenger collective. The phrase went straight to the dock. For a moment, the hearing was suspended. The judge rang the bell and struck the gavel to restore silence. The accusation was far more powerful than any testimony. The people, in their very being, had just delivered their verdict. The prosecution, still standing, lowered their eyes to their notes, leaving it to the Court to hear what no audit could quantify: the voices of the victims rising up to condemn voracious and corrupt leaders.

In the heavy silence that followed the insulting remarks spat in the face of Martelly and his accomplices, the public prosecutor resumed, in a grave voice, the presentation of the facts, bringing the debate back to the field of squandering.

Construction of the Île-à-Vache Airport Terminal

—"The Ministry of Public Works, Transportation and Communications (MTTPP) signed a contract with a private firm for the construction of the Île-à-Vache airport terminal. It appears that the project was not managed according to recognized rules and standards, or according to sound management principles. The supplier was selected through a request for a technical and financial proposal without a competitive bidding process, which represents a significant deficiency in project management given its complexity."

- The Court noted that the work stopped after using 38% of the allocated budget, or $10,088,137.63. No formal rules govern the decision to proceed with or halt this project, which was launched without a formal implementation plan.

- At the time work was halted, 46% of the advance payment for commencement had been disbursed. A balance of $3,582,805 remained to be recovered. Taking into account the 25% advance payment not yet recovered and the invoices already paid for work completed, the Court estimates that the MTPTEC has paid a total of $13,166,535.75, representing 49.8% of the contract amount. The last invoice received covers the period from July to August 2015, with the project being in its 17th month out of the 18 months stipulated in the contract.

- The Court made the following observations after visiting the construction site:
- The progress of the work has eaten up approximately 26% of the initial project cost.
- The findings from the sites visited indicate:
- that the runway built is in a more pronounced state of disrepair than the Cayes airport;
- that there is no infrastructure (guardhouse, waiting room and other service buildings);
- that, given the deterioration of the premises, a resumption of work would require a budget greater than the remaining balance of the budget initially granted (approximately $14 million);
- Given its isolation, it does not appear that the facility is being used by the island's inhabitants.

- The appointed experts visited the public squares built or developed on the island. In most cases, these are non-functional; only the concrete structures have been completed. Their landscaping remains to be done, and the planned street furniture is not yet in place.

The Île-à-Vache airport terminal

The public prosecutor closes his eyes for a second. He went there during the investigation to see the state of the site. This visit took place long after the work had been abandoned. He can still see himself standing on the cracked runway, the salty wind stinging his face. He encountered no living soul there, only absurdity frozen in concrete. Construction less than 30% complete. This modern infrastructure was promised as a hub to attract investment. Instead, it looks more like a scar, tangible proof that the country can be betrayed even in its most remote corners. The figures on the screen – 10 million, 38%, and 49.8% – are the geographical coordinates of this betrayal.

Île-à-Vache, once hailed as a symbol of tourism revival, reappears here as a most eloquent metaphor: a crumbling runway, unfinished structures, a future hanging in the balance. The prosecution believes that the entire country sometimes resembles this airport terminal, barely built, abandoned too soon, and more expensive to repair than to construct. The prosecution's objective is to uncover the secrets of the Petro Caribe affair, and it is with this objective that it continues its closing argument.

Construction of the premises for the Intervention and Law Enforcement Corps (CIMO)

—"A contract has been signed between the Ministry of Planning and External Cooperation (MPCE) and a private firm for the construction of the premises of the Intervention and Law Enforcement Corps (CIMO).

- The Court's analysis of the disbursements for this project revealed an amount of $1,058,487.65, representing 25% of the initial advance. Of this amount, less than 50%, equivalent to $500,000, was paid to the firm. However, the Court found no supporting documentation proving the use of the remaining balance. Furthermore, the Court notes that an amendment for $934,581.52 was signed by the parties, bringing the total project cost to $5,168,532.22.

— Regarding contract management, the Court notes the following irregularities in relation to the regulatory framework: the project amount exceeds the threshold for awarding a public contract, which normally requires an open tender, taking into account the provisions relating to public contracts (Article 2 of the decree of May 25, 2012, setting the thresholds for awarding public contracts and the intervention thresholds of the National Commission for Public Contracts). Instead of a tender, a negotiated contract was signed following the activation of the emergency law of April 17, 2010.

— By referring to the nature of the market and the absence of needs analysis, it appears that the officials of the MPCE (Ministry of Planning and External Cooperation) have abused the use of the state of emergency to justify their lack of foresight, their negligence or solely for the purpose of evading their obligation to resort to competition (Art. 107 implementing decree of October 26, 2009).

Construction of the Port Margot High School

- A contract worth 27,830,785.15 HTG was awarded by mutual agreement on September 22, 2010, between the Ministry of Planning and External Cooperation (MPCE) and BEC ENGINEERING for the construction of the Port Margot High School. This is in addition to another contract worth 4,000,000 HTG signed with the supervision firm J&J Construction and an addendum worth 5,565,761.34 HTG.

- This contract refers to the decree of April 21, 2010, declaring a state of emergency for a period of eighteen months. The decree is based on the Law on the State of Emergency of September 9, 2008, as amended by Parliament on April 15, 2010.

- An advance payment of 1,915,392.57 HTG, representing 50% of the contract cost, was granted to the firm. This clause contradicts the provisions of the law of June 10, 2009, which establishes the general rules for public procurement and public service concession agreements. Article 83 of this law specifies that "advance payments may be granted for preparatory work related to the execution of the works, supplies, and services covered by the contract. The total amount of advance payments granted may under no circumstances exceed 30% of the initial contract amount." This breach constitutes an irregularity that has caused harm to the project and the community.

Responsibilities	First level • Laurent Salvador Lamothe: Minister (MPCE), Principal Authorizing Officer • Mr. Michel Présumé: Secretary of State for Planning at the MPCE • Jean Max Bellerive: Minister (MPCE), Principal Authorizing Officer • Jude Hervey Day: Minister (MPCE), Chief Authorizing Officer Second level • Paul-Erick Bruno (BECA Engineering) referred to as workforce Third level • Giovanni Dorélien, Deputy Director General (MPCE) • Engineer Hérode Thélusma (J&J Construction) for supervision

The prosecution is examining the defendants one by one. Misappropriating millions of dollars allocated for school construction in a country where 40% of the population is illiterate, and where the literacy rate is among the lowest in the Americas, constitutes a heinous act.

Staring at the large screen, he continues:

Emergency rehabilitation of the Colladère – Cerca-Carvajal road

- A contract was signed on February 22, 2013, between the Haitian government, represented by the Minister of Planning and External Cooperation (MPCE), and the firm HONGUYAN CONSTRUCTION COMPANY LIMITED for the emergency rehabilitation of the Colladère – Cerca-Carvajal road. The contract cost $20,894,909, funded by PetroCaribe.

- The Court reviewed the work and found that irregularities in the regulatory framework had harmed the project and the community. The $20,894,909 contract was awarded without competitive bidding, under the emergency law of April 15, 2010. This contract should have been subject to an open tender process, given the provisions of Article 2 of the Order of May 25, 2012, which set the threshold for public procurement of works at 40,000,000 HTG. It was signed by the Project Manager on February 22, 2013. This contract therefore does not fall within the scope of the emergency law, which was in force from November 5, 2012 to January 5, 2013. It consequently contravenes Article 34.2 of the law establishing the general rules relating to public contracts and concession agreements for works or public services, as well as Article 107 of the decree of October 26, 2009 specifying the terms of application of this same law.

- The Court also noted that the first payment was made on September 24, 2012, nearly 12 months after the contract was signed on October 20, 2011. It found that the emergency situation was invoked improperly, which constitutes an irregularity detrimental to the project and the community.

The state of emergency, designed to streamline disbursement procedures in cases of natural disasters, appears in this case as a convenient refuge for those who squander funds. The prosecution demonstrates, once again, how the exception has become the rule, how the emergency has served as a smokescreen for a lack of planning. In the silence of the courtroom, one certainty emerges: when the emergency becomes permanent, it ceases to be an excuse and becomes a wrongdoing.

The substitute continues:

- "The provisional advance payment of 2% required by article 4 of the last paragraph of the contract concluded between the MPCE and the firm HONGUYAN CONSTRUCTION COMPANY LIMITED and article 76 of the decree of 29 September 2005 (monitor of 5 October 2005, special no. 10) on income tax, equivalent to $501,979.08, has not been collected according to the Court of Auditors.

- The contract was signed without the National Commission for Public Procurement's (CNMP) no-objection notice, as it was not covered by the emergency law. This is further in contradiction with Article 107 of the decree of October 26, 2009, which specifies the implementing procedures for the law establishing the general rules relating to public procurement and concession agreements for public service works.

- The project was identified by the BMPAD board of directors and approved by resolution taken in the Council of Ministers on December 21, 2012. Its total cost (initial contract and amendment) is $23,598,685.73.

- The project was fully completed. However, its implementation did not adhere to best practices and sound project management. No preliminary studies were conducted, no project documents were submitted, and the assessment of needs, costs, risks, project profitability, and required funding was not rigorously documented.

Project Name

- Emergency rehabilitation of the Colladère – Cerca-Carvajal road section

  (13 km + 2 km)

- Audited institution: Ministry of Planning and External Cooperation (MPCE)

Responsibilities

First level Names, surnames and titles of responsible for the central administration	▪ Laurent Salvador Lamothe, (MPCE) ▪ Yves Germain Joseph, (MPCE) ▪ Aviol Fleurant, (MPCE) ▪ Marie Carmelle Jean Marie (MEF) ▪ Wilson Laleau (MEF) ▪ Yve Romain Bastien (MEF)

The names are lined up methodically, almost impersonally. Yet each defendant has their signature affixed at a specific moment to the bottom of a contract, sometimes in haste, sometimes indifference. In the dock, the accused avoid looking at the courtroom, aware that their name is no longer just an administrative identifier, but a marker in the narrative of an institutional collapse.

The public prosecutor's office continues:

Rehabilitation of the Freycineau Intersection section (Saint-Marc) – Bigot (Gonaïves) via National Route #1

—"Three contracts, including an addendum, were signed between the Ministry of Public Works, Transportation and Communications (MTPTC) and the Ingeneria ESTRELLA & EATT consortium for a total amount of $78,875,803.43. These contracts were defined in the resolutions of August 24, 2010; December 11, 2013 and finally January 6, 2016.

The Court found that the three contracts were awarded without competitive bidding. According to Haitian procurement regulations, these contracts should have been subject to an open tender process. The stated reason for circumventing the regulations was urgency. This reason is questionable. Minister Jacques Gabriel awarded these contracts without competitive bidding to a firm he had personally contacted beforehand.

The chronological sequence of decisions made in awarding the initial contract for the "Carrefour Freycineau (Saint Marc) – Bigot (Gonaïves) section rehabilitation project," valued at $51,452,645.35, leads the Court to suspect that there was an initial intention to award this significant contract without competitive bidding, in violation of public procurement rules. It also appears that the Ministry of Public Works simply took advantage of the situation created by the January 12, 2010 earthquake to finalize the project and award the contract under the provisions of the state of emergency declared on January 16, 2010.

— The reconstruction of the invoices revealed a discrepancy of $4,850,910.53 between the total amount of the invoices

($56,303,555.88) and the amount of the initial contract ($51,452,645.35). This represents a 9% overpayment compared to the contract.

— The work was scheduled to be completed within 12 months under the contract. The last invoice is dated February 10, 2014, which corresponds to 47 months since the contract was signed on January 28, 2010. Consequently, the work was completed 35 months late.

— Seven months after the initial contract, on September 28, 2010, Amendment #1 resulted from the desire of the Ministry of Public Works to expand the project for a total amount of $20,166,148.13:

- Rehabilitation of the slip road: National road n ⁰ 1 – Marchand;
- Construction of a variant of the RN1: bypass of the city of Gonaïves from Bigot to Carrefour Joffre;
- Rehabilitation of the slip road: National road n ⁰ 1 (Bienac) / K-Soleil)

— Amendment #1, totaling $20,166,148.13, represents 39% of the initial contract, equivalent to $51,452,645.35. This is contrary to public procurement regulations.

— Article 21 of the decree of October 26, 2009, specifying the terms of application of the law of June 10, 2009 on public procurement, stipulates that: the amendment may in no case exceed 30% of the initial contract, after application of any updating and revision clauses.

The contract amount exceeds the amount of the resolution by $3,472,907.84. The amount approved for the project in the resolution of August 24, 2010, after decommissioning, is $16,693,240.29, while the contract amount is $20,166,148.13. It is therefore clear that an incorrect assessment of the project's needs was made, since the amount authorized in the August 24, 2010 resolution would not be sufficient to fulfill the contract. In light of this, three additional resolutions were adopted to finance the projects carried out under the amendment (July 22, 2015, January 6, 2016, and September 28, 2016). Despite this, there is a funding shortfall of $492,138.61 to cover the needs outlined in Amendment #1.

—A second amendment was signed on August 2, 2015, extending the initial period from 10 months to 18 months and 17 days because the rehabilitation work on the bypass road around the city of Gonaïves, included in the first amendment, could not be completed within the period stipulated in the contract.

— Site visits by the Court's investigators revealed that the work is still incomplete. The connection between the Gonaïves bypass and National Route #1 has not been completed due to the lack of a bridge. Many sections of the road are unpaved.

On May 3, 2011, a contract for additional work was signed between the Ministry of Public Works, Transportation and Communications (MTPTC) and the consortium Ingeneria ESTRELLA & EATT on the Freycineau (Saint-Marc)/Bigot (Gonaïves) section for a total amount of $7,257,009.95 for the construction of the connections between the Gaudin and Mapou bridges and National Route No. 1 and the Freycineau drainage system (Part C of the January 28, 2010 contract). Performing additional work on a road that had already been built demonstrates a lack of planning and a poor assessment of needs.

The supervision contract signed between the Ministry and the BEJV-METRIC Group for $2,406,825 does not comply with current legislation because it contains an income tax exemption clause that is outside the scope of legal requirements. However, Article 2 of this contract stipulates that the amount for services does not include Haitian taxes, duties, and levies on the services provided by METRIC Engineering and on those of expatriate staff. Deductions of the 2% provisional advance payment on invoices 15 through 21, totaling $14,590.73, were made by the Ministry of Economy and

Finance when these invoices were paid. The BEJV-METRIC Group requested and obtained reimbursement of this amount. Invoice #22 totals $233,163.03, corresponding to payments for services from March 1 to 31, 2012, and contains the clauses for the reimbursement of the amount.

In a letter on October 12, 2012, Minister Jacques Rousseau asked the Minister of the Economy and Finance, Marie Carmelle Jean-Marie, to honor this debt. The bill was paid by the public treasury on October 16, 2012.

—The reconstruction of the invoices revealed a discrepancy of $1,296,924.24 between the total invoice amount of $3,703,749.24 and the amount of the additional contract valued at $2,406,825. This represents a 54% overpayment compared to the contract. This is a blatant violation of applicable regulations.

Contracts here and projects there, the public prosecutor, incredulous, shakes his head. While Haiti trembles on January 12, 2010 and natural disasters follow one after another, the accused, sitting in their air-conditioned offices, negotiate and sign lucrative contracts, awarded without competitive bidding, with close friends of those in power.

Casting a contemptuous look in their direction, he continued:

Construction of the Cayes Tourist Port

- "The Court conducted an audit of the Cayes Tourist Port construction project to determine whether it was implemented economically, efficiently, and effectively. It appears that several actions taken by the MTIC (Ministry of Tourism and Creative Industries) did not meet these three criteria."

- First, the contract, valued at 14,101,362.50 HTG, was awarded without competitive bidding on May 21, 2015, without any justification. However, for such a sum, the procurement method is inappropriate because it has not been established that the Ministry of Information and Communication Technologies (MTIC) used the supplier consultation or price request procedure required by Article 27-1 of the Law of June 12, 2009, on public procurement, and Article 115-3 of the Decree of October 26, 2009, which specifies the implementing provisions of the law establishing the general rules relating to public contracts and concession agreements for public service works. This decree requires that, for amounts below the established thresholds, the contract be awarded following the comparison of at least three proposals.

- In addition to this irregularity with regard to the regulatory framework and best management practices, the Court found that the invoicing and payment methods were inadequate with regard to Article 83 of the Law of June 12, 2009, on public procurement. Indeed, according to the provisions of this article, the advance payment may under no circumstances exceed 30% of the initial contract amount. However, in the implementation of this project, the Ministry of Information and Communication Technologies (MTIC) provided an advance payment of 40%. The Court considers that such an irregularity could have a negative impact on the community, especially since the contract does not include any penalty clause in the event of delays in the execution of the work.

Construction of the Reed Bridge

—"A contract worth $5,118,950.43 was awarded between the Ministry of Public Works, Transportation and Communications

(MTPTC) and a private firm for the construction of the Roseaux Bridge.

The Court of Auditors examined this project to verify whether the Ministry of Public Works, Transport and Communications (MTPTC) and other stakeholders managed it effectively, efficiently, and economically. It appears that irregularities occurred during the project's implementation.

- The cost of the completed project is $8,871,582.40, exceeding the amount planned in the adopted resolutions, which was $5,118,950.43.

- No justification is provided by the MTPTC.

- The project was completed in thirty-three months, compared to the ten months initially planned.

The public prosecutor's office is questioning the exorbitant cost of the project, which has cost over five million dollars to build a bridge over the Roseaux River in the Grand'Anse department and the Corail district. They are wondering why, instead of traditional bridge construction, modular bridges -a design and construction process using prefabricated sections and modules -were not considered. The modular approach not only streamlines the construction process but also allows for the integration of advanced technologies and materials, thus improving the overall performance and sustainability of the project.

Bellerive and his associates decided otherwise. The higher the cost, the easier it is to divert money through overbilling. What matters is the percentage to be earned: The bribes to be received. A practice often used by Senator Bautista to win contracts.

The prosecutor remains hesitant. Haiti is considered the poorest country in the Americas and one of the most impoverished in the world, with approximately 60% of its population living below the poverty line, often on less than $2 a day; the leaders are indifferent. Under their leadership, the embezzlement of public funds has become the highest in the world. Corruption is endemic.

The prosecutor continues:

BBQ work - Sports Centre - Thursday Market

- "An agreement was reached on July 3, 2015 between the Ministry of Tourism and a private firm for the BBQ - Sports Centre - Thursday Market work.

  —The Court conducted an audit of the project to determine whether it was implemented economically, efficiently, and effectively. It appears that several actions taken by the Ministry of Information and Communication Technologies (MTIC) did not meet these three criteria.

—The contract, valued at 34,174,593.75 HTG, was awarded without a negotiated procedure and without any documented justification. The awarding method for this contract is inappropriate because it has not been established that the Ministry of Information and Communication Technologies (MTIC) used the supplier consultation or price request procedure required by Article 27-1 of the Law of June 12, 2009, on public procurement, and Article 115-3 of the Decree of October 26, 2009, which specifies the implementing provisions of the law establishing the general rules relating to public contracts and public service concession agreements. This decree requires that, for amounts below the established thresholds, the contract be awarded following a comparison of at least three proposals.

— The Court found no progress reports on the work in the documents provided by the MTIC (Ministry of Tourism and Creative Industries). Such an administrative irregularity could impact the very execution of the project, and therefore the judicious use of public funds and the community.

The prosecutor's voice falls silent for a moment. In that silence, he dreams of another Haiti, a prosperous and developed country, one that would stand out in the Caribbean as the Pearl of the Antilles. The completed airport on Île-à-Vache would welcome visitors from around the world, breathing new life into the South Coast. In the port of Les Cayes, one would see sailboats and yachts, not abandoned docks. In primary schools, like the one in Débouchette, one would hear the voices of children echoing in new classrooms equipped with computers. Newly built roads would connect the regions and expedite the movement of both people and goods. Once finished, the public squares and markets would fully assume their role as the nerve centers of the communities. They would become spaces for living, exchanging, and celebrating. Streetlights would not only illuminate the streets but would also give rise to a vibrant nightlife. Petro Caribe money, if it had been rigorously invested in viable projects, instead of vanishing into opaque accounts, would have made it possible to build much more than infrastructure: it would have restored confidence, given back dignity, and offered the community hope for a promising future.

Chapter 13

CORRUPTION IS VISIBLE

The murmurs in the courtroom are not merely a sign of indignation; they are the cry of a people who are drowning and being despised...

The prosecutor pauses to review his notes and then continues:

— "Your Honor, allow the prosecution to display on the big screen the list of institutions involved, the nature of the projects, the location, and the amounts to be disbursed."

The president:

— "The Court grants the request."

The prosecutor states:

— "Resolution of February 28, 2012"

List of Projects	Amount ($)
PNH Reinforcement	$3,000,000
Electrification project	$11,280,000
Sub-programme for combating poverty and social exclusion	$30,000,000

Sub-project for the urban renewal of the city of Jacmel	$20,000,000
Urban renovation of Gonaïves (phase 1) (14km)	$5,000,000
Construction of the Jacmel Public Market	$400,000
Urban renewal of St Marc	$5,000,000
Sports Infrastructure Sub-Programme	$6,200,000
Rehabilitation of the Petit-Goâve Wharf	$2,300,000
Rehabilitation of the Wharf of Jeremiah	$2,700,000
Additional work on Frecyneau/St Marc	$7,450,000
RN1 Rehabilitation: Frecyneau Intersection (St-Marc) - Bigot (Gonaïves)	$19,750,000
Rehabilitation and maintenance of the Baie de l'Acul road	$3,000,000
Post-Earthquake Accommodation	$1,183,272
Support for the operation of the CNE	$8,000,000
Morne à Cabri Industrial Park	$10,000,000
Construction of the Miragoâne-Petit-Trou de Nippes road	$13,000,000
Infrastructure rehabilitation and maintenance Rehabilitation of the Carrefour 44/Côte de Fer road (36km)	$14,000,000 $12,500,000
Export fund for PetroCaribe-financed projects	$4,000,000
Rehabilitation of the Frères road	$3,500,000
Street rehabilitation in Cap-Haïtien	$1,012,500
Support for the SMCRS	$10,000,000
Rehabilitation of the Cul de Sac plain irrigation system	$8,000,000
Rehabilitation of the Rouyonne/Léogâne drainage infrastructure	$8,000,000
Rehabilitation of the Hasco/Boulevard la Saline/ Admiral Killick naval base road	$6,000,000

Social security pilot project	$3,000,000
Literacy	$6,000,000
Rehabilitation of the Jérémie airstrip	$3,000,000
31-Construction of 15 bridges in the Northwest	$863,500
Total	$230,139,272

Construction of a Bridge over the Rivière Grande in Marigot and Pérédo

— A contract has been signed between the MTPTC (Ministry of Public Works, Transport and Communications) and the firm WENLING HONGYAN for the construction of a bridge over the Grande River in Marigot and Pérédo. The project cost is $6,890,758.91. The Court examined irregularities that caused harm to the project and the community.

- US$9,662,423.57 has been disbursed for the project. This cost exceeds the adopted resolutions of US$6,890,758.91 and the amount authorized in the contract of US$8,557,634.32.
- No justification has been provided by the MTPTC.
- However, there remains a balance on resolutions of $961,538.46.
- There is no explanation for the payment of two invoices totaling $2,978,257.75, so
- The project is 86% complete.
- With the payment of these invoices, the amount exceeding the authorized limit for this contract will be exceeded of 25%.

INSTITUTION AUDITED
MINISTRY OF PUBLIC WORKS, TRANSPORT, ENERGY AND COMMUNICATION (MTPTEC)

PROJECT NAME	Construction of the bridge over the Grande River in Marigot and Pérédo
RESOLUTIONS	December 21, 2012: $4,500,000 11-12-2013: $1,402,102.81 July 21, 2015: $335,111 September 28, 2016: $653,545.10 Total: $6,890,758.91
TOTAL FINANCING	Petro Caribe Fund
PROJECT REVIEW	• Project completed with a significant delay of 31 months. • Project exceeding the authorized market cost by 25%. • Lack of documentation relating to provisional and final acceptance.

RESPONSIBILITIES

First level Officials of The Central Administration	1. Jacques Rousseau, Eng., Minister, Principal Authorizing Officer of expenses 2. Gaetan Youance, coordinator of the UCEA (MTPTC)

Second level Managers of The Louis Berger Groupe Inc. – CECOM Consultants for supervision and the technical inspection The Louis Berger Group Inc. – CECOM Consultants	3. Ariel Frank, legal representative of LBI-Cecom consultants 4. Mario Aldana, Eng., supervisor, LBI-Cecom consultants
Third level Company officials Wenling Hongyan	5. Mr. Wang Wentian, representative of WENLING HONGYAN 6. Mr. Yinkai Deng, project director, WENLING HONGYAN

Construction of a Bridge over the Left River

— A contract has been signed between the MTPTC and the firm WENLING HONGYAN for the construction of a bridge over the Gauche River. The cost of the project is $9,180,505.19.

The CSCCA noted the following irregularities:

- The project cost of $9,180,505.19 is in line with the resolutions adopted, namely $10,010,974.29, but exceeds the amount authorized in the contract, namely $8,682,772.
- The MTPTC has not provided any justification for this overrun.
- However, the cash receipts indicate a balance of $1,604,131.25.
- There is no explanation for the payment of 4 invoices totaling $1,064,977.06.
- With the payment of these invoices, the overrun of the authorized amount for this contract is 17.5%.
- The project was completed over 21 months compared to the planned 10 months.

- There was no indication as to whether any penalties were applied.

INSTITUTION AUDITED
MINISTRY OF PUBLIC WORKS, TRANSPORT, ENERGY AND COMMUNICATION (MTPTEC)/ DIRECTORATE OF PUBLIC WORKS (DTP)

Project Name	Construction of the bridge over the Gaul River
Resolutions	December 21, 2012: $5,000,000 11-12-2013: $1,884,011.74 July 21, 2015: $3,126,962.55 Total: $10,010,974.29
Total Financing	PetroCaribe Fund
Project Summary	Project completed with an 11-month delay. The project exceeded the authorized budget by 17.5%.

RESPONSIBILITIES

First level Officials of The central administration	1. Jacques Rousseau, Engineer, Minister, Principal Authorizing Officer of Expenditures 2. Garry Jean, coordinator of the UCEA (MTPTC)
Second level Managers of The Louis Berger Groupe Inc. – CECOM, Consultants for supervision and the technical inspection	5. The Louis Berger Group Inc. – CECOM consultants 6. Ariel Frank, legal representative of LBI-Cecom consultants 7. Mario Aldana, Eng., supervisor, LBI-Cecom consultants

Third level Company officials WENLING HONGYAN	8. Mr. Wang Wentian, representative of WENLING HONGYAN 9. Mr. Junin Wu, Project Director, WENLING HONGYAN

Acquisition of Equipment for the Urban and Rural Equipment Maintenance Service (SEEUR)

— A call for tenders was launched on February 11, 2010, to equip the CNE (National Emergency Operations Center) with civil engineering materials and equipment to strengthen its response capacity following the earthquake of January 12, 2010. A contract was signed between the MTPTC (Ministry of Public Works, Transport and Communications) and the Haytrac Company. The contract specifies that the acquisition of the materials and equipment was made on behalf of the SEEUR (State Emergency Operations Center).

The Court of Auditors examined this project to verify whether the Ministry of Public Works, Transport and Communications (MTPTC) and other stakeholders managed it effectively, efficiently, and economically. It appears that irregularities occurred during the project's implementation.

— The acknowledgments of receipt included in the file indicate that all the selected companies received their letter of invitation on February 11, 2010 and the date of signature of the contract between the MTPTC and the Haytrac Company, the successful bidder, is also February 11, 2010.

— Nowhere in the contract is there any provision for the deduction of the provisional advance payment of 2%, which represents derogation from article 76 of the decree of 29 September 2005 on income tax.

— In the absence of disbursement slips and credit advice certifying payment to the seller Haytrac, the Court attempted to reconstruct the chronology of expenses related to the contract from invoices, payment requests from the MTPTC and a global disbursement table transmitted to the CSCCA by the Ministry of Economy and Finance.

— This reconstruction is presented in the following table:

Breakdown of payments to the supplier HAYTRAC

Invoice No.	Disbursement date	Amount ($)
Starting advance 1	24/03/2010	$821,382
Invoice 2	15/04/2010	$490,000
Invoice 3	12/07/2010	$727,363
Invoice 4	18/08/2010	$220,167.50
Invoice 5	19/08/2010	$305,567.50
Invoice 6	23/12/2010	$173,460
Total		$2,737,940

Source: MEF disbursement schedule and HAYTRAC company invoices

PROJECT REVIEW

— According to available information, the execution of the amount of $2,737,940 adopted by the Resolution of 11-02-2010 has been fully completed.

- The amount allocated in this contract, $2,737,940, corresponds to the resolution authorizing the project. However, no documentation has been produced to guarantee the advance payment of $821,382 granted, which was part of the overall contract amount.
- The provisional advance of 2% on the amount of the contract was not provided for in the contract taking into account the irregularities affecting the process of awarding this contract, it goes without saying that the execution of this project does not seem to comply with either the sound

management of public funds or good project management practices.

INSTITUTION AUDITED
MINISTRY OF PUBLIC WORKS, TRANSPORT, AND COMMUNICATION (MTPTC)
URBAN AND RURAL EQUIPMENT MAINTENANCE SERVICE (SEEUR)

Project Name	Acquisition of equipment for the SEEUR
Resolutions	February 11, 2010: $2,737,940
Total Financing	PetroCaribe Fund
Responsibilities	

Hospital Construction and Rehabilitation Works

- The "Construction and Rehabilitation of Hospitals" project, under the authority of the MSPP (Ministry of Public Health and Population), has enabled the implementation of the following projects:
- The HUEH (State University Hospital of Haiti) construction project
- Bon Repos Hospital construction project
- The SIMBI Hospital construction project
- The project for the rehabilitation and construction of the "La Gonâve Health Center"
- The Port de Paix Hospital Studies and Supervision Project.
- Six resolutions have been adopted by successive governments to finance hospital reconstruction and rehabilitation projects across the Republic. The total amount of the resolutions adopted by the Council of Ministers is $53,656,843.

Resolutions	Amount Adopted
February 11, 2010	$3,223,885
December 21, 2012	$20,000,000
December 11, 2013	$8,500,000
April 15, 2015	$12,000,000
January 6, 2016	$9,932,958
Total	$53,656,843

— The funds used for the reconstruction of the HUEH come from these various Resolutions.

Reconstruction of the State University Hospital of Haiti

- A contract was awarded following an international call for tenders dated December 2, 2013, between the Ministry of Economy and Finance (MEF) and the Group International Santé pour Haïti (GISH), for the reconstruction of the State University Hospital of Haiti (HUEH). Several subcontracts were also signed within the framework of the same project.
- Six contracts were signed with qualified professionals such as project manager, project leader, and project coordinator. Their role is to assist the head of mission of the Technical Support Company and to oversee all activities related to the implementation of the State University of Haiti Hospital Reconstruction and Equipping Project. Of these contracts,

three were signed in US dollars for a total of $144,000; and the others, in gourdes, amount to 9,684,871 HTG.

- Five contracts have been signed with qualified professionals, including assistant accounting specialists, accountants, and project chief accountants, whose role will be to support the Accounting Specialist in all activities and stages of preparing the State University of Haiti Hospital's financial statements, in accordance with international accounting standards and the procedures required by the various donors for the implementation of the State University of Haiti Hospital Reconstruction and Equipping Project. Three of these contracts were signed in US dollars for a total of $75,600, and the others, in gourdes, amount to 2,298,000 HTG.

Four contracts were signed with qualified professionals, including a mechanical engineer, a social media design and management specialist, an architect for quality assurance, and an environmental affairs officer, for the project's implementation. Of these contracts, one was signed in US dollars for $6,000, and the other three, in gourdes, totaled 6,290,400 HTG.

— The Court of Auditors noted several irregularities in the execution of these contracts. Firstly, in accordance with Article 6 of the Decree of May 25, 2012 setting the Thresholds for Public Procurement and the Thresholds for Intervention of the National Commission for Public Procurement at 40,000,000 HTG for Works contracts, the amount of the contract for the first contract is $184,450 or 7,907,205.50 HTG, and was concluded through a negotiated procedure.

— The Court noted that this contract was signed without the validation of the CNMP. Furthermore, the 20% withholding tax required pursuant to Article 8 of the decree of September 29, 2005, concerning income tax, was partially deducted from the amount of the statements submitted by the firm GENIVAR INC / WSP CANADA INC.

— The value of the amount of the withholding tax not collected and paid to the DGI reached $85,967.27. The UTE is responsible for the payment of said tax to the DGI, in accordance with Article 8 of the decree of September 29, 2005 relating to income tax.

— Regarding the execution of the contract, the CSCCA noted, through the files submitted by the Ministry of Economy and Finance (MEF) via its Technical and Execution Unit (UTE), that the disbursements to the Georges Lescot firm had not been fully executed. The provisional or even final Certificate of Acceptance for this project was not provided by the MEF/UTE to the Court.

— As for the execution of the Technical Support contract for the management of the HUEH reconstruction and equipment project, the Court noted through the files submitted by the Ministry of Economy and Finance (MEF) via its Technical and Execution Unit (UTE), that the disbursements in favour of the firm WSP CANADA INC have not been completed.

Responsibilities	First level
	Dr. Florence Duperval Guillaume: Minister of MSSP, Principal Authorizing Officer;
	Yves Romain Bastien: Minister of the Economy and Finance;
	Pierre Erold Étienne: Director General of the MEF.

	Technical support to the management of the HUEH Phase II reconstruction and equipment project
	First level
	Michaël De Landsheer: Executive Director of UTE/MEF; Mathilde F. Mardy: Chief Financial Officer;
	Parnelle Boursiquot: Project Coordinator;

	Reynold Pauyo: Technical Director of UTE/MEF;
	Marie Neltha Féthière: President of the CSCCA
	Second level
	Gaétan Demers: Vice-President of WSP CANADA INC.

Haiti State University Hospital Rehabilitation Project

Names of Consultants	Contract No.	Date of Signature	Amounts
Alex Lorquet	SCI-CC-MEF-92	28/01/2013	$18,000
Parnelle Boursiquot	GG-CC-MEF-164	15/02/2013	$72,000
Parnelle Boursiquot	GG-CC-MEF-230	08/09/2014	3,276,000 HTG
Parnelle Boursiquot	GG-CC-MEF-301	04/05/2015	3,384,000 HTG
Parnelle Boursiquot	GG-CC-MEF-389	25/04/2016	3,024,871 HTG

Names of the various project managers

Names of Consultants	Contract No.	Date of Signature	Amounts
Claudie Meus	SCI-CC-MEF-107	19/04/2012	$24,000
Claudie Meus	SCI-CC-MEF-175	04/06/2013	$24,000
Claudie Meus	GG-CC-MEF-235	02/04/2014	$ 27,600

Claudie Meus	GG-CC-MEF-296	09/07/2015	1,380,000 HTG
Claudie Meus	GG-CC-MEF-391	06/05/2016	918,000 HTG

Project for the Reconstruction and Equipping of the State University Hospital of Haiti

Names of Consultants	Contract No.	Date of Signature	Amounts
Jean Yves Metellus	GG-CC-MEF-231	21/03/2014	$6,000
Farah A. Dorval	SCI-CC-MEF-293	27/04/2015	2,270,400 HTG
Louis Patrick Paul	SCI-CC-MEF-306	15/10/2015	2,820,000 HTG
Martine Clerrobrun	SCI-CC-MEF-303	21/03/2016	1,200,000 HTG

— In the context of the recruitment process for the management team of the Reconstruction and Equipping Project of the State University of Haiti (HUEH), the Court noted that the contracts signed in US dollars with the various consultants for this project did not receive the reasoned opinion of the Court of Auditors, in accordance with Article 5, paragraph 3 of the Decree of November 23, 2005, establishing the organization and operation of the CSCCA.

Recruitment of individual consultants who can join the HUEH Project Management Staff

Responsibilities	First level
	Florence Duperval Guillaume, Minister of Public Health and of Population
	André Lemercier Georges, Minister of the Economy and Finance
	Marie Carmelle Jean Marie, Minister of Economy and Finance
	Wilson Laleau, Minister of the Economy and Finance
	Yves Romains Bastien, Minister of the Economy and Finance
	Michael De Landsheer, director of the UTE
	Alex Lorquet, HUEH Project Manager
	Mathilde Fedelaine Mardy, UTE administrative
	Second level: The different consultants

While the public prosecutor lists the allocations – millions for the construction of roads, hospitals, and sports centers – the inner eye of each listener conjures not the fraudulent invoices, but the phantom structures themselves.

The prosecutor continues:

Construction of a transitional hospital on the site of the former military hospital

—"The Court of Auditors discovered that the firm Expert Concept SA received an overpayment of $9,225.80; this sum must be returned to the Haitian State. Furthermore, the Court noted that the required 2% provisional tax payment, pursuant to Article 76, second paragraph, of the decree of September 29, 2005, concerning Income Tax, was not collected, amounting to $11,653.64."

— Documents referring to supervision reports were noted by the Court. These documents were not signed by the heads of the supervision firm, Cabinet Georges Lescot. The provisional or even final acceptance certificate for this project was not provided to the Court by the MEF/UTE.

Construction of a transitional hospital on the site of the former military hospital

Responsibilities	First level
	Dr. Florence Duperval Guillaume: Minister of MSSP, Principal Authorizing Officer;
	Wilson Laleau: Minister of Economy and Finance, principal authorizing officer;
	Michaël De Landsheer: Executive Director of the UTE/MEF;
	Mathilde F. Mardy: Chief Financial Officer;
	Parnelle Boursiquot: HUEH project manager;
	Reynold Pauyo: Technical Director of UTE/MEF;
	Nonie Mathieu: President of the CSCCA.
	Second level
	Georges Lescot: CEO of the Georges Lescot firm
	Third level
	Monique Duperval, Eng.: President and CEO general of EXPERT CONCEPT SA

The prosecutor closes his notes. He glances around the audience before concluding:

"Your Honor, this audit is not a surprise. It confirms the two reports from the Senate committees presented in 2016 and 2017, which already highlighted irregularities in the management of PetroCaribe funds. These irregularities included improperly signed contracts, unfinished work, poorly archived files, and public institutions failing to protect the interests of the State (MTPTC, MPCE, MTIC, MEF, BMPAD, etc.). The audit by the Superior Court of Accounts and Administrative Disputes (CSCCA) is conducted by the highest administrative body in the country. The Court of Accounts identified several anomalies in the execution of projects riddled with irregularities: administrative irregularities that caused harm to the projects and the community, as well as those related to the regulatory framework and sound management practices." Project managers, directors of the implementing and supervisory firms, ministers, directors general, and members of the BMPAD are all implicated. Several are appearing before this Assize Court to answer for their dishonest actions.

The prosecutor continues:

— "Coming from a respected and less directly politicized state institution, the CSCCA report highlights the extent of the scandal. Contracts involving waste, corruption, overbilling, and the embezzlement of billions of US dollars are being executed in a scandalous manner."

— In addition to the three directors of the BMPAD, Michael Lecorps, Eustache Saint-Lot and Patrick Noramé, who were directly implicated in the three audits, the names of three presidents and six prime ministers, who held power from 2008 to 2016, as well as ministers and other senior public administration officials, numerous civil servants and business leaders, are also found.

"Corruption in the Petro Caribe program," the prosecutor stated, "remained a deep wound in Haiti for a long time, with persistent protests demanding justice for the billions of US dollars embezzled from a development fund. Despite investigations (such as the one by the Court of Auditors) and reports (such as those by the IMF), no legal proceedings had succeeded in prosecuting and punishing those responsible, despite irrefutable evidence of corruption (illicit enrichment, money laundering, overbilling, etc.). Today, justice is underway. Judicial independence has been achieved with the passage of anti-corruption laws and the governance of the country by competent and respected authorities. The fraudsters are being arrested and brought before the Assize Court. The time for accountability has arrived."

The room is taking in the significance of what has just been presented. The figures have drawn a precise map of the squandering. They are not contested, not negotiated, not defended against their obviousness. They are undeniable.

Me. Antoine sat down, his hands trembling slightly with adrenaline. As his colleague rose, his mind, for a moment, escaped the confined atmosphere of the courtroom. He revisited the road from Santo Domingo to Punta Cana, traveled last year during a regional conference. An image flashed through his mind, a violent one: the silhouette of the Punta Catalina power plant, a 770-megawatt complex built with Petro Caribe funds, its two chimneys dominating the coastline. He remembered the hundreds of social housing units in the Santo Domingo Oeste sector, the urbanized and inhabited blocks. He thought back to modern hospitals like the renovated and equipped Robert Reid Cabral. There, in the Dominican Republic, Venezuelan oil money had been transformed into concrete, steel, and turbines. It embodied the energy sovereignty and social progress of our neighbor. In Haiti, Petro Caribe funds were stolen by high-ranking state officials. The same agreement signed with two radically different fates. The comparison, as painful as it is unavoidable, strikes the prosecution at its core: in neighboring Dominican Republic, the money was used; here in Haiti, it was pocketed by these defendants, who leave behind only ghosts of projects and a nation's bitterness.

The prosecutor imperceptibly shakes his head, banishing this unbearable vision, and brings all his attention back to the facts of the accusation, to the present of the trial.

Proud of his work, he resumes his seat. He gives the floor to one of the deputies.

Chapter 14

WHERE IS THE MONEY GIVEN TO HAITI?

It is an angry and threatening public prosecutor who takes the floor to ask this question: where has the Petro Caribe money gone? The public prosecutor repeats the same phrase in Creole "kot kòb Petro Caribe a?" (Where is the Petro Caribe money).

The question travels through the courtroom walls to reach the ears of the accused. They tremble like leaves at the thought of being lynched. Outside, under a blazing sun, a dense crowd has gathered, some protesting with placards, others watching the trial on giant screens set up in the street. Each time the prosecution utters the phrase, "Kot kòb Petro Caribe a?" "Where is the Petro Caribe money?" the entire crowd applauds. The obsessive slogan spills through the doors and windows of the courthouse, making its way into the courtroom. This is no longer a simple legal process, but has become a collective movement, a national heartbeat punctuated by anger and anticipation. In the courtroom, the accused feel the muffled pressure of the public outcry. The accusation no longer comes solely from the prosecution; it also comes from the street, from a people demanding reparations for decades of suffering and abuse.

It is no longer just a prosecutor who is interrogating; it is an entire people demanding accountability. With each slogan, the courtroom seems to vibrate, as if the boundary between institutional justice and popular justice were dissolving; reminding the accused that this trial is not only taking place before a court, but before history and before the Haitian nation thirsting for justice.

The prosecutor nervously begins his closing argument:

"Your Honor, the massive embezzlement linked to the Petro Caribe program has been duly documented: that involving political elites under Préval and Martelly, and that committed by private company executives, especially after the 2010 earthquake. Several governments have been implicated, with corrupt officials transferring sums to offshore bank accounts under the guise of fictitious social programs or poorly managed projects. Millions of dollars have been siphoned from the national budget and international aid, amounting to more than 3 billion US dollars. Despite billions of dollars received in foreign aid, living conditions remain precarious due to this embezzlement and poor governance."

The figures resonate, stark and undeniable. Nearly four billion US dollars, Petro Caribe funds, squandered. The money, intended to pay off debts to the Venezuelan oil agency and invest in development, has been stolen. A heavy silence falls over the courtroom. The prosecution observes a calculated pause. Its strategy is to give the public time to digest these figures. Four billion dollars; a sum that defies comprehension, but which can, through thought, be forced into a tangible form. It is the equivalent of building 400 modern hospitals or 4,000 fully equipped schools, or the annual salaries of 200,000 teachers for ten years; double the operating budget of the Republic of Haiti.

The prosecutor pauses and then continues:

"This sum is not an accounting abstraction; it is the exact amount of money that was stolen, mortgaging the country's future. Every dollar embezzled is a day of school lost for a child, a day of medical care denied to a sick person, a bag of cement missing from a dike, a meter of road that will never be paved. The scale of the squandering is staggering, it revolts the conscience. It is a financial crime, certainly, but it is also a crime of bloodshed. The Haitian nation has been stabbed, symbolically, by the accused. Here, the court is faced with a simple yet monstrous equation: the astronomical sum that was supposed to lift Haiti out of underdevelopment has been squandered by unscrupulous officials in collusion with foreigners. The accused and their accomplices deposited the Petro Caribe money in offshore accounts. The question is: 'Where is the Petro Caribe money?'" This then transforms into another question: "What has become of the country that Petro Caribe was supposed to build?"

The prosecutor fixes his gaze on the accused, and pointing his index finger in their direction, declares:

— "Ladies and gentlemen, you corrupt officials who were in charge of the country: where did the Petro Caribe money go?"

Without waiting for a response, the chief prosecutor continued:

— "Your Honor, from its implementation in 2008 until March 21, 2016, the Petro Caribe fund generated $ 3,833,890,217.58. From this amount, the BMPAD paid $ 1,714,288,623.21 in short-term (30-day) debt for petroleum products received. The remaining $ 2,119,601,594.37 was allocated to the State's investment budget for this period."

Petro Caribe debt cancellation

— Following the earthquake of January 12, 2010, the Venezuelan government cancelled the debt of the Republic of Haiti. This debt, contracted under the Petro Caribe agreement, consists of a long - term portion and a short-term portion, totaling $396,073,224 or its equivalent in local currency, 25,957,371,000 HTG, converted at the BRH exchange rate of 65 HTG to one US dollar on September 30, 2016. All products benefiting from this measure have been sold, and the proceeds and related amounts are shown in the following tables.

Short-Term Debt

Item	Description – Amount ($)
1. Fuel	$27,564,721
2. Fuel oil	$7,760,369
Total short-term debt	$35,325,091
Long-term debt	
Item	Description – Amount ($)
1. Fuel	$354,895,130
2. Asphalt	$1,620,702
3. Fuel oil	$4,232,301
Total long-term debt	$360,748,133
Total amount of debt cancelled	$396,073,224

The prosecutor continues:

— "In 2008, partial debt relief took place, including a cancellation of the debt owed to the AFD/French Bank. France cancelled a debt of approximately 58 million euros (representing 4 million euros of the total debt) of Haiti to the French Development Agency (AFD) and the French Bank.

In 2023, Canada provided $100 million in funding to directly support the Haitian National Police. In 2024, Canada contributed over $86 million to support the deployment of the multinational security support mission.

— The United States remains the largest donor of humanitarian aid to Haiti. Since fiscal year 2023, USAID has committed nearly $146 million in emergency assistance, providing life-saving support to more than 1.5 million people across the country.

—In 2024, the United States provided substantial assistance to Haiti, totaling nearly $470 million or more, primarily for emergency humanitarian assistance (food, health, water) and security support, including funding for the Multinational Security Support Mission (MSS) to combat gangs, with funds going to USAID and the State Department.

—As part of bilateral cooperation, from 2010 to the present, Germany has invested nearly 115 million euros in Haiti in various projects and interventions, including 28 million euros for the rehabilitation of the Péligre hydroelectric power plant.

—Furthermore, four German NGOs (German Agro Action, the German Red Cross, Handicap International, and Caritas) received $7.4 million in 2017 for long-term projects in Haiti's Northern Department. During the same year, the German Embassy, in partnership with local authorities, funded micro-projects to the tune of nearly $250,000.

—The European Union provides substantial aid to Haiti, mainly humanitarian, allocating tens of millions of euros in 2024-2025 to respond to humanitarian crises, gang violence, food insecurity and natural disasters such as Hurricane Melissa, supporting emergency aid (water, shelter, and food), education, food security and disaster preparedness.

- 35.9 million euros allocated in 2025 (including 20 million in May 2024) for humanitarian aid, the response to cholera and Hurricane Melissa;
- an additional 21.5 million euros to be released in November 2025 for Haiti, Venezuela and the Caribbean affected by Hurricane Melissa;

- 40 million in initiatives for education, customs and development in the Northeast by February 2025.

—Taiwan provides millions of dollars in aid to Haiti. Taiwanese aid to Haiti focuses on strengthening historical diplomatic ties (since 1956), with cooperation in public security, education, health, food security and infrastructure, while providing financial support (such as loans) to address Haiti's security and economic challenges.

—Remittances from the Haitian diaspora constitute a vital economic lifeline for Haiti, representing billions of dollars (approximately 3.8 billion in 2023) and about 20% of GDP, mainly supporting consumer spending (food, health, education, housing), and coming primarily from the United States and Canada.

—Haiti has levied a $1.50 tax on diaspora remittances since 2011. This tax was implemented by Michel Martelly to finance the National Education Fund (FNE). Other taxes are levied on international phone calls and gambling.

The list continues, relentless. United States, Canada, France, Brazil, Chile... The amounts transferred by the diaspora accumulate, overlap, and reach dizzying heights. It is no longer a list of aid, but the evidence of a deadly hemorrhage: the Haitian people, their veins open, are struggling in their own blood. Every debt cancellation, every donation, every tax levied represents a maneuver by the authorities in power to pocket more money. As the country sinks, they rejoice: each natural disaster gives them an opportunity to embezzle even more money, taking advantage of the emergency and contracts awarded without competitive bidding. One horrifying truth is inescapable: this colossal sum has vanished. He became ensnared in a subterranean network of complicity, impervious to any progress, fueling the opulence of a few and strengthening the machinery of corruption that is eating away at institutions. The real scandal lies not only in the theft, but in this infernal mechanism that transforms hope into poison, destroys progress, and facilitates the enrichment of the accused.

Bilateral, multilateral, humanitarian, and security aid, along with remittances from the diaspora, accumulate year after year, decade after decade, forming an uninterrupted flow of money into Haiti. Listening to these figures, the Criminal Court grasps a troubling truth: Haiti's problem lies not in a lack of resources, but in their absorption by a system incapable –or unwilling– to use them to establish strong institutions, sustainable public services, and functional infrastructure. Every donor cited, every debt canceled, every tax levied, reveals a fundamental contradiction that the prosecution must address: the more money flows in, the more the state deteriorates.

In the tense silence of the room, this observation takes on the value of an implicit indictment not against international aid or foreign solidarity, but against those who, charged with making it a lever for development, have allowed it to dissolve into opacity, bad governance and systemic predation.

The burning question now on everyone's lips is no longer "where is the money?" but "how could such plunder have been carried out, right under the noses of institutions like UCREF (the Central Financial Intelligence Unit), ULCC (the Anti-Corruption Unit), the Senate's Ethics and Anti-Corruption Commission, CSCCA (Superior Court of Accounts and Administrative Disputes), and the Haitian judicial institutions?"

> "Where is the money given in the form of aid to Haiti?" the prosecutor insists.
>
> — "In January 2015, the situation of the public treasury was alarming, to say the least. The reserves of the BRH (Bank of the Republic of Haiti) to finance the public treasury and EDH (State Electricity of Haiti), which amounted to

US$12.4 billion for the 2013-2014 fiscal year, had already fallen to US$6 billion by December 2014."

The prosecutor continues with the same momentum:

— "Your Honor, we are talking about the Petro Caribe funds, which in recent years could have put the country on the path to development with the construction of schools, hospitals, modern infrastructure, hydroelectric plants, etc. Well, what have we done with them? What has been achieved? We have missed a historic opportunity to accomplish what we can never achieve on our own."

Why didn't the state authorities, instead of squandering these funds, use them for more impactful projects than simply building useless footbridges and beautifying public squares, which are quickly degraded by a population in distress? In short, no initiative has been undertaken to sustainably transform living conditions in Haiti, a country considered the most structurally underdeveloped in the entire Western Hemisphere.

—And not only have we invested these funds in projects of no fundamental value, but the contracts signed without competitive bidding have given corrupt officials the opportunity to divert millions of dollars from the public coffers each time.

"All the institutions involved in the use of Petro Caribe funds are bankrupt, leaving behind colossal debts that the Haitian state must assume. This is the case, for example, of FAES, which, in addition to having been the victim of embezzlement of several hundred million dollars under the regime of former President Martelly, is also being asked to repay 3 million dollars by the IDB (Inter-American Development Bank)."

The prosecutor pauses before continuing:

—"Where is the Petro Caribe money? How frustrating and outrageous the actions of the accused are. It is important that this case be treated with all the seriousness it deserves, so that the world can understand the schemes used by these high-ranking officials and their accomplices to embezzle approximately 4 billion dollars from the Haitian state coffers."

"The prosecution has always wanted a thorough investigation of all 409 projects, one after the other, to establish an indisputable balance sheet. This involves analyzing each contract and the amounts committed, then, by comparing the funds disbursed with the actual progress of the projects, demonstrating how Petro Caribe funds were misappropriated or mismanaged. The investigating judge issued a high-quality ruling, which was upheld by the Court of Appeal. He acquitted those questioned for whom there were no issues, and prosecuted those linked to potential waste of resources. This meticulous work was carried out by the various commissions that investigated the case."

A total silence falls over the courtroom, heavier than in a cemetery. The machinery of justice has just frozen, and in this void, the accusation finally takes on its purest form: these are no longer merely thieving defendants sitting in the dock, but architects of chaos. The link is established, irrefutable: the billions embezzled from funds meant for the future have been recycled into weapons, ammunition, and the power to terrorize. Every dollar stolen from a school or a road is transformed into a Kalashnikov in the hands of a child soldier. The Petro Caribe trial suddenly transcends the realm of financial corruption; it becomes the trial of violence itself, the trial of those who knowingly undermined the foundations of the Haitian state and nurtured the demons that tear it apart.

Committed between 2008 and 2018 by heads of state and government, ministers, business leaders and bank executives, Petro Caribe embodies an irreparable affront to public ethics, with a system of malfeasance orchestrated by accomplices scattered across at least five foreign countries: the Dominican Republic, Venezuela, Panama, the Cayman Islands, and the United States of America.

The prosecution's gaze shifts from one defendant to another. It is no longer the gaze of the law upon fraudsters, but that of history upon traitors. The judicial sentence remains to be pronounced, but in the heart of the courtroom, a deeper verdict has just been delivered: the defendants stole the money, and with that money, they contributed to precipitating the ruin of their own country.

The prosecution fell silent for a moment. A cathedral-like silence filled the courtroom, heavy with the weight of the obvious truth. The chapter closed on this terrible reality: it was no longer a question of determining the guilt of the accused, but of measuring the extent of the disaster they had caused.

The prosecutor looks at the defendants and adds:

> — "The investigating judge used data from the Court of Auditors and, after hearing witnesses and defendants, and conducting other investigative acts, often through letters rogatory, issued his order. Defendants against whom the investigation found no evidence were released, and others—like those sitting in the dock—were charged. Among the accused are those who are the direct perpetrators of the embezzlements and those prosecuted for their participation as masterminds or accomplices in the alleged crimes. They are all criminals. The majority of them are sanctioned by the international community for financing violence, particularly the distribution of weapons and ammunition to the bandits who terrorize the population."

Chapter 15

INTERNATIONAL SANCTIONS

(The eighth day of the hearing)

It is nine o'clock in the morning. The courthouse is already bustling, long before the city has fully recovered its composure. Groups are forming at the entrance gate, silhouettes emerging in the still-soft morning light. Lawyers, journalists, families of the accused, activists, and simply curious onlookers are passing through the courthouse doors, under the watchful eyes of security guards. Everyone is there to see, to hear, to understand—or simply to be able to say later that they were there.

Outside, the crowd thickens as the hour wears on. But very quickly, conversations drift away from the trial. They talk about something else. They talk about the World Cup. Haiti is playing its first match against Scotland, and this prospect spreads through the crowd like a rumor carrying joy. Between comments about the defendants or the length of the hearing, predictions are exchanged, players are discussed, and hopes are raised for a victory capable, if only for a moment, of making people forget the fear, the insecurity, and the uncertain future. That morning, justice and football vie for the attention of a people accustomed to living through several tragedies at once.

At 9:30 a.m., as the hearing was about to resume, another concern weighed heavily on everyone's minds: that of international sanctions. In the Haitian context, these sanctions consist of an arsenal of coercive measures imposed by the international community—the United States, Canada, the European Union, and the UN Security Council—to target individuals and entities accused of threatening security in the region, financing armed gangs, and perpetuating corruption. This primarily involves freezing assets abroad, travel bans, visa revocations, and arms embargoes. These tools aim to isolate the perpetrators of instability economically and diplomatically, to stem the flow of arms, and to exert political pressure to restore security and the rule of law.

Inside, the atmosphere is tense. The benches in the courtroom gradually fill with somber-faced spectators, gathered for the eighth day of a historic trial. The distant murmur of the crowd gathered near the courthouse reaches the interior, a reminder that life, with its simple joys and passions, continues its course alongside the legal proceedings. The presiding judge opens the hearing in a firm voice, and the floor is given to the prosecution to continue its closing arguments, which focus on a crucial instrument of international pressure: sanctions.

— "The hearing has resumed," declared the president, adding:

— "The Court gives the floor to the prosecutor to continue the presentation of the facts."

The prosecutor begins:

— "Your Honor, a major problem facing the country is gang violence. The spread of armed groups is a major risk for Haiti and the Caribbean region. It is sad to admit that several defendants have their names mentioned in reports from the United States, Canada, the Dominican Republic, the European Union, and the United Nations. These individuals are listed as those who finance the violence, particularly the distribution of weapons and ammunition to the bandits."

- The United States, Canada, the European Union, and the United Nations Security Council have implemented sanctions intended to deter those they accuse of threatening peace, financing the activities of armed gangs, and perpetrating acts of corruption. On October 21, 2022, the United Nations Security Council unanimously adopted Resolution 2653. This resolution established a sanctions regime for Haiti (travel ban, asset freeze, and arms embargo) as well as a committee of experts to oversee its implementation.

- In 2023, the United Nations Security Council imposed sanctions primarily against individuals and entities financing gangs. Specifically, Resolution 2700, adopted in October 2023, targets those responsible for violence and crime.

- Arms embargo: prohibition on importing weapons, ammunition and military equipment for all actors in Haiti, except for exemptions.
- Asset freeze: the funds and economic resources of the designated persons are frozen.
- Travel ban: Individuals named on the sanctions list are prohibited from traveling.
- Targeting: Sanctions specifically target individuals linked to gangs, corruption, arms trafficking, and other illegal activities.

- The Security Council voted on the afternoon of September 30, 2025, in favor of a draft resolution authorizing UN Member States to transform the Multinational Security Support Mission (MMAS) in Haiti into a Gang Repression Force (FRG) for an initial period of 12 months. This force, whose personnel costs will be funded by voluntary contributions, will have a total authorized strength of 5,550 personnel, including 5,500 uniformed officers and 50 civilians.

- By resolution 2793 (2025) (S/RES/2793), adopted by 12 votes in favor and 3 abstentions (China, Russian Federation and Pakistan), the Council, acting under Chapter VII of the Charter of the United Nations, authorizes UN Member States participating in the MMAS to conduct, independently or in cooperation with the Haitian National Police (PNH) and the Armed Forces of Haiti, "targeted anti-gang operations" in order to neutralize, isolate and deter armed gangs.

- The Security Council further authorizes them to ensure the security of critical infrastructure and transit points; to complement, enhance and support the operational capacities of the Haitian National Police (PNH) and the Armed Forces of Haiti; to support the PNH, the Armed Forces of Haiti and national institutions in order to guarantee security conditions conducive to holding free and fair elections; to contribute to the creation of a safe environment enabling the population to access humanitarian aid; to assist the PNH and the Armed Forces of Haiti in combating the trafficking and diversion of weapons and related materials; and to improve Haiti's management and control of its land, sea and air borders and ports.

- The text, supported by the United States and Panama, also calls on the Secretary-General to create the United Nations Support Office in Haiti (BANUH), whose mission will be to provide support to the FRG, the United Nations Integrated Office in Haiti (BINUH), the PNH and the Armed Forces of Haiti.

— "The Haitian people could wait no longer."

Panama stated that the multidimensional crisis facing Haiti demands the Council's "determined attention." "You are not alone," its representative told the Haitian people, before highlighting the support given to the text by some fifty countries. Speaking again after the vote, the Panamanian delegate expressed the hope that this resolution would restore the security necessary for holding elections, reviving the economy, and creating opportunities that would give hope back to the population.

"The Haitian people could no longer wait," he insisted, welcoming the fact that the Council was fulfilling its role by sending a very clear message to actors in the region and the world. This resolution shows that the Council "continues to assume its responsibilities," the United Kingdom added.

"The UN can still contribute to international security," the US representative declared after the vote, adding that he was "proud" to have supported the resolution. He argued that gang violence, which the MMAS lacked the resources to combat, had jeopardized the very existence of the Haitian state and threatened to trigger a migration crisis in the region. "Today's vote rectifies this situation."

—After thanking Kenya for its actions and "sacrifices" in leading the MMAS (Multinational Security Support Mission), the American delegate stated that the new Anti-Gang Force could help Haiti reverse the trend. He nevertheless emphasized that any lasting solution could only be based on the restoration of the rule of law and stable institutions "by the Haitians themselves," as established in the resolution.

The prosecutor reflects and says to himself:

Behind the solemn words and diplomatic congratulations, the reality remains stark: the MMAS (Multinational Security Support

Mission) failed to fulfill its mission of restoring peace. Conceived as a support mission, it arrived without a clear offensive mandate, without sufficient resources, and without a nuanced understanding of local dynamics. On the ground, the gangs did not retreat; they adapted, moved, and strengthened. The population, for its part, quickly perceived the gap between international pronouncements and the persistence of daily insecurity. The MMAS protected certain routes and provided occasional security for strategic sites, but it was unable to dismantle the armed groups permanently or restore state authority in neighborhoods controlled by violence.

This failure was not merely military; it was political and symbolic. By limiting itself to a support role, the MMAS projected the image of a cautious international presence, almost paralyzed by the fear of failure or unpopularity. It depended on a weakened, fragmented Haitian state, often absent where force should have been deployed. Thus, the mission became a reflection of a paradox: it was called upon to reinforce a sovereignty that was no longer able to assert itself. It was in this void, between immense expectations and limited capabilities, that the MMAS was exhausting itself. Its announced transformation into a force for gang repression then appeared less as a strategic choice than as the belated admission of a failure that no one, until then, dared to name.

The prosecutor stares at the presiding judge for a moment. With the same energy, he continues his presentation: his face shows no sign of fatigue.

— "Your Honor, by unanimous vote of its fifteen members, the United Nations Security Council adopted, on 20 October 2025, resolution 2794 (2025), extending the arms embargo, travel bans and asset freezes targeting individuals and entities that threaten the peace, security or stability of the country.

—The decision also extends, for 13 months, the mandate of the group of experts tasked with supporting the sanctions committee established by resolution 2653 (2022), according to a UN note.

This new resolution, presented by Panama and the United States, reaffirms that all member states must prevent the direct or indirect supply, sale, or transfer of arms, ammunition, and related materiel to Haiti. It emphasizes the need to strengthen border controls to prevent arms trafficking and diversion, a major concern in a context where gang violence continues to escalate.

— The text encourages better coordination between UN bodies – notably the United Nations Integrated Office in Haiti (BINUH), the United Nations Support Office in Haiti (BANUH), the United Nations Office on Drugs and Crime (UNODC), and Haitian structures, such as the Gang Repression Force (FRG) and the Haitian National Police (PNH), to ensure the effective implementation of sanctions.

—The council further calls for increased support to the PNH (National Police of Haiti), the Armed Forces (FAD'H) and border authorities to strengthen the management of seized weapons and ammunition, improve the marking, storage and destruction of stocks, and intensify the fight against diversions.

—The United Nations has sanctioned Jimmy Chérizier, leader and spokesperson for the Viv Ansanm group. A 2023 United Nations report mentioned accusations that Michel Martelly had financed armed gangs, particularly those based in Pétion-Ville and Port-au-Prince.

December 15, 2025, the European Union officially announced targeted sanctions against former Haitian President Michel Martelly, his former advisor Youri Latortue, and former Senator Rony Célestin for their direct involvement in financing armed gangs, serious crimes, and repeated human rights violations in Haiti. According to the

EU, Michel Martelly and Youri Latortue are accused of arming and supporting criminal groups for political and economic gain.

—Rony Célestin, for his part, is presented as a major player in armed violence, involved in smuggling activities and the assassination of journalist Néhémie Joseph, who was killed after denouncing his alleged links to criminal networks. Furthermore, the 5 Segond gang has also been sanctioned for a long list of atrocities, including murders, kidnappings, rapes, extortion, and obstruction of humanitarian aid.

These measures entail the freezing of assets, a ban on funding by European nationals or entities, and a travel ban within the European Union for the individuals concerned. Through these sanctions, the EU states its intention to put pressure on those responsible for insecurity and impunity, while supporting efforts to restore peace, stability, and the rule of law in Haiti.

A hush fell over the room. Gradually, it thickened, becoming almost oppressive, as if everyone were inwardly weighing the weight of the words that had just been spoken. Sanctions were no longer a diplomatic abstraction; they now drew a clear line between words and deeds, between yesterday's impunity and today's stated intention to coerce. Behind every asset freeze and every travel ban loomed the same question: how far can the international community intervene when the Haitian state no longer has the means to impose its authority?

In the courtroom, all eyes slowly turn toward the defendants. The prosecution pauses briefly, and then continues. After Europe, another player enters the scene. Another jurisdiction, another legal framework, but the same logic of targeted pressure against those designated as responsible for insecurity and chaos. Then, from outside, a clamor erupts, so vast and sudden that it seems to shake the windows. At that precise moment, something has transpired on a football field thousands of kilometers away, and the wave of emotion has just crashed against the courtroom walls. The prosecution, interrupted in its flow, closes its eyes for a moment. In this brutal context, between the cold mechanics of sanctions and the feverish pulse of a nation, lies the entire Haitian tragedy: the quest for justice is an exhausting marathon, while hope lives to the staccato rhythm of matches. The prosecution resumes its account of the facts, turning the case over and over in its mind. Another page, another international actor enters the scene. The attention of the room gradually returns to the prosecution's case, while the echo of the clamor fades in the streets, giving way to a new expectation.

At that moment, the president rang the bell and struck the gavel, saying:

- "The hearing is suspended and will resume this evening at 6 a.m."

During the break, a crowd gathers. The prosecutor stands in the middle of a group of journalists who are asking him questions. A few meters away, television cameras are filming the scene. The trial is being broadcast around the world. In the space of a week, Me. Antoine has become a star. A journalist known for his controversial statements approaches the group. He waits for the other colleagues to give him a chance, and then addresses the prosecutor directly. He speaks loudly, not to provoke, but to be heard, and above all, so that the discreet microphones around him will capture every word.

— General prosecutor, we have heard the charges against the accused in your indictment, now what do you intend to do to freeze their assets? What mechanisms are in place to recover Petro Caribe funds for the benefit of the Public Treasury?" the journalist said.

The prosecutor listens without responding. He remains committed to the principle of the investigation. He quickly leaves, and followed by three deputies, he takes refuge in his office.

Chapter 16

CANADIAN/AMERICAN SANCTIONS

- "The hearing has resumed. The prosecution has the floor," declares the presiding judge.

The prosecutor casts a brief glance towards the accused and continues:

— "Your Honor, the Canadian sanctions related to Haiti were adopted under the Special Economic Measures Act and the United Nations Act in response to the activities of criminal gangs and those who support them in fomenting violence and insecurity. On November 3, 2022, the regulations concerning Haiti entered into force."

—The Special Economic Measures Regulations for Haiti impose restrictions on transactions, effectively freezing assets, involving any person whose name appears on the list established for this purpose. The regulations prohibit any person residing in Canada and any Canadian abroad from:

- to carry out a transaction relating to property, wherever it may be, belonging to a person whose name appears on the list or held or controlled by or on behalf of that person;

- to conclude a transaction related to a prohibited transaction described above or to facilitate its conclusion;
- to provide financial or related services in relation to all transactions described above;
- to make all goods, wherever they may be, available to a person whose name appears on the list or a person acting on his behalf;
- to provide financial or related services to or for the benefit of a person whose name appears on the list.

—It is also forbidden to cause or facilitate the perpetration of prohibited acts described above.

—Individuals designated in the schedule to the regulations are also prohibited from entering Canadian territory under the Immigration and Refugee Protection Act.

—The Regulations for the Implementation of United Nations Resolutions on Haiti were adopted under the United Nations Act to give effect to the resolutions of the Security Council of the United Nations. Subject to certain exceptions, the measures imposed against Haiti are as follows:

- a freeze on all funds, other financial assets and economic resources located in Canada and owned or controlled, directly or indirectly, by any designated person or entity, or by any person or entity acting on their behalf or at their direction, or by entities owned or controlled by them; and
- a ban on exporting weapons and related equipment to Haiti or any person located there.

—In accordance with resolution 2653 (2022), Canada imposes travel restrictions on persons whose names appear on Security Council lists, which are implemented in Canada under the Immigration and Refugee Protection Act.

—Resolution 2653 (2022)! The numbers resonate like technical jargon, almost abstract. Yet, in Haiti, 2022 also held another coded hope: the Grenadières' qualification for the World Cup. Two committees met that year: one at the Security Council, which decided to sanction and freeze the assets of those in Haiti associated with gangs; the other, the Haitian Football Federation, which was preparing the roster for the world's biggest competition. The same nation, torn between two destinies: that of an orderly space where the rules of the game apply to all, and that of chaos in the streets of Port-au-Prince where armed gangs rule. The Security Council's Sanctions Committee sits in order and silence; Port-au-Prince screams under the bullets. And this ban on exporting weapons... what bitter irony, when shipments of weapons for the criminal group "Viv Ansanm" have never stopped arriving, escaping all border controls.

The prosecutor is turning the page. It continues:

—"Your Honor, Canadian media reported on Thursday, February 16, 2023, that two members of the Haitian elite, former interim president Jocelerme Privert (February 14, 2016 – February 7, 2017) and lawyer Salim Succar, former chief of staff to former prime minister Laurent Lamothe, have been added to a list of individuals barred from doing business with Canada. Both are alleged to have ties to armed gangs that have taken control of a large part of the capital and several other geographic departments of the country."

Jocelerme Privert; for some, the name remains synonymous with a brief and singular interlude in the electoral process. He, the former president of the Senate, served as interim president after the chaotic departure of Michel Martelly. In 2016, in a country already in turmoil, he achieved the improbable: organizing presidential elections, ensuring their success, and transferring power to an elected president: Jovenel Moïse. It was a technical, almost an administrative act that seemed miraculous at the time. For a while, he was believed to be the temporary guardian of a republican rule of the game that everyone claimed to uphold. Today, that same name appears on a list of sanctioned individuals. He is now presumed to be a troublemaker, associated with those who have made any new elections impossible. History thus closes, cruelly: the man who had, for a time, managed to keep the electoral machinery running is now lumped in with those who rule by force of arms. His legacy is a bitter paradox – the president of a successful transition, now the *chairman* of a morally bankrupt board. The nation watches him, and sees in him not proof of virtue, but perhaps the opposite: it sees in him an illustration that professed legality is merely a clever way to conceal one's true intentions.

The prosecutor continues:

—"On November 20, 2022, Canada imposed sanctions on former President Joseph Michel Martelly and former Prime Ministers Laurent Lamothe and Jean Henry Céant. Canadian Foreign Minister Mélanie Joly stated in a press release that these individuals directly benefit from the work of gangs and are linked to a system of corruption."

—These sanctions bring to about thirty the number of people sanctioned by Canada for financing gangs, corruption and money laundering, including money from drug trafficking.

—Joseph Lambert, Youri Latortue, Gary Bodeau, Hervé Fourcand, Rony Célestin, Michel Martelly, Jean Henry Céant, Laurent Lamothe, Berto Dorce, Liszt Quitel, Nenel Cassy, Steeve Khawly, Arnel Bélizaire, Charles (Kiko) Saint-Rémy, Gilbert Bigio, Reynold Deeb, Sherif Abdallah, Jocelerme Privert, Salim Succar, Marc Antoine Acra, Carl Braun, Jean-Marie Vorbe, André Apaid, Jimmy Chérizier, Lanmo Sanjou, Vitel'Homme Innocent, Johnson André (alias Izo), Marc Antoine Acra, Carl Braun…".

The prosecutor sets the list of sanctioned names displayed on the screen. This list illustrates the fact that the scourge of corruption plaguing Haiti and its institutions is the greatest challenge to building a democratic society.

Indeed, the list is long. It unfolds like a counter-history textbook, unflinchingly exposing the true image of the political and economic class in Haiti. "The most repugnant elite in the hemisphere," Bill Clinton called them. Former presidents, senators, deputies, ministers, chiefs of staff, lawyers, businessmen, and gang leaders… Their common denominator, according to the indictment, is having transformed Haitian territory into a bloody playground where power is measured in dollars and corpses. They all have participated, in one way or another, in this rigged game. Some acted from the air-conditioned halls of power, others from the wastelands of armed insurrection. Their proclamation of innocence, discordant like a choir with out-of-tune voices, crashes against the wall of these sanctions which, like an irrevocable verdict, exclude them from the legal game. The trial, for its part, seeks to establish the degree of their responsibility in the squandering of Petro Caribe funds.

The prosecutor said:

—"All these people have proclaimed their innocence. Even assuming that the international community could be criticized for sanctioning the accused for complicity with armed gangs, the fact remains that the latter do indeed form a criminal organization."

The prosecutor pauses. He says to himself:

"We want to rebuild Haiti, and the challenge is to establish a rule of law where the rules are respected by everyone. It is certain that this cannot be done overnight, as it requires a functioning justice system. It is up to the Haitian government to demonstrate, through strong initiatives, its stated commitment to resolutely combat impunity by helping the justice system fulfill its mission. The Petro Caribe trial is a step in the right direction."

The prosecutor continues. Regarding judicial transparency, it is understood that, for the public to have confidence in the State's will and ability to punish abuses, it is essential that the authorities make the results of investigations public. He adds:

— "That said, the Court of Auditors' audit report on the management of PetroCaribe funds was an unprecedented decision in a country where the obstruction of investigations is one of the biggest challenges to be solved in the Haitian administrative/judicial system."

The prosecutor takes some time to consult his notes.

This suspended, almost imperceptible moment is not a mere technical gesture. It is the breath of a public official gauging the gravity of what he is about to say. In the courtroom, it becomes clear that the debate is leaving the confines of the tribunal and entering the international arena. Haitian justice, long confined within its crumbling walls, suddenly finds itself observed, connected, embedded in a global system where foreign powers appoint, designate, and punish.

The silence is heavy. It serves as a reminder that, for far too long, Haiti's sovereignty has been expressed more through decisions imposed from elsewhere than through the strength of its own institutions. The prosecution pauses to reflect, then says: "The PetroCaribe trial is the first step toward a second independence." It continues: "By bringing to justice those responsible for the misappropriation of Petro Caribe funds, Haiti will return with its head held high to the community of nations where justice prevails."

The prosecutor continues:

— "Your Honor, like the United Nations Security Council and Canada, the United States has taken sanctions against several individuals in the political and economic class in Haiti for their role in supporting and arming gangs.

In 2024, the United States supported and implemented targeted sanctions measures (asset freezes, travel bans) against individuals and entities linked to gangs, in accordance with UN Security Council resolutions. The US approach in 2024 was multifaceted: financial and humanitarian support combined with targeted sanctions against violent actors, while also implementing a stricter immigration policy.

Indeed, the United States announced on Wednesday, September 25, 2024, $160 million in aid to Haiti, where an international police force has been deployed for two years in an attempt to stabilize the gang-ridden country. US Secretary of State Antony Blinken, who visited Port-au-Prince in early September 2024, made the announcement during a ministerial meeting on Haiti on the sidelines of the UN General Assembly in New York.

—This aid would be used for development, the economy, health and security for the Haitian people, according to a statement from the State Department, which specified that this brings American aid to the country to $1.3 billion since 2021.

— Washington announced sanctions targeting former Congressman Prophane Victor for his role in training, supporting and arming gangs, and Gran Grif gang leader Luckson Elan for his involvement in serious human rights abuses related to gang activity.

—In October 2025, the United States, through the U.S. Treasury Department and the United Nations, imposed sanctions on two Haitian figures, namely, former presidential security chief Dimitri Hérard and Bel Air gang leader Kempes Sanon, for their involvement in the Viv Ansanm gang network.

The United States and the UN accuse the two men of providing material and logistical support to Viv Ansanm. Dimitri Hérard, a former police officer imprisoned in connection with the 2021 assassination of former President Jovenel Moïse, is a prison escapee. He left the National Penitentiary during Viv Ansanm's attack on the building. The bandits used a drone on the night of Saturday, March 2, 2024, to attack the Port-au-Prince Civil Prison and free inmates.

The prosecutor stares at Martelly, a protégé of Dimitri Hérard, for a moment, and continues:

—“Former head of President Jovenel Moïse’s close protection detail, Dimitri Hérard is a central figure in the unanswered questions surrounding the president’s assassination on the night of July 6-7, 2021. Tasked with coordinating presidential protection, he was on duty at the time of the attack on the president’s private residence in Pèlerin #5. No significant armed resistance was offered to the assailants. According to investigative reports, Hérard allegedly maintained close ties with criminal networks operating in Port-au-Prince. American and UN authorities suspect him of having played a leading role in the president’s assassination.”

The prosecutor continues:

“Dimitri Hérard directly supports Viv Ansanm’s coordinated attacks against state institutions,” the U.S. Treasury Department said in a statement. The State Department added that Hérard had supplied firearms and provided training to gang leaders operating in Port-au-Prince. Sanon, for his part, has been accused of using his influence in Bel-Air to extort money from residents, kidnap civilians, and impose illegal taxes. The UN describes him as maintaining a network of individuals within government institutions, including security agencies, which allows him to evade arrest and continue his criminal activities. Sanon also escaped from prison in 2021 while being held on charges of kidnapping and robbery.

—Bradley T. Smith, director of the Office of Foreign Assets Control at the U.S. Treasury Department, said in a statement that the sanctions “underscore the crucial role of gang leaders and facilitators like Hérard and Sanon, whose support enables Viv Ansanm to carry out its campaign of violence, extortion, and terrorism in Haiti.”

—The United Nations Office on Drugs and Crime, following a report by the DEA (Drug Enforcement Administration), indicated that weapons originating largely from the United States, particularly Florida, are supplying Haitian gangs. Hérard is accused of facilitating the clandestine smuggling of weapons and ammunition into the country, thereby fueling violence.

According to the United Nations Office on Drugs and Crime, the Viv Ansanm criminal coalition, a powerful alliance of armed groups that emerged in 2023, uniting Haiti's most notorious gang leaders in an informal coalition is fueled by a constant influx of firearms from the United States, particularly via Florida. The group's leaders, including figures such as Kempes Sanon, Johnson André alias Izo, Joseph Wilson alias Lanmò San Jou, Jeff Gwo Lwa, Vitel'homme Innocent, and Jimmy Cherizier alias Barbecue, operate with near impunity, thanks to connections within the central government.

—Berto Dorce and Liszt Quitel, respectively Minister of Justice and Minister of the Interior in the government led by Prime Minister Ariel Henry, were sanctioned by the United States in 2022. During the same period, the United States sanctioned two other Haitian political figures – Rony Célestin and Richard Lenine Hervé Fourcand – who allegedly abused their power to promote drug trafficking.

On December 2, 2022, the U.S. Treasury Department's Office of Foreign Assets Control (OFAC) froze the U.S.-based financial assets of Célestin, a former Haitian senator, and Fourcand, another former senator. According to OFAC, Célestin used his political position to smuggle drugs from Venezuela to Haiti, and then to the United States and the Bahamas. Fourcand used his own plane to transport drugs across southern Haiti and placed individuals in government positions to facilitate the trafficking activities.

The United States regularly sanctions Haitian businessmen, often linked to corruption, drug trafficking, or gang support. Among them are Reginald Boulos, Dimitri Vorbe, as well as political figures like former president Michel Martelly, and officials connected to drug trafficking and human rights abuses. Reginald Boulos and Dimitri

Boulos, two powerful Haitian businessmen, were arrested and imprisoned in the United States in 2025 for their alleged support of gangs. They are considered terrorists by the U.S. State Department. Former president Michel Martelly was sanctioned in 2024 for his involvement in drug trafficking. Joseph Lambert was sanctioned in 2022 for cocaine trafficking and corruption.

—In total, the United States revoked the visas of 50 former Haitian officials. These individuals were suspected of involvement in street gang activities and other criminal organizations through financial and other forms of material support, including facilitating the illicit trafficking of weapons or narcotics.

"There are consequences for those who support and finance gangs and other criminal organizations, and we will continue to use all available means, including visa restrictions and sanctions, to promote accountability for those involved in such activities. These measures, along with those implemented by our partners, are designed to lead Haiti toward a more prosperous and stable future," the U.S. Embassy in Port-au-Prince announced in a statement.

The United States has sanctioned individuals such as Youri Latortue, Joseph Lambert, Laurent Lamothe, Rony Célestin, and Hervé Fourcand. These sanctions focus on accusations of corruption and supporting criminal activities. The U.S. government has also imposed sanctions on Joseph Michel Martelly, accusing him of international drug trafficking and responsibility for Haiti's security and political collapse. "Today's action against Martelly underscores the significant and destabilizing role he has played, along with other corrupt officials, in perpetuating the current crisis in Haiti," said Bradley T. Smith, the acting Under U.S. Secretary of Terrorism and Financial Intelligence.

—For its part, the Dominican Republic has imposed sanctions on a long list including Claude Joseph, former prime minister, Gracia Delva, politician, and Liszt Quitel, former interior minister. Other notable names include Rodolphe Jaar, Kesner Normil, and Arnel

Bélizaire. Many of the individuals sanctioned by the Dominican Republic are also sanctioned by other countries and organizations, which underscores the scale of the accusations against them.

The list of those sanctioned is growing. The names of ministers, senators, former presidents of the Senate, and businessmen appear alongside the names of gang leaders, in the same paragraph, under the same seal of infamy. This administrative equivalence, this leveling down by the international community, is the most damning observation imaginable. It signifies that the line between statesman and criminal, between guardian of public order and destroyer of it, has dissolved.

The suit and tie and the assault rifle now sit at the same negotiating table and share in the spoils. In the historical memory evoked by this trial, such a blurring of distinctions is not unprecedented; it recalls the darkest hours when militias established themselves as a parallel power, with the tacit blessing of a segment of the elite. Yet, seeing this stark reality, laid bare in black and white in communiqués from Washington or the UN, is dizzying. It is an admission that the Haitian state project has, in some of its critical areas, capitulated to the logic of the mafia. The Petro Caribe trial, in its judicial ambition, attempts to re-establish this abolished boundary, to restore the rule of law. The weight of international sanctions serves as a reminder that the world has already drawn up its own indictment, without distinction of title or attire.

At this stage, the prosecution closes its notes and requests a suspension of the hearing.

— "The Court grants the request," declares the president, who adds:

— "The hearing is suspended and will resume at ten o'clock."

Chapter 17

CORRUPT OFFICIALS

(The ninth day of the hearing)

The courtroom is full early in the morning, but the judges are not yet present. The defendants are there, motionless, frozen in a posture of waiting that conveys as much fatigue as fear. Whispers rise slowly, as if each person is weighing the weight of what is about to be said.

This ninth day of hearings is unlike the previous ones. Corruption, the term that will be at the heart of the debate, will no longer be discussed as a rumor or an abstraction. The prosecution enters the courtroom with evidence, figures, and names.

The court resumed its work in an atmosphere of exceptional gravity. The debate opened with an examination of a phenomenon that transcends individual cases. The prosecution questioned the very functioning of the state. Corruption, far from being an accident or an isolated aberration, appeared here as a mode of governance, an organized system, with profound consequences for public finances, democracy, and the fundamental rights of the Haitian people.

This is an exceptional day. The prosecution is not simply presenting the charges. In its presentation, it will examine the gap between the principles proclaimed by the institutions and the practices observed within the administration. What are at stake are not only the legality of actions taken, but also the morality of public action and the credibility of the Haitian state in the eyes of its citizens and the international community.

In the courtroom, every word spoken carries more weight than a last-minute goal in the World Cup. It commits generations. The ninth day of hearings thus opens, under the watchful eye of history, as justice attempts, once again, to reclaim the ground that has been taken from it.

- “The hearing has resumed,” the president declared, adding:

- “The prosecutor always has the floor.”

When the judge gives the floor to the prosecution, everyone understands that the trial has just entered another phase. What is about to be said can no longer be ignored or concealed.

The prosecution takes a moment to review its notes and begins:

- “Your Honor, we are bringing the facts back to the issue of corruption. We begin with a broad definition of the phenomenon to arrive at the situation in Haiti.

—Corruption is a phenomenon as old as the world. For almost a decade, this phenomenon has become an important theme in political, socio-economic and legal debates at both the national and international levels, and has taken on an intense media dimension.

—In December 2018, the International Monetary Fund (IMF) presented extraordinary figures in its report on corruption, estimating the cost of bribes paid worldwide each year at between $1.5 trillion and $2 trillion. This represents nearly 2% of global GDP. The World Bank estimates that investing in a relatively corrupt country can cost up to 20% more than in a non-corrupt one.

The prosecutor continues:

—"Corruption does not have a single definition. The most common is that of the World Bank (IDB), which defines corruption as 'the abuse of public office for the purpose of obtaining a private advantage.' The definition given by the Council of Europe (EC) broadens its scope to include the private sector and civil society: it encompasses kickbacks and all actions or other behaviors involving individuals holding public or private office who have violated their duties arising from their status as public officials, private employees, independent agents, or in other similar relationships, in order to obtain illicit advantages of any kind, for themselves or for others. The same definition is adopted by the Canadian International Development Agency in a study entitled 'Fighting Corruption – An Introductory Guide.'"

—Corruption is "the politics of the belly," as a Cameroonian expression goes. It is a widespread practice, present across the globe. It has always existed and remains present in every place and time. Corruption can take many forms: bribes or kickbacks (under-the-table payments) or gifts, fraud, bribery, influence peddling, nepotism, illicit enrichment, embezzlement, or even drug trafficking. Whether large or small, active or passive, limited to a vote, linked to a small local arrangement or a larger market, whether it involves a dubious commission or the massive embezzlement of funds through companies, corruption, always contrary to morality, profoundly harms a country. Its effects affect everyone, but hit the poorest hardest.

— According to legal terminology, corruption constitutes any criminally incriminated behavior by which offers, promises, and gifts or presents are solicited, accepted or received, for the purpose of performing or refraining from particular favors or advantages.

—The fight against corruption is nowadays the credo of international institutions. In recent years, organizations such as the International Monetary Fund (IMF), the World Bank (WB), the Organization of

American States (OAS), the Inter-American Development Bank (IDB), the Organization for Economic Co-operation and Development (OECD), the United Nations, Transparency International (TI) have intensified their efforts in this fight because they have all realized that the consequences of corruption are disastrous for developing countries.

—As a major global concern today, the fight against corruption is a priority for the 25 signatory states of the Inter-American Convention against Corruption of the Organization of American States (OAS). Entering into force on March 6, 1997, it is the first multinational convention negotiated worldwide. It aims to strengthen cooperation among the states of the Americas in the fight against corruption.

Adopted by the United Nations General Assembly on October 31, 2003, at the organization's headquarters in New York, the convention was signed by 114 countries on December 9, 2003, in Merida, Mexico. It provides for the adoption of preventive measures and the criminalization of the most widespread forms of corruption in the public and private sectors. It marks a decisive turning point in that it requires states to return the proceeds of corruption to the defrauded country.

—According to Transparency International, the leading international non-governmental organization dedicated to fighting corruption, the United Nations Convention is a very important step in the international effort to combat this scourge. For the second time, a multinational instrument establishes, in a binding manner, the principle of the restitution of illicitly acquired assets and also provides for the establishment of an effective system of mutual legal assistance.

The prosecutor pauses and, in a firm and authoritative voice, declares:

— "Your Honor, let's now talk about the phenomenon of corruption in Haiti."

At these words, a gasp of astonishment swept through the room, immediately followed by a brief, nervous, almost irrepressible laugh. A laugh that was not joyful but that sprang from the audience's cruel lucidity. For here in Haiti, corruption is neither a phenomenon to be demonstrated nor a theory to be introduced: it is a lived reality, an imposed habit, a parallel language that everyone learns without a manual. The judge banged his gavel to restore order. Silence returned, even heavier, as the impassive prosecutor prepared to bring this bitter laughter back within the strict framework of the law.

The prosecutor continues:

—"Corruption is a phenomenon found today in all sectors of public and private life in Haiti. However, it is at the level of public administration that the phenomenon is much more perceptible and its consequences are felt much more acutely. At the level of public finances, it takes on disproportionate dimensions and constitutes a serious threat to the establishment of a democratic state committed to respecting fundamental human rights."

The prosecutor continues:

Reading the two reports from the Court of Auditors, corruption clearly emerges as a political phenomenon in Haiti. Beyond the issue of embezzlement in the management of the Petro Caribe program, architecture of corruption in Haiti is taking shape and developing like a cancer within the Haitian social fabric, particularly among the ruling class. This corruption does not affect a specific set of public or private institutions implicated in the misappropriation of Petro Caribe funds. "The entire project implementation chain, from planning to supervision and final delivery, was not so much flawed as simply circumvented and diverted." What is alarming is that, beyond the rules and conditions that were violated, all the control mechanisms and bodies, all the checks and balances, and first and foremost the Court of Auditors itself (but also Parliament and the judiciary), failed.

The prosecutor glances around the room, points at one of the defendants, and declares:

- — "Your Honor, the Anti-Corruption Unit (ULCC) has recommended criminal proceedings against former President Michel Joseph Martelly for serious irregularities in his asset declarations. The ULCC accuses him of having deliberately falsified his declarations upon entering and leaving office."

Indeed, in a report published on Monday, December 8, 2025, following a complaint filed by the organization *Together Against Corruption* (ECC) in September 2024, the ULCC accuses the former president of false statements, omissions, and blatant inconsistencies. Martelly's financial declarations "were incomplete, inconsistent, and deliberately misleading."

The investigation, commissioned by the Director General of the ULCC, Hans Jacques Ludwig Joseph, covers Martelly's presidency, from May 14, 2011, to February 7, 2016. Its aim was to verify the accuracy of the declarations of entry into and exit from office, required by the law of February 12, 2008. The ULCC uncovered official, banking, and administrative data revealing that Martelly's declarations were not only late but also incomplete and false. His wife, Sophia Saint-Rémy Martelly, and his son, Olivier Martelly, both presidential advisors, failed to comply with this legal requirement.

—The main allegations against former President Martelly include:

- Undeclared bank accounts: The investigation revealed 17 active individual and institutional bank accounts, as well as three credit cards, which were not mentioned in his exit statement, unlike the two term deposits and six accounts that were declared.
- In his 2011 entry declaration, Martelly declared four term deposits and four accounts at Capital Bank, totaling

approximately US$168,000 and 98,000 gourdes. However, bank statements obtained from several institutions, including Capital Bank, BNC, Sogebank, and Unibank, show 20 accounts in the name of the Martellys or related entities, 12 of which were undeclared assets. Twelve bank accounts, both personal and institutional, not mentioned in the entry declaration of assets, were nevertheless active at that time. Several of these accounts are directly linked to Michel Joseph Martelly's election campaign and to the Rose and White Foundation.

- The Commission of Inquiry did not find, in the statements provided by Capital Bank at the request of the ULCC, the term deposit (DAT) no. 448953 or the current account no 458316, despite these being declared by Martelly in her official declaration upon assuming office. Furthermore, a bank loan contracted with Capital Bank by Sophia Saint-Rémy Martelly, in the amount of thirty-nine thousand nine hundred twenty-one US dollars and sixty-nine cents ($39,921.69), registered on August 10, 2007, and maturing on September 19, 2011, appears in the bank statements, even though it was not declared in the declaration form.
- Missing and inconsistent assets: vehicles listed in 2011 reportedly disappeared from his 2016 declarations without proof of sale, while new acquisitions appeared with no link to declared income.
- Hidden business companies: Several business entities registered in the name of Martelly and his wife, Sophia Martelly, were not mentioned in his asset declarations.
- Unjustified income: income from artistic activities under his alias "Sweet Micky" and conference fees were not tax-documented.
- Former President Martelly's exit declaration, filed in January 2018, nearly two years after the end of his term and in violation of legal deadlines, is equally fraudulent. In the declaration form, Mr. Martelly listed two term deposits at Unibank and six accounts at Capital Bank, totaling

over $560,000 and 5 million gourdes. However, the banks identified 17 accounts and three credit cards, several of which were undeclared. Some of the listed accounts have not been located, reinforcing suspicions of falsification.

- Michel Martelly declared a monthly presidential salary of 242,400 gourdes, annual artistic earnings of $100,000, and $60,000 for his wife. However, the family's net income is listed as $529,000, with $348,000 attributed to Sophia Martelly, leaving an unjustified discrepancy of $288,000. Public payments to Sophia Martelly, totaling over 10 million gourdes in her capacity as an advisor, are not mentioned. Upon leaving office, artistic and speaking income is reported as $370,400 (a 270% increase), without any evidence of activity during his term. Rental income of $138,000 appears, linked to undeclared connections.
- Real estate holdings raise further questions. In 2011, Michel Martelly declared four properties, including an apartment in Miami and three in Haiti, valued at $2.25 million. In 2018, he listed six, with values reaching as high as $3.6 million for a house near Saint-Marc acquired in 2012. A property on Villate Street disappears without explanation, while others, such as an apartment in Puits-Blain acquired in 1991, appear only later. No source of financing is provided for acquisitions during his term, the ULCC emphasizes in its report.
- The vehicles follow the same pattern. Two Toyota Land Cruisers registered in 2011 disappeared without a trace in 2018, without any sales agreement. The Third-Party Vehicle Insurance Office confirms the existence of unregistered vehicles registered in Sophia Martelly's name.

The prosecutor pauses. He raises the glass of water to his lips and continues.

- "A look back at the facts is necessary, using rigorous figures. Before coming to power, Michel Martelly lived off the stage,

> his musical fame, irregular fees dependent on the seasons, and invitations to perform in Haiti and the diaspora. His name circulated, his songs shocked or amused, but his financial situation remained that of a popular artist, without a structured industry, without a known economic empire, without a constant stream of income capable of justifying a rapid accumulation of wealth. Nothing in this recent past foreshadowed the explosion of wealth that would follow his entry into the National Palace."

In the courtroom, this unsettling report, though simple in its nature, is disturbing. It stems neither from rumor nor ideology, but from common sense. Faces harden. Each person mentally weighs the pros and cons, the differences between the stage and the state, between the microphone and the public treasury.

This unease becomes more acute when it clashes with the daily reality of the Haitian people. While the majority live in precarious conditions, counting every penny for food, walking for miles due to a lack of transportation, and surviving without decent public services, the state devotes colossal sums to Carnival. The deployments of floats, stages, sound systems, exorbitant fees, booked hotels, and exceptional budgets, mask the misery for a moment, but it never makes it disappear.

In the collective imagination, Carnival is supposed to be an outlet for the people. Here in Haiti, it becomes a symbol of a reversal of values: a people invited to dance while their resources are being depleted. Public money flows freely for the spectacle, but is scarce for education, healthcare, agriculture, and electricity. The celebration repeats itself, but poverty remains.

In the courtroom, no one speaks, but everyone understands. This contrast is not a matter of partisan politics, but of decency. The prosecution pauses, takes a moment to breathe, and then immediately resumes its presentation. The legal proceedings continue, but the memory of the events remains vivid.

The prosecutor continues:

—"The ULCC (Anti-Corruption Unit) recommends the initiation of public action against Mr. Michel Joseph Martelly for false declaration of assets, in accordance with the provisions of Article 17 of the Law of February 12, 2008 relating to the declaration of assets by certain categories of political figures, officials and other public agents ; combined with Articles 107, 108 and following of the Haitian Penal Code relating to the crime of forgery and use of forged documents.

"These measures are motivated by the discovery of an incomplete, false, inconsistent, and late declaration, which compromises transparency and administrative integrity," the ULCC concluded.

Leaning over to speak with one of the deputy prosecutors, the public prosecutor glances towards the dock. He sees former president Michel Martelly and several accomplices weeping, and he knows he has just scored a point.

In the same vein, he continues:

— "Your Honor, it seems essential to me to reiterate here certain statements made by former President Martelly. When responding to journalists regarding the misappropriation of Petro Caribe funds, he stated:

—"In his statements on Thursday, February 1 , 2018, during the program "Mise au point," hosted by Jean Serginho Lindor on Haitian National Television, when questioned about the Petro Caribe affair, Michel Joseph Martelly did not mince words and did not utter any profanities. He stated that he was in favor of holding all those who managed the money accountable."

"Regarding the Petro Caribe case, I'm sure there are people who have stolen, whether at the state level or in the private sector," Martelly concluded.

The prosecutor remains serious. He was thinking. Returning to the Petro Caribe case, he declared:

— "Your Honor, the Senate Ethics and Anti-Corruption Commission, during its investigation, received accounting documents attesting that three Dominican companies, Hadom SA, Rofi SA and Construcciones y Diseños RMNSA belonging to Senator Félix Bautista, made financial contributions to Michel Martelly's campaign and then continued to give him kickbacks on contracts awarded by the Haitian State.

— International sanctions:

— In addition to the ULCC's recommendations at the national level, Michel Martelly is subject to separate international sanctions:

- Canada: The Canadian government sanctioned Martelly in November 2022 for his alleged involvement in corruption and the financing of armed gangs.
- United States: In August 2024, the US Treasury Department imposed sanctions on Martelly for his alleged role in international drug trafficking and money laundering, as well as for financing Haitian gangs.
- European Union: The EU has also adopted sanctions, including an asset freeze and a travel ban, against Martelly and other figures for their role in financing armed groups that are destabilizing Haiti.

The prosecutor casts his gaze once again towards the dock. He points his index finger towards Martelly Sr., and declares:

"Your Honor, Mr. Martelly is an insensitive individual. Not only is his hand in the misappropriation of Petro Caribe funds, but he also mocks the Haitian people, who are the greatest victims in this affair. Let us never forget this appalling reality: throughout his musical career, Martelly consistently displayed vulgar and depraved behavior. A disreputable artist, he uses music to spread his repugnant and obscene message. He calls himself a legal bandit, also known as Ti Simone. It is no coincidence that his time as head of state was marked by banditry, cronyism, and the embezzlement of colossal sums from the public treasury. Sanctioned by the United States for his affiliation with armed groups, he plays a major role in the misappropriation of Petro Caribe funds." Two-thirds of the projects financed with these funds were signed under the Martelly government (2011-2016), and the majority of them under the Martelly/Lamothe administration. Furthermore, in most cases, the investigation found that the funds were invested in non-revenue-generating instruments. For example, 56% of the projects were implemented by the Ministry of Public Works, Transport and Communications (MTPTC) and the Ministry of Planning and External Cooperation (MPCE).

The prosecutor is once again turning its attention to Martelly. He saw him cry just a moment ago. He sees him now, head bowed, neck exposed. And yet, the sight of "Micky" in the dock inspires neither pity nor triumph. It awakens in him a cold, controlled anger, fueled by files, figures, and anonymous faces. He sees not just a fallen former head of state, but the embodiment of an era when the state became synonymous with spectacle, when vulgarity served as a political platform, and when impunity became the norm. Every time his gaze falls upon the hunched figure of the accused, the prosecution thinks of hospitals without medicine, roads never finished, children deprived of schooling, of everything the former head of state promised but never delivered.

The chains on the accused's feet are not, in his eyes, a personal humiliation. They are a brutal reminder that public service is not a stage and that power is not a fleeting carnival. He remembers that

Martelly once laughed at institutions, defied them with derision. Today, the laughter has shifted. But the prosecution is not pleased. It knows that justice is not vengeance. It is a belated duty. He then straightened up, gathered his voice, and transformed this suppressed emotion into accusatory rigor. The court did not need visible anger. It needed the truth.

The prosecutor states:

—"Your Honor, some of the accused are implicated in the *Dermalog* scandal. According to Gride, Citizens without Borders (CSF), and several other national organizations, between forty and one hundred and twenty million US dollars from the Local Government Management and Development Fund (FGDCT) were withheld or embezzled. The corruption is blatant. A German company was appointed by the former president of the Republic, in violation of public procurement rules, to produce voter cards. This decision is difficult to explain, according to the report of the Senate's Ethics and Anti-Corruption Commission (May 24, 2019), which attests that the previous card production system was beyond reproach. It was in Cannes, France, at an international trade show on new technology in 2018, that the Director General of the National Identification Office (ONI), Jude Jacques Philippe Elibert, accompanied by First Lady Martine Moïse, signed the contract with the Dermalog Company.

The purchase of fifteen armored vehicles for the Haitian National Police is another scandal. Each of these vehicles cost the Haitian state US$143,581, with transportation costs accounting for 40% of the purchase price. The state incurred a loss of US$1.1 million in this transaction, according to Senator Youri Latortue, who alleges overbilling.

The prosecutor casts a contemptuous glance at Martelly and continues:

—"Your Honor, is it possible that an individual without academic preparation, without management experience, a self-proclaimed legal bandit, who in all areas advocates "Ki te Melem" (I don't give a damn), can manage an economy as complex as Haiti's in the light of the principles of a good family man and in the direction of collective interests? (dixit Professor Leslie Péan)."

The prosecutor, continuing in the same vein, states:

— "Your Honor, for years Haiti has been mired in serious political, economic, health and security crises, which have fueled increasing violence and paralysis.

—President Jovenel Moïse was assassinated on July 7, 2021, at his home. Public outcry proclaims that those who squandered the Petro Caribe funds were among those who ordered the assassination.

The prosecutor smiled inwardly. Without a gesture of pity for the accused, and in the same breath, he continued:

—"Can we deny, Your Honor, the impact of the 'Bautista affair' on the Haitian conscience? On March 31, 2012, Dominican journalist Nuria Piera presented bank statements and account numbers of Dominican construction companies on Dominican television. She revealed money transfers totaling $ 2,587,000 given to Michel Martelly up until November 2011, after his inauguration, as bribes. These bank statements presented by the journalist are irrefutable proof of the transfers made between Banco Reservas and Banco Popular in the Dominican Republic and Unibank in Haiti to Michel Martelly's account."

The journalist's investigation revealed certain practices confirmed by a series of financial statements from companies affiliated with Senator Bautista. These statements contained relevant details that the investigation was subsequently able to verify. These verifications confirmed the embezzlement and suspicious transactions.

Information also obtained from data in the possession of Dominican journalist Faust o Rosario helped the investigating judge determine the relationship between Haitian officials and international businesspeople.

—The U.S. Treasury Department's Office of Foreign Assets Control (OFAC) accused Senator Bautista of receiving a $10 million contract to build the Ministry of Foreign Affairs in Haiti but failing to complete the construction. Senator Bautista's bank accounts and assets, including the companies Rofi and Hadom, were confiscated. U.S. authorities estimated Bautista's net worth at over $1.5 billion.

The mere mention of Bautista's name provokes consternation among the audience. For behind the Dominican businessman's name, everyone understands that it represents a system that transcends individuals. A system where Haiti's already scarce public funds are siphoned off into international circuits, while the country sinks deeper into dependency and poverty.

Bautista, summoned by the commissions working on the Petro Caribe affair, never responded to the summonses. He sent emissaries, lawyers, and businessmen with shifty eyes. He himself remained at home in San Juan de la Maguana, safe from awkward questions. But today, in this courtroom, his Haitian accomplices have nowhere left to hide. And every minute of the hearing is an ordeal, a humiliation they can no longer endure.

The prosecutor presents the testimonies gathered by the Ethics and Anti-Corruption Commission headed by Senator Latortue:

—"Your Honor, through Bautista, it is not only funds that are being transferred, but also powerful arms abroad that are participating in the plundering of these funds. The accomplices are everywhere. The revelations show how infrastructure projects, presented as symbols of regional cooperation, are in reality becoming vehicles for predation."

—In the Latortue Commission report, several former employees of Dominican firms spoke out. They described how money was handed over, in cash, to intermediaries. They quantified the commissions. Ten percent of the total contract value was given to local authorities to secure their signature, and another ten percent was given to consultants and other intermediaries for fear of being exposed.

This connection between Haitian and Dominican authorities to embezzle funds is summarized by Dominican journalist Rafael Percival as follows: "The deep internal crisis in Haiti has no basis in its neighbor, the Dominican Republic, because it is a blatant conspiracy. The only one trying to extend his influence is himself, the Haitian president. Their corruption scandals are disrupting ethics and morality and shaking the foundations of Haitian society. Martelly and his friends are favored and sponsored by his business cronies and Dominican politicians, among whom stands out Senator Félix Bautista, none other than the Secretary of Organization for the ruling party, the Dominican Liberation Party (PLD), playing a leading role in the Haitian scenario. Félix Bautista is the mastermind of corruption. Now, let's not fool ourselves: who put Martelly in power? Who provided the economic resources?" Don't we Dominicans know better? Just like Trujillo did with Stefano Vicente.

The prosecutor pauses and declares:

—"Your Honor, in June 2018, the U.S. government confiscated Bautista's assets to punish him for his dishonest actions in Haiti. The powerful Dominican senator and businessman became the first person accused of corruption and the first to be sanctioned in the Petro Caribe case. After the January 12, 2010 earthquake, the Haitian government attempted to rebuild public buildings destroyed by the quake. The construction firms Rofi and Hadom, owned by Bautista, a close associate of then-Dominican President Leonel Fernández, won contract after contract. A powerful and generous man, the Dominican senator's name was cited in connection with the financing of the campaigns of the main candidates in the 2010-2011 elections in Haiti."

—In the list of restricted tender contracts, six contracts were signed with the firms Hadom SA, Rofi SA, and Constroccionnes y Diseños RMNSA. The investigation noted that these six contracts were not the first projects between the Haitian government and firms affiliated with Bautista. In fact, firms affiliated with the senator had already benefited from contracts for debris and excavated material removal. Two contracts, for the respective amounts of ten and five million dollars, were signed in February 2010.

—Regarding the 6 contracts signed following restricted tenders, they are:

- $ 33,765,366.08
- $ 135,309,218.65
- $ 178,951,296.90.

—Rofi and Hadom later became Haitian companies, but nothing changed in their modus operandi: simplistic contracts were signed but not signed, generous advances were disbursed, and the work was never completed. In Haiti, two complaints were filed on Friday, August 3, 2018, with the investigating magistrate's office against Senator Félix Bautista for his involvement in the misappropriation of PetroCaribe funds and the distribution of bribes to Haitian authorities.

—Senator Félix Bautista, of the Dominican Liberation Party (PLD), suddenly became the richest legislator in the Dominican Republic thanks to these contracts in Haiti. Based on data provided by the Civic Movement of Citizens Against Corruption, Dominican journalist Nuria Piera reported that "engineer and entrepreneur Félix Bautista, PLD senator, allegedly paid $2.5 million, $250,000, and $1.2 million to Michel Martelly, Myrlande Manigat, and Alejandro

Toledo, the 2011 presidential candidate in Peru, respectively, for their election campaigns."

The Legislative Ethics and Anti-Corruption Commission verified the veracity of the payments made between companies, as presented by the Dominican journalist. The documents confirmed that high -ranking Haitian state officials received bribes from Félix Bautista. Ms. Manigat, Mr. Salim Succar, and Mr. Jean Henry Céant confirmed the payments received, respectively, for campaign contributions, legal fees, and notary fees. Meanwhile, Michel Martelly, Jean Max Bellerive, and Thierry Mayard Paul categorically rejected the documents presented by the journalist.

"The question is why these individuals—Michel Martelly, Jean-Max Bellerive, and Thierry Mayard—rejected the journalist's accusations without ever taking legal action against her. Yet, she maintains the veracity of her statements and the authenticity of these documents?"

As he uttered these final words, the prosecutor's piercing gaze fell upon the defendants. Embarrassed, they avoided the prosecutor's eyes. Hearing the charges against them, knowing the trial was being broadcast worldwide, felt like a slap in the face. It was as if they had been spat upon. They were overwhelmed with remorse.

Outside, the cries of the demonstrators grow louder. The slogan "Kot kòb Petro Caribe a" (Where is the Petro Caribe money?) permeates the walls of the courthouse building, reaching the ears of the defendants who remain frozen in their seats. They fear being lynched. The fate of Vilbrun Guillaume Sam resurfaces in their minds. The former Haitian president was lynched in Port-au-Prince on July 28, 1915, after seeking refuge in the French delegation. His violent death led to the immediate landing of American troops and the occupation of Haiti.

It was a difficult period in the country's history. The public prosecutor pauses, quickly consults his notes, and adds:

—"Your Honor, the crime is appalling. The accused who squandered the Petro Caribe funds are ruthless criminals, concerned only with stealing money that the Haitian state should be investing in key areas of development: agriculture, education, health, roads, electricity, and many others.

—Of the forty-one contracts signed by Prime Minister Bellerive, twenty-three, although awarded through private negotiation thanks to exceptions in the emergency law, concern municipalities that were not affected by the earthquake. These are: Pignon, Ranquitte, Saint Raphaël, Limbé, Grande Rivière du Nord, Hinche, Maïssade, Ennery, Saint Michel de l'Attalaye, and Côte de Fer. In addition, contracts for 13 other municipalities could not be identified.

The prosecutor continues:

—"Your Honor, we are making a national appeal to combat corruption. This cancer weakens governance, hinders development, and undermines social justice. The example must begin now with the conviction of all those involved in the misappropriation of Petro Caribe funds. They are present in the dock and await their sentence."

Applause greeted the prosecutor's final sentence. Aware of the impact his plea had on the audience, he continued in the same vein:

"Nothing positive has been done with the Petro Caribe funds, except for shady dealings that have allowed legalized criminals to become millionaires in US dollars at the expense of the Haitian people. Furthermore, the corruption surrounding this affair is driving away other donors and discouraging them from supporting any investment projects. The Petro Caribe experience is closing doors for Haiti to receive new loans and grants."

On August 27, 2014, the disastrous nature of Petro Caribe's management was strongly emphasized by several senators during the presentation of the 2014-2015 budget bills by Finance Minister

Marie Carmelle Jean-Marie. At this event, Senator Steven Benoît criticized the government's use of the funds. According to him, they would have been better used for sustainable development projects. "Petro Caribe is a real free-for-all," he lamented. "You're playing politics with this money, and our children will have to pay it back."

The Special Senate Commission of Inquiry (CSSE), headed by former Senator Evalière Beauplan, is denouncing those who profited from the $188 million squandered under René Préval's administration and those who benefited from the $2 billion during Joseph Michel Martelly's presidency. Jude Célestin is among those implicated, having received millions of dollars from Préval. This sum was drawn from Petro Caribe funds to finance Célestin's presidential campaign. Tania Chihimie, a prominent figure in the Haitian upper class of Italian descent, played a significant role in facilitating the embezzlement of these funds. She is reportedly the mother of one of Jude Célestin's daughters.

—There's also talk of Moïse Jean-Charles. The former senator from the North, an advisor to René Préval, received PetroCaribe funds to finance his Senate campaign. Jonas Gay's name has also been mentioned. Gay, a minister under Préval, owns a hotel in Mirebalais. Reliable information indicates that Petro Caribe money was used in the construction of this hotel. Under Jocelerme Privert, the government disbursed the modest sum of $33 million from Petro Caribe funds.

The Senate's Special Commission of Inquiry investigated part of Jocelerme Privert's administration, up to September 30, 2016, and asked the Senate to rule on the remainder of the interim president's term, who led the country from February 14, 2016, to February 7, 2017. The Public Prosecutor's Office confirms that the report contains a partial conclusion regarding Patrick Noramé, the former Director General of the BMPAD during the transition period. Patrick Noramé has been accused of complicity in the misappropriation of Petro Caribe funds.

—According to Carl Murat Cantave, this appointment was proposed by Nenel Cassy, a member of the Commission. The Commission accused Senator Cassy of increasing the parliament's operating fund to 437 million gourdes, whereas from 2008 to 2015, this fund had never exceeded 131 million gourdes.

Looking at the defendants, the prosecution adds:

"Your Honor, the accused are both roguish and cunning." At a press conference on Tuesday, November 28, 2017, former Prime Minister Laurent Lamothe criticized the Beauplan-Latortue report. According to him, the senators falsified and fabricated information in the report to destroy not only his reputation but also the reputations of a dozen other ministers in the Martelly administration. "The Beauplan/Latortue Report is nothing more than a political attempt to destroy honest public servants and prevent future competition in the upcoming elections." Laurent Lamothe cries conspiracy. He accuses the Speaker of the National Assembly, Youri Latortue, of orchestrating a corruption campaign against him to prevent him from receiving a clearance certificate that would allow him to participate in the next presidential elections.

Without a second thought, Lamothe called upon allies who came to his defense. Kedler Augustin, a close associate, declared: "The Beauplan Report is illegal, inadmissible, and scandalous. The Senate is barred from further investigation; only the Court of Auditors is authorized to conduct post-audit reviews. Furthermore, this process constitutes a violation of the Constitution. The clientelism and overtly political nature of the investigation prove that it is an abuse of power for the purpose of political persecution, and therefore a violation of human rights, which is punishable by the Inter-American Court of Justice."

—Contested by those involved, the Petro Caribe case was referred to the Court of Auditors, which conducted an audit of the funds' management. The CSCCA's ruling revealed serious irregularities and the misappropriation of significant sums of money disbursed for projects that were never initiated.

—Your Honor, the investigating judge's order, upheld by the Court of Appeal, has the merit, thanks to the Senate committee reports and the three audit reports from the Court of Auditors, of outlining the main disbursements and analyzing the accounting of the funds disbursed. In short, it helps to understand how the funds were used and misappropriated.

"This investigation aimed to determine the effectiveness of investments and the validity of allegations of mismanagement as presented by various sources. It also sought to verify compliance with standards and procedures."

The prosecutor continues:

— "Six senators make up the Ethics and Anti-Corruption Commission:

- Senator Youri Latortue, President;
- Senator Jacques Sauveur Jean, Vice-President;
- Senator Onondieu Louis, rapporteur;
- Senator Richard Lémine Hervé Fourcand, member;
- Senator Ronald Larèche, member;
- Senator Andris Riché, member.

Turning his gaze towards Senators Evalière Beauplan and Andris Riché, who were present in the courtroom, the prosecutor declares:

"On behalf of my colleagues who support the prosecution, I take this opportunity to thank the two senators present. Their investigation into the Petro Caribe funds constitutes the foundation and driving force of what could be the first step toward a state governance where waste has no place. The referral of the accused to this Assize Court, based on the investigating judge's order, is the second step toward uncovering the truth. The presumed culprits in the squandering of Petro Caribe funds have been found. They must be punished now."

The prosecutor glances around the audience, then turns his gaze towards the defendants and continues:

"Your Honor! The Petro Caribe funds that were misappropriated are enormous. They amount to nearly four billion US dollars. This sum, granted by Venezuela in the form of a loan on very favorable terms through the sale of fuel on credit, is repayable over a period of twenty-five years with an interest rate not exceeding 1% per year. What an opportunity Petro Caribe provides to the various Haitian governments (2006-2016) for the economic recovery and development of Haiti within the framework of structured and planned projects and programs!"

"Almost all major public contracts awarded in Haiti over the past ten years are overpriced. The evidence is there. In other words, the state is enriching a minority and impoverishing the community, according to the confessions of the assassinated former president Jovenel Moïse."

The prosecutor consults his notes and continues:

— "Your Honor, the criminal acts committed under the Martelly-Lamothe government are so numerous that it is impossible to list them all. However, the prosecution will take a few minutes to list some of them."

— Under the Martelly-Lamothe regime, Haiti has a whole graveyard of unfinished or unexecuted projects, even though all the disbursements have been made. A contract was signed by Minister Florence G. Duperval with a deceased person. Regarding this, the second Senate Commission, headed by Senator Beauplan, stated: "As for the first Commission's criticism of her having signed a contract with a dead person, Ms. Duperval replied that she knew the person was deceased, but since the contract was already at the ministry, she signed it thinking it wouldn't be a problem."

—Other instances of embezzlement are linked to measures taken by the Martelly regime. One example is the fees collected on money transfers entering Haiti. From July 2011 to September 12, 2018, the money collected by the Haitian state, the historical origin and date of introduction of the $1.50 tax, totaled 120,130,745.50, according to the report published by the Bank of the Republic of Haiti.

—Your Honor, the record of the five years of governance of the Haitian state by the Martelly regime is catastrophic. The absence of values is the defining characteristic of his regime, known as "Tèt Kale" (Bald Head). Michel Martelly is a stupid, ignorant, and vain tyrant, modeled after dictators who have turned power into a den of gangsters, with the aim of destroying all human capital and leading minds to complete submission to absurdity and stupidity.

The 2017-2018 budget report, published in May 2019 by the Court of Auditors, examined the operating budget of the state apparatus under the Martelly governments and revealed a record increase of 63%. Of the 80.5 billion gourdes allocated, 91.7% was dedicated to the administration's operations. Only 8.3 billion gourdes were earmarked for social projects. In short, 60% of the budget was allocated to the Executive's administrative operations and 32.7% to civil servant salaries.

Public opinion is constantly denouncing the privileged situation of people receiving salaries without ever setting foot in a public office. The issuance of "zombie checks", (actually fictitious jobs), siphons millions of dollars from public funds every month. Each minister legally has at least four all-terrain vehicles in their motorcade. The prime minister has approximately ten Toyota Land Cruisers and several escort vehicles used by his security detail. During his presidency, Michel Martelly had about twenty vehicles in his presidential motorcade.

—Under Martelly, the Haitian state was even described as a mafia state, with a corrupt and debauched president at its head. The former president himself called his cronies "legal bandits," the title of a song he composed in 2008. The former president was subject to international sanctions due to allegations that he maintained ties with armed gangs and financed violence in Haiti.

In uttering these words, the prosecution is not merely condemning a man, but revisiting a chain of consequences. In its view, the insecurity plaguing Haiti did not emerge spontaneously with the arrival of armed coalitions. It is the product of years of tolerance, encouragement, and strategic blindness. Under the Martelly regime, gangs were not considered a threat to the Republic; they were normalized, exploited, sometimes courted, and often ignored. Neighborhoods were abandoned to armed groups who filled the void left by a failing state.

The prosecutor reflects and declares to himself:

—Before the arrival of the Gang Suppression Force (GSF), the country had already crossed a point of no return. Weapons circulated freely, territorial control had slipped from the state's grasp, and criminal leaders gained legitimacy through their proximity to power. This climate did not arise by chance. It was cultivated by a style of governance that prioritized immediate political control over lasting national security. By weakening institutions, ridiculing authority, and blurring the lines between the state and organized crime, the "Tèt Kale" regime paved the way for the explosion of violence that would follow.

In this sense, Martelly is not accused of firing the first shot, but of completing the work of weakening the state. He can be seen as the partial but decisive architect of the chaos; a man who allowed insecurity to reign to the point where repression became the only remaining option. The GSF (Gang Suppression Force) did not arrive as a solution born of force, but as a desperate response to years of neglect, complicity, and abdication of responsibility.

On April 2, 2013, engaged citizens filed a complaint with the Port-au-Prince prosecutor's office against Michel Martelly for the US$2.5 million he received from Félix Bautista in November 2011, after his inauguration. These events demonstrate that corruption is a phenomenon that permeates all levels of power in Haiti. There is a close link of complicity between Haitian leaders and other leaders around the world, particularly those of the Dominican Republic.

—The phenomenon of corruption is no longer merely a societal issue specific to each country, but has become a strategic phenomenon extending across the globe. All over the world, movements, generally originating from civil society, are mobilizing against corruption, primarily that of political leaders. This dynamic affects every continent, without distinction political regimes, elected officials and those who have come to power through other means. (Pascal Boniface, Mobilization against corruption,*La Croix,* March 23, 2016.)

Outside, the summer night has already fallen, although it is only six o'clock. The president looks at his watch and declares:

—"The hearing is suspended and will resume tomorrow at 10 a.m."

Chapter 18

PUNISH THE CRIMINALS

(The tenth day of the hearing)

Outside, the June sun beats down on Port-au-Prince. In the courtroom, the air is heavy, thick with heat and palpable tension. The prosecutor adjusts his tie, his right hand resting on a pile of files that grows larger each day, like an abscess he is trying in vain to lance.

The prosecutor didn't sleep. He spent the night rereading police reports, analyzing witness statements, verifying dates, names, and locations. At dawn, a power outage plunged his house into darkness. He sat there, listening to the city awaken, the dogs bark, the first motorcycles pass by. His son slept in the next room. He, on the other hand, was thinking about the trial and about his family's safety.

Two stories are unfolding simultaneously. One plays out during the World Cup, under the floodlights of American stadiums, before millions of television viewers. The other unfolds here, under the pale fluorescent lights of the courthouse, amidst the dust of archives and the scratching of pens. One is swift, dazzling, and instinctive: a ball that flashes across the penalty area, a cry of joy that rips through chests. The other is slow, methodical, and obstinate: a signature negotiated at the bottom of a contract, a bank account in Grand Cayman, a commission hidden away in the labyrinth of a shell company.

The people outside chant both: *Go Grenadiers!* And also: *Kote kob PetwoKaribe a?* (Where is the Petro Caribe money?). Same voice, same anger, same mingled hopes. As if justice and victory were two sides of the same coin that destiny, at last, had deigned to offer them.

The public prosecutor closes his file. He thinks of what his father told him one evening in 1986, when Duvalier had just fled and the country was awaiting a revolution: "Justice, my son, is like football. There are matches you win on the field. And there are championships you never win. In both cases, until the very last second, you always have to chase the ball."

The court is being convened.

"The hearing has resumed," the president declared:

- "The prosecutor has the floor."

The prosecutor begins:

"Your Honor, all these measures taken by the international community, primarily by the United Nations Security Council, the United States, Canada, the Dominican Republic, and the European Union, have the same objective: to force the Haitian state to enforce the law and punish criminals, the corrupt, and outlaws. Haiti is a country where the state is absent. The insecurity caused by the fighting between armed gangs puts the lives of residents in danger every day. In Martissant, Grand-Ravine, Cité Soleil, Croix des Bouquets, Pernier, and several other places in the West and Artibonite departments, there is total chaos. Gangs are everywhere, heavily armed, and perpetrate uncontrolled violence. The United Nations Development Programme (UNDP) and the United Nations Integrated Office in Haiti (BINUH) have identified approximately 162 armed groups operating in Haiti. These armed groups are financed by actors from the Haitian public and private sectors." Several defendants present here support these bandits.

In the dock, some faces remain impassive. Others avoid eye contact. The silence becomes accusatory. The prosecution speaks of gangs, but everyone understands that it is also talking about certain defendants, once protected by their positions. The courtroom remembers that crime in Haiti always has an invisible hand behind it: the true perpetrators are sometimes those in power. They finance from the shadows. They hire criminals to eliminate the adversary.

The prosecutor takes a moment to see his notes, in the same breath, continues:

PHTK (Pati Haïtien Tèt Kale) regime seized power in 2010 under the presidency of Michel Martelly, residents of impoverished neighborhoods have been living in a truly terrifying situation. Abandoned by the government, these poor people are subjected to repression by armed groups who hold them hostage in lawless zones. The misuse of central power for criminal purposes has led to a complete breakdown of the state apparatus and, consequently, has facilitated the control of the capital and its surrounding areas by armed groups."

—The gangs control areas that are primarily agricultural. They control irrigation systems, including the main reservoir on the Rivière Grise, which irrigates 7,000 hectares, and the Source Zabeth system, which irrigates nearly 2,000 hectares. They control the Malpasse road, preventing trade with the Dominican Republic. Farmers from Forêt-des-Pins, Thiotte, Cornillon, and Belle-Anse are unable to use this road to reach the Croix-des-Bouquets market, a merchant confided.

Croix-des-Bouquets and its surrounding areas continue to be plagued by a senseless nightmare. This situation is stifling economic activity in the region. For many residents, it means total insecurity. Fear is forcing the majority to flee amidst the closure of farms, stores, and shops. This state of affairs is suffocating neighboring communities like Thomazeau and Ganthier. The northeastern outskirts of Port-au-Prince have been at the mercy of the 400 Mawozo gang for years.

This armed group carries out disturbing kidnappings, including of Haitian, American, French, and Canadian citizens. The bandits demand ransoms sometimes exceeding one million dollars. The vast majority of the women held captive are sexually abused and victims of gang rape.

—The crisis is widespread. After the assassination of President Jovenel Moïse, insecurity intensified. Gangs took advantage of the state's weakness to extend their control over several regions of the country. The Central and Artibonite departments are attacked by the gangs of Savien, Gran Grif, and Jeff Gro Lwa. The Pernier, Torcelle, and Tabarre areas are occupied by Vitel'homme's "Kraze Baryè" group, the Cul-de-Sac Plain area (Croix-des-Bouquets and its surroundings) by Lanmò San Jou, and the south of Port-au-Prince by Krisla, Izo, and others. These armed bandits control a large part of the national territory, particularly the southern and northern parts of the capital, and a significant portion of the Artibonite region. They block the roads leading to oil terminals and prevent fuel from reaching service stations. This situation has serious consequences for institutions such as hospitals, media outlets, and telecommunications companies, among others.

—Benefiting from the unconditional support of the central government, gang violence exploded after July 7, 2021, the date of President Jovenel Moïse's assassination. This violence has caused thousands of deaths, with few punitive actions against the perpetrators, who enjoy widespread impunity.

At the subject of Jovenel Moïse's assassination: Port-au-Prince awoke that morning as if after a silent explosion. On July 7, 2021, at dawn, the news spread faster than lightning: the president was dead, riddled with bullets in his private residence. The streets froze. Radio stations broadcast the news continuously. Phones buzzed incessantly. No one understood yet, but everyone knew that something had just been irrevocably shattered.

Very quickly, the capital descended into a state of shock mixed with fear. Roadblocks appeared. Armed men moved about freely. The state seemed absent, as if dissolved in the stupor. The hunt for Colombian mercenaries began in utter confusion: hasty arrests, summary executions, bodies paraded, contradictory accounts. Justice stalled while rumors spread like wildfire. The crime was supposedly linked to the president's stances against certain influential figures in the business sector, a journalist commented on the radio.

The prosecutor paused to reflect on the tragedy. He shook his head. He continued his presentation:

"Your Honor, for the past five years, Haiti has experienced an explosive security and political crisis, indirectly fueling financial crime through chaos, corruption, and gang control. This has resulted in massive bank losses, increased credit risk, the financial exploitation of the population (arms, drug, and human trafficking), and a financial exodus. Gangs linked to elites have rendered the system vulnerable to embezzlement and economic instability. These gangs facilitate money laundering and tax evasion through kidnappings and racketeering, affecting both businesses and citizens. They assist the mafia in drug and organ trafficking. They infiltrate the economy, exploit the vulnerability of citizens, and undermine financial institutions, exacerbating poverty and instability.

The gangs are at the heart of power. They are financed with money and weapons by the political and economic elite. They are protected by the very same people who squandered the Petro Caribe funds. They are the armed wing of the mafia that uses Haiti as a free and open territory for illegal activities such as drugs, money laundering, organ trafficking, and others."

The prosecutor adjusts his glasses and continues:

— "Besides the violence, the Even worse is the poverty that affects the majority of people in the population. Indeed, 60% of families in the country live on less than $2 a day. Haiti is among the poorest countries in the world, ranked 168th out of 189 by the UNDP on its Human Development Index. Due to corruption and bureaucratic red tape, *Forbes magazine* ranked Haiti among the worst countries to do business in 2018 (151st out of 153 countries).

The prosecutor continues:

"Your Honor, poverty in Haiti is a reality that cannot be ignored. It manifests itself in the precarious living conditions of many Haitians and encompasses various aspects. Therefore, it is important to address the harm caused by the squandering of Petro Caribe funds. The society we represent demands accountability. The defendants present here must be condemned. They bear primary responsibility for the scourge plaguing the country. They must be severely punished to set an example. They must be tried to send a clear message to the international community, demonstrating that Haiti is determined to break with impunity once and for all. For if the country wants to attract foreign investors and reassure donors, the first obligation of those in power is to combat corruption and ensure the proper use of public funds."

A heavy silence fell over the courtroom. The prosecution paused for a moment, as if to give the Assize Court time to grasp the significance of what had just been said. It was no longer simply a matter of denouncing a crime and punishing those responsible, but of achieving a much more important objective: to finally break with impunity. He briefly consults his notes. The hearing continues. The anger in his voice mingles with the hardness of his gaze. What he is about to say is no longer a conclusion, but a further elaboration. Behind the corruption he denounces lies a broader, even more brutal reality: that of a country plunged into a structural crisis whose poorest pay the price every day.

Chapter 19

THE CRISIS IS SEVERE

The courtroom is stifling. It's not just the June heat that makes the air heavy and humid; it's the weight of what is about to be said. For seven days, words have been piling up like stones on a grave. Today, the grave is opened.

The courtroom is silent. What is at stake here is not just the fate of a few defendants, but the exposure of a country on its last legs. Haiti stands here, both upright and unsteady, like a nation tested by a succession of shocks, broken promises, and emergencies that have become commonplace.

The crisis is no longer an episode; it is a state of affairs. It is seeping into institutions, eroding public authority, and fracturing the social fabric. The state is retreating while fear advances. Roads are closing, schools are falling silent, and hospitals are emptying. In besieged neighborhoods, survival becomes a daily act of courage. The country is shifting, going into exile, crumbling.

While the nation sinks, billions disappear; funds intended for reconstruction, dignity, and the collective future are diverted from their purpose.

The humanitarian crisis is intertwined with the moral crisis; material misery reveals an ethical failure. It is no longer just sums of money that are disappearing, but lives that are being turned upside down.

It is in this context of widespread collapse that the voice of the prosecution is raised. It does not fill the void, but illuminates it. Here, in the heart of the courtroom, the crisis takes on a face, names, dates, and responsibilities. The trial reflects back to the entire nation its own image, the moment when history holds its breath to demand accountability.

Sweat trickled down his temple, along his jaw, and disappeared into the collar of his already damp white shirt. The prosecution recalled a sad, old story: the face of a little girl whose small legs had been painstakingly freed from the rubble after the earthquake. She died from the shock of the trauma. Lost in thought, the prosecution considered the countless victims—dead, injured, and amputees—of the disaster that devastated half of Port-au-Prince and severely damaged several other cities in the west and southeast of the country. He had seen people running, narrowly escaping their collapsed homes. He had seen dump trucks filled with corpses destined for Titanyen. While refugee camps at the Champ de Mars sheltered thousands of refugees, the defendants had exploited the situation to unlock enormous funds for the Petro Caribe program. While the country is on its knees, while children are dying of hunger, the emergency law becomes the norm, a strategy used by former Prime Minister Bellerive and associates to embezzle funds.

The prosecutor wipes his face and continues:

— "Your Honor, all this waste of money was orchestrated in the name of fighting poverty and social exclusion. The most vulnerable populations were supposed to be the beneficiaries of the Petro Caribe-related programs. But what is the reality while billions are being embezzled?"

Haiti is facing the most serious crisis in its history. Institutional collapse is complete, not to mention devastating humanitarian disasters. Dominated by extreme insecurity caused by armed gangs that control the capital and other regions, the humanitarian crisis in Haiti is complex and multidimensional. This crisis is causing massive displacement (more than one million people) and widespread violence, particularly against women and children. This situation compromises access to basic needs (water, food, healthcare) and leads to the closure of essential services (schools, hospitals). Sexual violence has exploded, targeting displaced women and girls living in precarious conditions. We see a population in despair, facing hunger and a lack of access to vital services.

The prosecutor wipes his face again and continues:

—"Your Honor, the squandering of PetroCaribe funds is directly linked to the increase in poverty in Haiti (one in four Haitians lives on less than a dollar a day). Growing inequality, the exodus of the population abroad, unemployment, and underdevelopment are shocking facts that outrage the human conscience. On the other hand, while living a comfortable life, the accused have spent exorbitant sums acquiring luxury villas and residences, modern private amenities, financed through kickbacks and the overbilling of work carried out on behalf of the State."

The prosecutor consults his notes and, in a strong and reassuring voice, concludes:

—"Your Honor, what is the conclusion?"

The Petro Caribe program, established by President Chávez and to which Haiti was admitted in 2006 should have been a unique opportunity to invest in sectors capable of creating a favorable environment for the country's economic takeoff. This money could have been used to rebuild Haiti and help the population meet basic needs: schools, hospitals, roads, electricity, etc. But it is clear that the money was embezzled or mismanaged. Billions of dollars were squandered by high-ranking state officials and their accomplices.

At this point, a profound silence falls over the courtroom. The prosecutor glances once more at the defendants and continues:

– "Your Honor, the first human rights violation suffered by the vast majority of the Haitian people is poverty. Part of the answer lies in the mismanagement and embezzlement of Petro Caribe funds; all facilitated by the law on public procurement, particularly negotiated contracts, and the two emergency laws (2008 and 2010)."

Under the state of emergency, decision-makers opted for negotiated agreements, granting them considerable autonomy in selecting projects and signing contracts without adhering to the legally prescribed protocol. Under the administrations of Préval and Martelly, the emergency law became a license to override administrative regulations. Its use was misused; it was left to the discretion of the executive branch, which took advantage of it to incur expenses unrelated to the emergency.

From the Préval administration to that of Martelly, the emergency law was repeatedly abused. The first emergency law, passed on September 8, 2008, after Hurricanes Gustav and Hanna struck Haiti on August 25 and September 6, 2008, respectively, was used as the cornerstone of a parallel system. The BMPAD's procedures allowed the government to bypass formal public administration oversight mechanisms. The use of the emergency law became the norm and the preferred method for Haitian governments to circumvent procurement regulations. Under this law, the CSCCA's signature did not occur at the time contracts were signed. It came afterward, in its capacity to exercise control. This law was reactivated with some modifications after the 2010 earthquake and remained in effect for many months. It was reintroduced in response to Hurricane Sandy in 2012.

—The investigation by the investigating magistrate's office uncovered a troubling fact: almost all of the Petro Caribe funds were committed under the guise of the emergency law. All sorts of contracts were signed, some genuinely related to the emergency, and many others, including some of the most important ones, that had no connection whatsoever to the emergency situation.

The last state of emergency ended on December 30, 2012, yet most of the contracts signed based on resolutions passed in 2013, 2014, and 2015 (Toussaint Louverture High School and Pétion High School) were clearly backdated to take advantage of the flexibility afforded by the emergency law. These contracts were not subject to any competitive bidding process. This maneuver is an attempt by successive governments after 2010 to violate procurement rules for the benefit of patronage.

The state of emergency, initially declared for one month on January 26, 2010, was extended for an additional eighteen months, beginning March 26, 2010. This allowed the Préval-Bellerive administration to make a number of commitments at its discretion, without being bound by the provisions and limitations of the law regarding contracts. Analysis of the signed contracts referring to the state of emergency revealed that this exceptional duration of the state of emergency paved the way for certain abuses.

— Under President Préval's administration, the investigation found that the objective was to develop road infrastructure. In addition to road rehabilitation work and equipment purchases, budget lines included "supervision" and "construction of social housing." The majority of disbursements were made under emergency provisions.

The prosecutor glances at his notes before continuing:

"Your Honor, while the emergency law streamlines public administration procedures, it does not authorize the unconstrained execution of projects outside the framework of the emergency.

This reasoning stems from the spirit of the law, whose wording, 'emergency law,' refers to the specific circumstances to which it applies. The investigation has found that the projects benefiting from the considerations of urgency are not generally those requiring rapid execution due to the urgency. Rather, they are projects requiring long-term planning and studies. These types of projects, which should be subject to formal and regular procurement structures, have benefited from the exceptional procurement provisions facilitated by the emergency law."

The investigation therefore concludes that if the execution of certain projects is initiated several years after the events that granted them the simplified contractual status under the emergency law, it is because they were not truly urgent; or, alternatively, it is because there was a clear intention to portray them as urgent when they were not. This is yet another strategy used by certain administrations to embezzle funds, particularly from PetroCaribe accounts.

—In conclusion, the emergency law of September 8, 2008, and that of April 19, 2010, which stemmed from a desire to allow the government to quickly alleviate the suffering of a population ravaged by cyclones, provided an ideal legal loophole to conceal and reinforce reprehensible practices within the state apparatus.

The prosecutor turns his gaze towards the presiding judge and declares:

—"Your Honor, the report from the Court of Auditors is categorical:

—Based on the foregoing considerations, the CSCCA believes it can declare that Petro Caribe funds were the subject of embezzlement, bribery, malfeasance, and prevarication by those named in this report. The specific cases that drew the attention of the investigating judge, and to which the committal order is particularly relevant, revolve around the following issues:

1- The mandatory deductions of the 2 % advance payment for the benefit of the DGI (General Directorate of Taxes) have not been made in almost all cases;

2- Not all Dominican firms and some Haitian firms were eligible at the time the contracts were signed.

Taking a few seconds to organize his papers, the public prosecutor stated:

— "Your Honor, from September 2008 to September 2016, the country had six Ministers of Economy and Finance: Daniel Dorsainvil, Ronald Bodin, André Lemercier Georges, Marie-Carmelle Jean-Marie, Wilson Laleau and Yves Romain Bastien.

— In our indictment, we asked the investigating chamber to open an investigation into the squandering of Petro Caribe funds. The investigating judge's committal order lists the following individuals presumed to be involved: former President Michel Joseph Martelly, former Prime Minister Laurent Lamothe, former Prime Minister Jean-Max Bellerive, Marie Carmelle Jean-Marie (former Minister of Economy and Finance), Olivier Martelly (son of the President), former President Jocelerme Privert, Félix Bautista (Dominican Senator), Sophia Martelly (wife of President Michel Martelly), Stéphanie Balmir Villedrouin (former Minister of Tourism), Yves Germain Joseph (former Secretary General of the Presidency under Jovenel Moïse), Florence Duperval Guillaume (former Minister of Public Health), Jacques Gabriel (former Minister of Public Works, Transport and Communications), Jude H. Day (Minister of Commerce and Industry), Nonie Mathieu (Judge of the Superior Court of Accounts and Administrative Disputes), Arold Élie (President of the Superior Court of Accounts and Administrative Disputes), and Max Rodolphe St-Albin. (former Minister of the Interior), Michael Lecorps (former Director General of the Bureau for the Monetization of Development Assistance Programs, BMPAD), Eustache Saint-Lot (former Director General of the Bureau for the Monetization of Development

Assistance Programs, BMPAD), Patrick Noramé (former Director General of the Bureau for the Monetization of Development Assistance Programs, BMPAD), Joséfa Raymond Gauthier (former Minister of Social Affairs), Jacques Rousseau (former Minister of Public Works, Transport and Communications). Around fifteen businessmen and women are also suspected in this case.

The prosecutor opens the documents (Latortue/Beauplan report/ CSCCA/order from the investigating judge) from which he draws the information, he identifies the accused, and declares:

— "The investigation began in 2018. The dean of the Port-au-Prince civil court, Mr. Bernard St Vil, appointed Judge Ramoncite Accimé as the investigating judge in the case. For months, the judge investigated the Petro Caribe affair. The order issued by the investigating judge's office, through a new investigating judge, brought the main defendants before this Assize Court."

The prosecutor continues:

— "Your Honor, the commission tasked with further investigating the report of the Ethics and Anti-Corruption Commission led by Senator Youri Latortue recommended that legal action be taken against two former prime ministers, a number of former ministers, directors general, and numerous private firm executives for their alleged involvement in the misappropriation of Petro Caribe funds. At least 30 public figures in the country are named in the report for the entire eight-year duration of the Petro Caribe program."

The prosecutor continues:

"Your Honor, many are wondering why, for all these years, the Petro Caribe trial has not been held. Despite three administrative reports citing the names of high-ranking officials responsible for managing these funds, there has been no judgment to date. The truth is simple. Holding such a trial requires the establishment of a government with recognized legitimacy and a body that rigorously and authoritatively ensures the application of the rule of law. For the trial to be fair and equitable, it must first have the support of Haitian institutions that want to see Haiti break free from the reign of impunity, and second, it must have the support of the international community, which must understand that instability in Haiti stems from the negative economic effects of corruption. The squandering of Petro Caribe funds is the most egregious example of this."

"The Petro Caribe case is a highly political matter. When one considers the major political issues at stake, and knowing that these questions are being raised publicly in a court of assizes, holding such a trial requires political will at the highest level. Because by deciding to hold this trial, one is not only touching on the most sensitive political and financial interests, but also opening a case that shakes the foundations of the Western political system. Petro Caribe has made corruption the modus operandi of Western capitalism, which allows itself to be guided by profit at the total detriment of human well-being, particularly that of the Haitian individual."

The prosecutor continues:

—"Your Honor, hundreds of individuals are implicated in the misappropriation of Petro Caribe funds. Around twenty of them bear direct responsibility in the affair; however, they are not all equal in terms of the degree of corruption involved. Those who were and are at the highest levels of government, members of private companies and international actors are primarily responsible and, as such, must be the first to be held accountable. Martelly, Lamothe, Bellerive, Laleau, Bautista… are at the top of the list."

Chapter 20

THE ACCUSED ARE CRIMINALS

(The eleventh day of the hearing)

They are called decision-makers, high-ranking officials, and elites. That morning, the accused were brought before their judges, before the people, before history. They were brought before this Assize Court as criminals, delinquents, usurpers, forgers… In the case, now, it's no longer just about numbers. It's about corpses. It's about stray bullets. It's about embezzled funds. In short, it's about sham contracts…

The hearing opens with a truth the prosecution is determined to stop ignoring: the defendants are not merely incompetent managers or reckless politicians; they are at the heart of a structured criminal system where financial and physical violence feed off each other. Here, the embezzlement of public funds is not a simple accounting infraction; it is the fuel for a deadly mechanism that has disintegrated the state and unleashed chaos.

The financial crimes the defendants are accused of are varied: emptying public coffers, sabotaging development projects, and diverting funds intended for schools, hospitals, roads, and national security. But these crimes do not stop at collective impoverishment. They extend their effects to bloodshed. To protect impunity, stifle investigations, and silence witnesses, this system resorts to organized terror. Gangs have been financed, equipped, protected, and used as the armed wing of political and economic interests.

So when the prosecution rises to speak, it's not just to demand an accounting of the missing money. It's to make the connection between the signature at the bottom of a contract and the gunshot in the night; between the tax haven and the hell of the working-class neighborhoods. The defendants emptied the coffers. And with that money, they filled the gangs' arsenals. They created a system where corruption fuels violence, and where violence protects corruption. It is this system, in all its horror, that this eleventh day of the hearing will expose.

Thus, economic crime transforms into physical crime. Squandered funds become weapons, ammunition, and death contracts. Gangs don't emerge from nothing: they thrive in the shadow of fraudulent administrative decisions, rigged public contracts, and complicity at the highest levels of government. Every embezzled gourde loads a rifle, every fictitious contract strengthens an armed network, and every silence bought paves the way for new assassinations.

The defendants took Venezuelan oil money. They squandered this money, which should have been used to build schools, hospitals, electricity, roads, and infrastructure. Billions of US dollars were embezzled. The defendants signed rigged contracts, inflated invoices, and created shell companies. They transferred the country's future into private accounts in the United States, Canada, the Dominican Republic, Panama, African countries, and elsewhere. This is the financial aspect of the crime; the part that takes place in air-conditioned offices, with ties and smiles.

But the embezzled money has another use. It buys silence. It pays masked men. It kills opponents. The gangs called "*Viv Ansanm*" who terrorize neighborhoods, rape women, kill, and burn, were protected in the past by the accused. These men, present here today, are not mere fraudsters. They are criminals. They order assassinations and kidnappings. Petro Caribe money paid for the ammunition that plunged Port-au-Prince into fire and bloodshed.

It was in a courtroom shaken by strong emotions that the public prosecutor continued his plea.

"Your Honor, the defendants are criminals. They form a criminal organization. Their hands are stained with numerous murderous acts: violent crimes and others. As part of their operations to conceal the truth, they have assassinated several prominent figures. Robert Marcello, the coordinator of the National Commission for Public Procurement (CNMP), was kidnapped on January 12, 2009, while Alix Mary Junior Gassant, the director of a construction firm, was killed on February 24, 2012. These two murdered individuals were the first two victims of Petro Caribe. Klaus Eberwein, former director of the Economic and Social Assistance Fund (FAES), committed suicide on July 12, 2017, in a Florida hotel, after agreeing to testify before the Senate committee investigating the use of Petro Caribe funds. It is claimed, however, that he was assassinated."

—Another death, to say the least suspicious, was that of Caroline Estimé, who was in charge of the Petro Caribe file at the Prime Minister's office. She was also scheduled to testify before the Senate Committee, and she took her own life in Florida on August 2, 2018.

—Mr. Guitau Toussaint, Chairman of the Board of Directors of the National Credit Bank, was assassinated on Sunday, June 12, 2011, following a gunshot wound at his residence in Vivy Michel (Frères). According to the investigation, the assassination is linked to the Petro Caribe affair, particularly the launch of the "*Kay Pam*" housing loan program. Unidentified armed individuals entered the victim's home, overpowered the household staff, and shot him at point-blank range in the face. He was pronounced dead at the Haitian Community Hospital in Frères.

—Those who embezzled Petro Caribe funds attempted to assassinate former Senator Evalière Beauplan, president of the report of the Special Commission of Inquiry into the Use of Petro Caribe Funds. Unidentified armed individuals attacked the senator's residence on the afternoon of Wednesday, June 7, 2023, in Tabarre 60. He survived thanks to his vigilance and the intervention of neighbors. The Movement to Liberate Haiti (MOLHA), of which Beauplan is the national coordinator, attributes this attack to those who embezzled Petro Caribe funds, who want to silence him.

— "We expected them to react, but we didn't think they would go so far as to want to physically assassinate the former senator, after having assassinated his character," said MOLHA.

"We urge those who embezzled Petro Caribe funds to prepare to face justice instead of engaging in unhealthy practices such as paying gangs to carry out dirty work for them," the statement reads.

The prosecutor continues:

"Your Honor, mistrust remains ever-present whenever the Petro Caribe affair is discussed, because those who have an interest in silencing the truth are still lurking. They wait in the shadows to strike. In 2018, Prime Minister Jean-Henry Céant attempted to establish a Truth Commission on the management and use of the funds. No sector agreed to participate in this body. Representatives of the sectors who met with the Prime Minister formally requested that their names not be mentioned. The Core Group acknowledged this in a press release on November 2, 2018."

The prosecutor glances at the defendants and declares:

— "Your Honor, the defendants exerted physical pressure on the investigating judge in charge of the case. As a result, Judge Ramoncite Accimé decided to suspend the investigation. This decision was vehemently condemned by the plaintiffs, who immediately announced their intention to appeal. In a press conference on Thursday, June 24, 2021, the lawyers representing the civil parties in the case denounced "the investigating judge's attempt, which, according to them, is a malicious attempt to exonerate those who embezzled Petro Caribe funds." According to the lawyers, the order issued on June 21, 2021, by Judge Accimé declaring the investigation premature due to the absence of a debit ruling from the Court of Auditors is a subterfuge.

This order had an immediate consequence: the lifting of the freeze on the assets of companies suspected of involvement in the Petro Caribe scandal. Local banks were now required to unfreeze their accounts. This decision came the day after the Anti-Corruption Unit (ULCC) took action against businessman Réginald Boulos. As a precautionary measure, the ULCC ordered financial institutions operating in Haiti to freeze 260 million gourdes belonging to Boulos and his associates. According to the ULCC's director general, this sum represents the embezzled funds plus a fine equal to three times the value of the misappropriated assets.

The prosecutor continues:

— "Your Honor, between 2016 and 2017, the Senate Ethics and Anti-Corruption Commission produced two reports highlighting irregularities in the Petro Caribe program. By Senate resolution of August 1, 2018, these reports were transmitted to the oversight body for the potential prosecution of state officials: "The Senate requests the Court to conduct a thorough analysis, verification, and review of the management of Petro Caribe funds for the period from September 2008 to September 2016, in accordance with Article 200 of the Constitution." (Senate Resolution: Article 1).

In January 2019, an initial report by the Superior Court of Auditors and Administrative Disputes (CSCCA) revealed disastrous management of public funds related to Petro Caribe and suggested widespread corruption within the Haitian public administration. The Court's second report was submitted to the President of the

Supreme Court, Carl Murat Cantave, on Friday, May 31, 2019. On August 18, 2020, a third report was submitted by the President of the Court, Rogavil Boisguéné, to the President of the Senate, Pierre François Sildor.

— Like the first two reports, the latest report from the Court of Auditors reveals irregularities that have caused harm to the community. This report implicates two other governments in the squandering of funds and recommends a judicial inquiry to recover the misappropriated funds, the majority of which were lost under the Martelly/Lamothe government.

The prosecutor pauses to review his notes, and then continues:

—"Your Honor, one fact is undeniable, with the force of irrefutable convergence. Three separate investigations, conducted by different institutions, at different times and under their own mandates, nevertheless arrive at the same conclusions. The Senate of the Republic, through its Commissions of Inquiry, the Court of Auditors in the exercise of its constitutional mission of oversight, and the investigating judge within the framework of criminal prosecution, follow separate institutional paths but all lead to the same factual truth."

The methods differ in form but share the same rigor. The Senate conducts witness hearings, analyzes supporting documents, and confronts public officials. For its part, the Superior Court of Accounts and Administrative Disputes (CSCCA) examine financial statements, contracts, procurement procedures, and the traceability of disbursements. The investigating judge, meanwhile, cross-references data, contextualizes the facts, and assesses the evidence related to individual and collective criminal liability. Yet, at the end of these independent investigations, the diagnosis is identical: systematic irregularities, repeated violations of legal standards, a lack of transparency, and the misuse of emergency legislation.

Even more troubling, the three investigations reveal the same patterns of operation. The same institutions appear, the same practices are repeated, the same companies benefit from preferential treatment, and the same authorizing officers reappear as central players in the squandering of funds. Far from being isolated errors or administrative blunders, these facts reveal a coherent, structured, and persistent organization.

"The convergence of the findings rules out any possibility of coincidence. It lends the alleged facts greater evidentiary weight and places the court before a historical responsibility. When three independent bodies, with distinct jurisdictions, produce a convergent interpretation of the same reality, the judicial truth ceases to be hypothetical and becomes demonstrable."

The prosecution rallies. The floor is once again open. The trial continues, now illuminated by this damning convergence of evidence.

One of the substitutes takes the floor.

— "Your Honor, The irregularities in question include the misappropriation of funds allocated to certain projects, the payment of unjustified invoices, the falsification of payroll records, and a number of projects undertaken without a needs assessment or cost estimate. Deficiencies in the supplier selection process, as well as expenditures not included in contracts or not covered by any signed contracts, were also observed.

— At the Ministry of Defense, 5 million gourdes were embezzled, while accounting and contractual documents could not be found to justify several expenditures by the Ministry of Justice. This is the case, for example, with approximately 11 million dollars disbursed for the acquisition of equipment, ammunition, and accessories for the National Police, as well as another tranche of approximately 300 million gourdes, also intended to strengthen the Haitian National Police (PNH).

The Ministry of Social Affairs was unable to provide supporting documentation to demonstrate a discrepancy of over 60 million gourdes, representing the balance in the budget for the Bel Air special plan. The investigation also denounces the misappropriation of funds from Petro Caribe. According to the investigating judge's order, these funds were used for operating expenses instead of investment expenditures.

At the Ministry of Planning and External Cooperation, the investigation found no reliable accounting documents to justify certain expenditures. The investigating judge noted that at the Ministry of Tourism, expenditures were either not stipulated in contracts or not covered by any signed contract. The case of the Ministry of Agriculture appears even more serious, as the Superior Court of Auditors and Administrative Disputes (CSCCA) reported non-compliance with the law on public procurement in the awarding of 15 negotiated contracts and the failure to optimize spending of just over $4 million. The Court also noted the disappearance of delivery slips and delivery notes for purchased products, as well as for other projects.

As for the Ministry of the Interior, no contract could be found for the disbursement of three million dollars committed under the "Support for the Restructuring of the Passport System" project, while another expenditure of 2 million gourdes for the acquisition of water filters was not justified. The Superior Court of Accounts and Administrative Disputes (CSCCA) also denounces favoritism in the awarding of contracts to the Housing and Public Buildings Construction Unit (UCLBP), as 6 out of 12 contracts awarded were granted without competitive bidding to a single firm: the IBI/DAA Group Inc. Furthermore, for all the contracts signed, there was neither a public nor restricted call for tenders, or approval from the Court of Accounts.

Cases of embezzlement were also found in the accounting records of the Economic and Social Assistance Fund (FAES), amounting to

169 million gourdes, while 12 million dollars allocated to the FAES under the Petro Caribe program could not be located, even though this money was intended for the social protection and promotion program. The court order also reports discovering that electrification work in the municipality of Terrier Rouge, for which 18.2 million gourdes were disbursed to EDH (Électricité d'État d'Haïti), was not carried out, as well as a cost overrun of 24.4 million gourdes between the amount received by EDH (681.3 million) and the amount spent (705 million) on capacity building work at the Carrefour power plant.

— Other significant sums could not be traced by the investigation, notably 369.8 million gourdes received by the Office of the Minister Delegate to the Prime Minister in charge of Energy Security and 84 million gourdes allocated to DINEPA (National Directorate of Drinking Water and Sanitation) for the implementation of a development program, which were misappropriated. Other infractions are common to almost all the institutions audited. These include failure to comply with several initial parameters in the execution of projects, such as the nature and scope of the work, cost estimates, and timelines. The Court of Auditors audited a total of 92.1% of the total amount of resolutions adopted by the Council of Ministers from September 2008 to September 2016. The remaining 7.9% relates to undisbursed funds as well as allocations and reallocations resulting from the resolutions in question.

The prosecutor pauses. He looks at the defendants and declares:

— "Your Honor, based on these considerations, we ask the criminal court to convict these authorizing officers who have succeeded one another at the head of the institutions and who are involved in the management of Petro Caribe funds for having committed the State to irregular transactions in the context of the development and/or management of the projects.

—Alongside this criminal trial, it is necessary to conduct national and international investigations in order to recover sums hidden in banks and deposited in accounts belonging to these high officials accused of squandering Petro Caribe funds.

— Your Honor, an international investigation to identify the accounts into which the misappropriated Petro Caribe funds were deposited is essential. This trial must be used to tackle the scourge of corruption. An investigation by the Bureau of Research in Information Technology and Economic and Social Development (BRIDES) reveals that "the payment of bribes to obtain basic public services or licenses, to influence judicial decisions or the awarding of public contracts and other state functions remains a significant problem in Haiti. The 2018 Corruption Perceptions Index (CPI), published by Transparency International, ranks Haiti 161st out of 180 countries with a score of 20 out of 100."

The prosecutor continues:

— "Your Honor, with the failure of the Interim Haiti Recovery Commission (IHRC), the Haitian state established mechanisms to manage aid funds and the public development and investment projects resulting from these funds. It is therefore pertinent to ask this question: how can we understand that, despite the institutionalization of these mechanisms, projects financed by Petro Caribe funds have been subject to so many irregularities?"

—Here, it is important to emphasize the approach used by the Court of Auditors and the Senate to arrive at the audit results. The CSCCA established audit committees. These committees conducted interviews with managers and then analyzed documents from the institutions. The Senate's methodological approach primarily involved: organizing working sessions with ministers and directors general and analyzing documents (reviewing supporting documents, verifying internal controls, and confirming the existence of reports).

"Thus, the charges against the accused are based on projects financed by the audited funds. Therefore, it remains relevant to declare that all the crimes attributed to the accused in the investigating judge's committal order and the facts mentioned in the indictment are just and well-founded."

The prosecutor continues:

— "Your Honor, our role as the public prosecutor, coupled with twenty years of experience in the Haitian judiciary, makes us understand that organizing such a trial to recover the funds squandered and illegally misappropriated by political authorities and figures in the private sector is a difficult undertaking. The involvement of high-ranking state officials in the case as well as the inherent weaknesses of the Haitian judicial system, make the process even more complicated."

- A competent judge with specialized training in financial crime investigations is needed to uncover the elements of this case. Not just any judge can handle a trial of this magnitude. First, you need the necessary experience in financial crime trials; you also need a judge who has courage and is free from any political influence. A magistrate above suspicion, who refuses to be corrupted.

Even before the prosecution calls his name, the presiding judge knows. This demand for courage is not foreign to him. It took hold of him long before the trial began, long before the closing arguments and the intense gazes of the millions of people following this historic trial, especially those in the courtroom. He remembers his family's anguish, the nighttime calls filled with fear, the words repeated like a plea: leave, flee the country, save his life before it's too late.

The threats are specific, insistent, sometimes whispered, sometimes brutal. They have forced him to relocate his family, change his address, and abandon his routines. Yet, every morning, he puts his robes back on. Not out of heroism, but out of loyalty to a simple idea: if the judge flees, only the law of the strongest remains.

The prosecutor continues:

"This magistrate is you, Your Honor, who bears the responsibility of judging and convicting those who embezzled billions of dollars from Petro Caribe funds. You are the blindfolded woman who symbolizes justice (an allegory of the goddess Themis) and represents impartiality, objectivity, and equality before the law, signifying that justice must be served without distinction of wealth, power, or status, judging solely on the facts, without prejudice. In your right hand, you hold the scales of justice, which symbolize fairness, balance, and the measurement of arguments for a just decision, inherited from the Greek goddess Themis, representing impartiality and divine order, where you weigh the facts to determine the truth and the just punishment."

The prosecutor wipes his face, drinks some water, before continuing.

—"This trial concerning the misappropriation of Petro Caribe funds, Your Honor, is a remarkable contribution to ethical governance in Haiti. As sociologist Antoine Augustin pointed out: 'The conclusion of the Petro Caribe case has an ethical and political dimension with societal and strategic implications. In short, the Petro Caribe trial, through the restitution, damages, and fines it will result in, must contribute to the repayment of Haiti's debt to its creditors.'"

The prosecutor continues:

"Your Honor, it is often said that justice elevates a nation. This means that the moral rectitude, integrity, and fairness of its citizens and leaders elevate a people, fostering its prosperity and honor. This is why the Petro Caribe trial is so important. It will mark history with its societal, legal, and political impact. Like the great criminal trials of history, such as the Nuremberg Trials, the Tokyo Trials, the trials of Slobodan Milošević, and Klaus Barbie, which served to uphold the rule of law and protect fundamental human rights, the Petro Caribe trial will shape legal memory in its own way, strengthening the fight against corruption and impunity throughout the world."

As someone once said: "This trial opens the path to hope for those who, through false promises, have lost faith, for the new generation adrift, for those who say and repeat that we Haitians are strong in words but weak in actions."

The prosecutor takes a break. He breathes a little and declares:

—" Your Honor, at the end of the in-depth investigations carried out around the use of Petro Caribe funds, the investigating judge's inquiry has confirmed the facts of wrongdoing in the two Senate investigation reports. Indeed, the 5 senators of the Special Senate Commission of Inquiry (CSSE), [Senator Evalière Beauplan (PONT), Senator Nenel Cassy (Fanmi Lavalas), Senator Antonio Cheramy (VERITE), Senator Richard Lénine Hervé Fourcand (PHTK) and Senator Onondieu Louis (KID)], based on the documents inventoried and analyzed, from the data provided and examined by the audit firm that the Commission had engaged for the purposes of this investigation, came to the conclusion that the management of Petro Caribe funds was marked by serious anomalies, irregularities, acts of malfeasance and prevarication which attest that those who had the responsibility of executing the programs and projects related to the resolutions concerning Petro Caribe funds did not respect the standards and legal provisions in the awarding of contracts and did not have the concern to protect the interests of the Haitian State.

The report indicates that the facts revealed in all the operations prove that the majority of those with the authority to authorize disbursements acted with laxity, which the CSCCA was able to deduce in almost every case: negligence, inconsistencies, and other irregularities were repeated. In such cases, the investigating judge asserts that these could no longer be considered simple clerical errors, but rather acts likely to mislead and facilitate illicit practices, collusion, and influence peddling.

The investigating judge's order, for its part, states that the review of the contracts demonstrated that more than half of them were signed outside of public procurement procedures (lack of transparency, good governance, etc.) and in violation of contract awarding standards (fairness, equal treatment, free competition, free access to public procurement, etc.). The emergency laws adopted by governments between 2008 and 2016 allowed public officials and state accountants to exercise their power with an excess that sometimes bordered on indecency. Under the cover of these laws, both irrational and illegal acts were carried out in violation of regulations and laws on public accounting and finance.

— In his committal order, the investigating judge concluded that all the investigations conducted with the organizations concerned revealed weaknesses of such magnitude that it was necessary to consider each case individually and place them within a broader context in order to establish individual and collective responsibilities. It became clear during the course of the investigation that Petro Caribe was the victim of large-scale fraud. The most blatant example is that the current status of the funds and the disbursements made through the 13 resolutions for the period from September 2008 to September 2016 are so tainted by irregular, even fraudulent, acts that it was necessary to analyze the financial statements of BMPAD, the principal and primary actor in the management of Petro Caribe funds. It is difficult to determine the accuracy and reliability of the fund balances, the disbursements, and the management of the contracts. The management of the funds, according to what was submitted by the BMPAD, in no way reflects the financial situation of this fund.

The prosecutor continues:

— "Your Honor, in light of all this data, allow me to point out that the guilt of the accused can hardly be doubted. All the irregularities noted in the various reports – that of the Senate Ethics and Anti-Corruption Commission, that of the Special Senate Commission of Inquiry, the audit of the Superior Court of Accounts and Administrative Disputes (CSCCA), and finally the order of the investigating judge – all these reports attest that the accused present here are either perpetrators or accomplices in the squandering of PetroCaribe funds.

—The Court of Auditors analyzed the transactions carried out by the Préval/Pierre-Louis administrations (September 2008-October 2009) totaling US$197,500,000, Préval/Bellerive (November 2009-May 2011) US$348,240,830.01, Martelly/Conille (November 2011-May 2012) US$210,303,222.68, Martelly/Lamothe (May 2012-December 2014) US$668,315,429.20, and Martelly/Paul (January 2015-March 2016) US$280,003,698.66. No administration was overlooked. The obligation to give an account concerns all those who have had the privilege of being in charge of state affairs.

The prosecutor opens the new 2025 Penal Code, looks at the defendants for the umpteenth time, before declaring:

— "Your Honor, our conclusions are simple, the prosecution requests the application of Articles 130, 137, 224, 225, 226, 324, and 334 of the Haitian Code, which provides a maximum penalty of 10 years. That is the sentence that our society expects from the Criminal Court against the accused."

Comments

In many countries, governing involves planning and managing available resources to ensure the well-being of citizens. In underdeveloped countries like Haiti, however, governing is more about accumulating wealth, protecting oneself from poverty, and ensuring the affluence of one's family. This is done with utter disregard for the citizens. The Petro Caribe affair perfectly illustrates this trend.

In 2005, Venezuelan President Hugo Chávez, as part of a regional integration strategy (Thomas, 2019), concluded an energy agreement with 15 Central American and Caribbean countries, including Haiti. The agreement involved selling oil to the signatory states at low prices. These states were granted sufficient repayment periods to avoid disrupting their balance of payments. According to Antonin (2018, cited in Thomas, 2019), the profits generated were to be invested in development projects.

The Haitian authorities established the Bureau for the Monetization of Development Assistance Programs (BMPAD) to manage the funds generated by Petro Caribe. The Superior Court of Accounts and Administrative Disputes (CSCCA) presented a report on the subject on January 31, 2019. According to this report, from 2008 to 2018, 219 shipments of oil from Venezuela were sold to Haiti. These shipments totaled 43.9 million barrels of oil and were sold for over $4.237 billion (CSCCA, 2019). What about social projects?

That's another debate. The CSCCA report exposes irregularities in the management of Petro Caribe funds. This damning report severely damages the reputation of the highest-ranking officials of the time. And since there is no accountability without responsibility, they are obligated to provide explanations to the nation. Otherwise, history will remember their time at the helm of the state with a bitter taste.

Moreover, this affair sparked several violent protests across the country. Ordinary citizens accused the leaders of the time of squandering Petro Caribe funds. Six years after this report, the Haitian population seems to have already forgotten these moments of intense tension, with the deteriorating security situation in the country becoming the primary source of concern. For their part, the leaders implicated are taking advantage of the situation to increase their ill-gotten gains.

Thus, minds have partially shifted away from the Petro Caribe affair. This observation is symptomatic of the perpetual corruption that characterizes governance in Haiti. Its corollary is impunity. Leaders are accustomed to playing for time. It's an easy way for them to restore their image. They are confident that people will soon forget everything. They will then be able to rebuild a good reputation.

It is in this climate of moral lethargy that Judge Jean Sénat Fleury's book, "Petro Caribe: The Prosecutor Speaks," has emerged. The author envisions the opportunity to close the case with a fair and equitable trial. For justice is the path laid out in a law-abiding society to resolve disputes. By initiating this trial, Judge Fleury also reignites the mobilization against the alleged embezzlers of Petro Caribe funds. At the same time, he invites the accused to take the path of justice to prove their innocence, if necessary. They will also have the opportunity to seek forgiveness should they be found innocent.

References

Superior Court of Accounts and Administrative Disputes (CSCCA, 2019). Specific Audit of PetroCaribe Fund Management: Management of Projects Financed by the

PetroCaribe Fund. Report 1 https://www.haitilibre.com/docs/PETROCARIBE-31-01-2019.pdf

ThomasFrédéric(2019).Haiti:TheScandaloftheCentury.Corruption, Neoliberalism, and Popular Revolt . *Conjoncture* . https://www.contretemps.eu/haiti-petrocaribe-corruption-neoliberlaisme/

Jean Elifaite Gué

Postdoctoral researcher in educational sciences

University of Quebec at Trois-Rivières

Master's degree in criminology

Bachelor's degree in social communication

Member of the laboratory: language, discourse and representation (LADIREP, UEH)

Member of the international research and expertise laboratory on educational relations and masculinities in educational contexts (LIRE-RÉMCÉ)

Professor at the State University of Haiti (UEH)

Professor at the Institute of Science, Technology and Advanced Studies of Haiti (ISTEAH)

A Criminal Court for History

PetroCaribe: The Prosecutor Speaks of Jean Sénat Fleury is much more than a book: it is an act of literary justice and an exercise in national catharsis. In this fictional trial of astonishing power and precision, the magistrate-writer summons public and private officials, interrogates them, exposes their methods, and reveals the staggering scale of the plunder.

PetroCaribe: The Prosecutor Speaks is not just a book; it is a tribunal where history and justice meet. Judge Fleury here performs the foundational act that reality has denied the people: to investigate, judge, and symbolically condemn the largest plundering of funds in Haitian history.

In this rigorous fictional account, the former magistrate gives substance to the missing money. He names those responsible, establishes a procedure for the chaos, and gives voice to the stifled collective indignation.

This trial was necessary because it establishes the truth as a national heritage. It documents, with supporting evidence, the mechanisms of an economic crime that has generated the current misery and security crisis in Haiti. It shows how systemic corruption is not inevitable, but a series of criminal choices that must be called into question.

Finally, this book-trial is an act of resistance to memory. It prevents forgetting, that accomplice of impunity. It offers Haitian youth a clear account of what was stolen from them, and future generations a solemn warning about the cost of tolerating predators in suits.

PetroCaribe: The Prosecutor Speaks is therefore much more than a novel. It is a duty of justice fulfilled through words where institutions have failed. It is an essential work for anyone who believes that the first step in rebuilding a nation lies in the courage to confront its history head-on, without compromise.

A book that anyone should be read.

Prof. Amerigo Bernadel

I wish to thank my friend **Jean Sénat Fleury** for giving me this opportunity to comment on what constitutes one of the biggest scandals involving the embezzlement of public funds in Haitian history. I also wish to congratulate the author for his commitment to preventing the Petro Caribe scandal from being forgotten. This commitment places him on the path of the great **Imhotep**, whose light shines through him and his entire body of work. "May this light illuminate you from the primordial ramp leading to the summit of the pyramid of existence, my dear Jean?"

Reflecting on this work, I wonder where to begin. But first and foremost, I hope my commentary will shed new light on the subject, helping the reader to better grasp some of the hidden facets of this major transnational crime. In this regard, I do not intend to elaborate in depth on the transnational dimension of this financial crime, but rather to highlight it in order to emphasize a fundamental fact: the Haitian banking system is incapable of absorbing more than $500 million. Consequently, the vast majority of these funds were necessarily transferred to foreign banks. It will be up to specialists in international law to delve deeper into this aspect.

From a distance, one might wonder how international involvement in the laundering or absorption of these embezzled funds could influence or compromise the trial. This is precisely one of the reasons why this work can be considered a classic: all those potentially implicated are, in a way, virtually put on trial. For my part, my commentary will focus on the issue of Haitian identity from the perspective of the citizen.

When one observes the decline of Haitian society on social, economic, and institutional levels, it becomes clear that the country is facing a crisis of citizenship. But what is a citizen? Generally speaking, a citizen is a person who, by virtue of their place of birth, the nationality of one or both parents, or by naturalization, is recognized as having the full range of rights and responsibilities as a member of a nation or political community.

However, this notion was understood differently in the first Haitian constitution, where the concept of citizen was conflated with the actions and conduct of the individual. In other words, according to the Dessalinian constitution of 1805, being Haitian depended primarily on the person's behavior.

In light of this understanding, it is clear that the actions of Haitians today differ profoundly from those adopted by the Founding Fathers of the nation. Politically, leaders cannot act without following the agenda of their local and foreign patrons. Economically, those who enjoy a monopoly on wealth increase its primarily through imports. Meanwhile, a youth abandoned by these same groups faces two tragic alternatives: leaving the country for an uncertain adventure abroad or joining armed gangs to survive.

At this level, the crisis of citizenship is more easily understood from the perspective of young people, even if there is no guarantee that they will behave differently from their predecessors when they gain power and wealth. One thing remains certain: these young people are suffering, lacking direction, which makes them vulnerable and deeply anti-Haitian in their behavior.

As for the current politicians and oligarchs, they demonstrate no genuine sense of belonging to the country. This is why, from 1986 to the present day, these groups have governed and conducted business without even living alongside their immediate families, the vast majority of whom reside abroad. This crisis of citizenship was, however, clearly addressed in Haiti's imperial constitution of 1805, Article 9 of which stipulates:

"No one is worthy of being called Haitian unless they are a good father, a good son, a good husband, and above all, a good soldier."

Nevertheless, we must acknowledge that more than two centuries ago, our ancestors had already established criteria for identifying what constitutes a true Haitian citizen. Therefore, how could a son of Haiti, meeting the requirements of Article 9, have embezzled public funds and acted against him and against all the families of the country?

In this sense, neither Bellerive, nor Laleau, nor Martelly, nor any of those involved—including the Prévalists (Lespwa and Unité), the PHTK, and so many others—in the misappropriation of Petro Caribe funds are truly Haitian in the sense of this constitution. This is why all those implicated in this embezzlement should be tried twice: first for the misappropriation of these public funds, and second for violating Article 9 of the 1805 Imperial Constitution. In any case, they will not be able to hide: even if human justice fails, their names will remain banished from the history of this country.

Conclusion

Ultimately, the Petro Caribe scandal cannot be reduced to a simple case of financial corruption or just another administrative failure. It represents the most complete expression of the breakdown of the moral and civic pact that was supposed to bind the Haitian individual to the nation. By squandering resources intended for collective development, the perpetrators of this crime have not only materially impoverished the country, but they have also, and more importantly, emptied the very notion of Haitian citizenship of its meaning.

In light of the 1805 imperial constitution, it is clear that Haitian identity is not defined solely by birth certificate or legal nationality, but by conduct, commitment, and a sense of duty toward the community. Therefore, those who have consciously worked against the vital interests of the Haitian people have excluded themselves from this citizenship, regardless of their position, political affiliation, or social standing.

This observation imposes a dual imperative: that of criminal justice, which must establish responsibility and punish the guilty, and that of historical and moral justice, which must inscribe these acts in collective memory so that they are neither trivialized nor forgotten. For a people who forget their crimes against themselves condemn themselves to relive them.

Thus, the real issue, transcending the Petro Caribe trial, is the reconstruction of Haitian citizenship, founded on ethics, responsibility, and a sense of the common good. Without this refunding, no political project, no institutional reform, no development plan can pull Haiti out of the abyss in which it finds itself. The country's future depends less on its resources than on the moral character of those who claim to lead it.

Jacques Arnaud Démézier – Sociologist

Petro Caribe: The Public Prosecutor Speaks

The Petro Caribe scandal is one of the biggest financial scandals on the long list of embezzlements of public funds committed by high-ranking officials in Haiti. Despite their highly reprehensible and disastrous actions for the Haitian state and their social disengagement from the people and the socio-economic fabric of the country, these high-ranking officials have enjoyed complete impunity due to their "privileged" relationships with foreign diplomats who wield considerable influence in Haiti's internal affairs.

This particular saga began with René Préval's unequal selection of candidates, to the detriment of Leslie Manigat in the first round of the 2006 presidential election, leading to the cancellation of the second round that should have taken place. René Préval subsequently signed the Petro Caribe agreement with Venezuela, which included particularly advantageous economic terms for Haiti.

Despite a number of rumors circulating regarding the misuse of funds, the Préval administration—based on available data and information—was not generally accused of involvement in the misappropriation of Petro Caribe funds. This is evidenced by the relatively positive record it left to its successor administration.

The government that succeeded René Préval's was installed and put in place by the US State Department following a fraudulent election in 2010, according to Préval's own testimony. An individual well-known for his lack of qualifications and respectability, his farcical actions, misogynistic views, and documented affiliations with the far right, was chosen under international pressure, to the detriment of far more serious and qualified candidates.

This individual, in concert with his family, friends, allies, and personal supporters (that is, those who supported him during his periods of hardship and uncertainty), acquaintances, political allies, and others, oversaw the near-complete squandering of Petro Caribe funds. He used these funds to justify unnecessary expenses for frivolous activities such as frequent carnivals, lavish parties, and frequent trips abroad accompanied by an impressive entourage, costing the Haitian treasury millions of dollars. He also purchased numerous luxury homes in Haiti and abroad, yachts, and other such items. The mission entrusted to him—to improve the living conditions of the population—instead amounted to squandering public funds by hindering the Haitian government's investments in agriculture, infrastructure, higher education, and industry.

Consequently, Haiti's reconstruction was never possible. The economy quickly fell into decline, generating exponential poverty and absolute distress among the lower classes of society.

Twenty years later, following the initial signing of this agreement, Haitian society found itself in such a state of decay that it allowed the beginnings of delinquency and banditry to manifest themselves and subsequently to be imprinted by acts of gangsterism (kidnappings, rapes, robberies, crimes), to become entrenched and part of everyday life.

The worsening financial distress plaguing Haiti naturally contributed to the country's near collapse. And, supposedly, to complete a cycle that had already reached its breaking point, the American government decided, as an extreme measure, to impose sanctions on a group of individuals for the atrocities committed against their own country.

Too late!

Most economists wonder what Haiti would be like today if the money and profits derived from the Petro Caribe program had been used for the purposes intended in that agreement. What would have happened if the United States hadn't intervened to place an unconventional, utterly incompetent person at the head of the country at a critical moment in its history, when Haiti needed serious and competent leadership more than ever?

Just recently, a government audit report was finally released, accusing numerous high-ranking officials of involvement in the scandal. But most of the perpetrators are protected by a weak and corrupt judicial system, as well as by the U.S. government's disinterest in a corruption trial that would implicate many American citizens and entities. It is in this context that Susan D. Paige, a highly respected diplomat who had advocated for a trial following the release of the latest audit report, was unceremoniously removed from her senior position with MINUJUSTH (United Nations Mission for Justice in Haiti).

We are greatly pleased to see that, through a mock trial, Judge Fleury has decided to judge these monstrous figures who shamefully squandered the Petro Caribe funds. What an excellent idea to invent a criminal trial in which the case is presented before a Court of Assizes where high-ranking officials in the public and private sectors are tried for embezzlement, misappropriation of funds, abuse of power, and fraud ! I sincerely congratulate the author for the work accomplished and for his contribution to the cause, ensuring that collective memory does not forget, but above all, that it acknowledges and becomes aware of the situation.

Eng. Luckner Bayas

Boston, MA

A Brief Commentary on the Book

My dear Jean! I've read the preliminary draft of a potential trial concerning "Petro Caribe funds squandered" by politicians and business leaders in the private sector, against the Haitian state, under the *Petro Caribe label: The Prosecutor Speaks*. This mock trial will take on great importance when it's published. It will allow younger generations to reflect on the consequences for the management of public affairs. My initial observations leave me somewhat doubtful about a fellow Haitian understands of this matter. If we want to discuss the "Petro Caribe Fund" solely to seek the truth and punish the guilty, historical truth must not be sacrificed on the altar of passion and self-interest. We must also try to eliminate random data, as well as the lingering political biases designed to capture the imagination and amplify the absurdity. The truth is singular; it doesn't care about a door being ajar; for it, a door is either open or closed. And, if we were to go back only to those who squandered "state funds" during the so-called "democratic" period, 2008-2016, a trial seems to me politically motivated, because selective justice will always have regrettable consequences.

That said, a technical report must accompany the administrative report for the trial to proceed. Do we have this technical report? The current level of corruption leaves very little room for maneuver for a judge, however competent, to render a fair decision. The judicial system lacks credibility; the rot has set in. However, I believe that with positive political will, guaranteed by an honest executive branch and an independent court, this trial could take place without getting bogged down in the intricacies of politics. "Force without law is dangerous, but law without force is a pipe dream," as the saying goes.

Between 2008 and 2016, politicians and business leaders embezzled funds estimated at $4.2 billion (some say $3.8 billion) under the guise of sham projects, only 30% of which were completed. Where do these figures come from? Given this situation, amidst this political and administrative chaos, the Haitian state can still salvage what it can, without targeting political adversaries or enemies in a spirit of revenge. In my humble opinion, the solution is simple: "If the administrative files concerning these projects still exist, we simply need to follow them and trace them back to those responsible for the projects and their funding. Once the projects are verified, those responsible will be ordered to complete them, reimburse the remaining amount, or face imprisonment along with the seizure of their assets." I believe it would be better to seek a peaceful solution, rather than stirring up trouble between Haitian families. The "Petro Caribe" affair is more of a political than an administrative episode, directly linked to "PAYS LOCK", the assassination of Me Monferrier Dorval, the "Dermalog Affair", and even the assassination of Jovenel Moïse; and that is why it fizzled out like a straw fire...

Finding those responsible in the Petro Caribe affair is not complicated; one simply needs to review the profile of the ringleaders of this affair.

Harold Gresseau

Social justice and equity: the unmissable event of the Haitian nation with history.

Dr. Josué Pierre, sociologist

The Petro Caribe trial, all things considered, appears as a major event that will demonstrate the future of the Haitian nation in the near future. Therefore, the foundational act, which often takes the form of a land claim—"on concrete"—proves to be just and reasonable. However, the ordinary language of a gathering in the streets by a group of men and women, commonly called a public demonstration, seems to appeal to the eye, but not to the heart, much less to the mind. This is why it seems essential to approach this case from another angle: that of militant writing demanding social justice. It is also evident that the challenge of highlighting the Petro Caribe trial through an ingenious legal scenography is the work of a practicing legal artist with an unwavering determination to place Haiti among the respectable nations.

It is important to remember that the squandering of Petro Caribe funds by Haitians, both men and women, members of various successive governments, and third parties previously unknown to the global community, has placed the entire society in a position of international vulnerability, where the Haitian nation appears less credible in the eyes of the world. Therefore, translating the legal system into a dramatic form gives rise to a new trend. It is a different kind of art. It is an articulation of the sociological, the legal, and the raison d'état at the crossroads of a need for enlightenment, justice, and definitive redress. It is also a way of restoring human social reason to its genuinely hoped-for elevation. It is, therefore, a rediscovery of social morality and, by way of opportunity, a start to the mental re-education of Haitian society through the symbolic power of criminal justice.

It's fashionable to speak one's mind, but speaking truthfully about justice is worth more than ten tons of gold. This leads us to believe that bringing justice to a suffering and unhappy people are the work of divine liberation. For God the Creator is the just judge and He is truth. Thus, one can subscribe to the view that comprehensive societal healing can only be effective when those innocent in this affair can finally say to those who betrayed and delivered the nation to suffering: "Your time has come; accused, rise for your judgment!"

It is entirely speculative to imagine that this day will ever come, as Judge Jean Sénat Fleury demonstrates, who, in the annals of cosmic justice, believes that good must triumph over evil. Therefore, three concepts appear essential: truth, social equity, and the reconstruction of the people's spirit through the revival of a social psychology of trust. For the deep wounds inflicted on the Haitian people, a consequence of the suffering caused by injustice can only be healed if justice finally prevails within society.

Indeed, in artistic literature, thinkers and literary figures conceptually define it as follows: "Theater, or the dramatic genre, is simultaneously the art of representing a drama, a specific literary genre, and the building in which theatrical performances take place." This single idea, translated into social ergonomics, readily demonstrates the diversity and complexity of the masterpiece accessible to lovers of fine works. It is a trial, for the moment fictional, in which Judge Jean Sénat Fleury, a man of great historical and legal scholarship, delivers a message where impunity is finally and vigorously punished in its absolute audacity. It is a work that offers Haitian justice an unstoppable scenography roadmap that sends chills down the spines of potential perpetrators. Therefore, if the grieving people, preoccupied with their daily struggles, forget the historical account of this trial as presented in *Petro Caribe: The Public Prosecutor Speaks,* it is there to remind them of their duty to remember and their timeless need for justice in all respects, which must truly be achieved. For this is about putting into action Dessalines dream of comprehensive justice.

Dr. Josué PIERRE, independent sociologist and researcher - Social fact analyst- Didactician/methodologist, specializing in local and socio-professional development.

PetroCaribe: An Inevitable Trial

Anne-Edeline François

It is absolutely essential to revisit the Petro Caribe case, to discuss it, to bring it to the forefront, to investigate it, to dissect it thoroughly in order to eradicate this phenomenon that is so pervasive that the disappearance of such a considerable sum of money still does not result in any convictions, any imprisonment, and any serious legal proceedings. Would we, therefore, become complicit, through our silence and indifference, in such a grave crime? Do we not understand that this sum of money could, as in any other country, and even more so in Haiti, reverse many situations that today constitute breeding grounds for poverty and crime? We understand this, and this case will be resolved. The perpetrators must be condemned. This book exposes a scandal that, by its very nature, calls for a reconsideration of our social norms, the adoption of new laws, and the criminal prosecution of the guilty parties, serving as an example for the building of a new, more just and inclusive Haitian nation.

This squandered sum of over 4 billion US dollars is equivalent to several decades of loans granted by international organizations (World Bank and others) under conditions that only exacerbate our structural problems and increase our financial burden. For the years 2023-2024, the amounts disbursed total approximately 180 million. These are supplemented by annual donations of between 20 and 30 million. Furthermore, and adding insult to injury, the criminal industry has flourished thanks to Petro Caribe funds, which these corrupt officials have used to arm young people and train gangs to maintain their grip on power. And so, have we embarked on this downward spiral of fear and decay?

Certainly, the rule of law should provide the solution. However, the concept of the rule of law, disseminated globally in the 1980s by the former colonial powers, has not proven its relevance in our country. It is defined as a legal order in which the state is called upon to submit to the law and to defend fundamental rights, including subjective rights. It is based on a liberal ideal that emphasizes individual rights and limits the role of the state in public activities. But since legal pronouncements are not inherently effective, their content and implications must be carefully considered. Thus, Haiti, for its part, must link the rule of law to an ideal of justice and equality inherited from its history and its own vision of development.

The judicial system is the backbone of the rule of law. Like any other institution, it is in crisis due to endemic corruption and limited public resources. Those who championed the rule of law as a universal value are the very same ones who will destroy the institutional foundations upon which the concept of the rule of law could have become a reality in our country. The structural adjustment policies of the Bretton Woods organizations, the International Monetary Fund and the World Bank, have advocated underfunding institutions and adopting laws that are too liberal for our economy.

The disastrous consequences that ensued were such that these organizations followed up their adjustment programs with the creation of a new category of poor: the extremely poor. Haiti was the prime example. The country, in fact, still suffers from the disintegration of numerous sectors and the opening of its borders. Often, these dictates from dominant countries are unfortunately unavoidable, as are the ensuing scourges and crises.

Moreover, situations of political and economic crisis and instability tend to exacerbate the asymmetry in power relations, creating fertile ground for the expansion of corruption. The prevailing extreme precarity grants those in power and the privileged class far more power and audacity in their immoral actions. As early as the 1890s, a member of the Mews family, of Dutch and Haitian origin, arrested for flagrant acts of smuggling, document forgery, black marketeering, obstruction of justice, and circulation of counterfeit currency, was released shortly afterward and faced no punishment. Yet his smuggling operations were so extensive that the president had issued a decree prohibiting the circulation of certain coins. His status and connections allowed him to escape justice, and he was able to peacefully pass on his fortune acquired under these conditions to his descendants, who benefit from the same social status, protecting them from their possible or proven wrongdoing.

Many notorious acts of corruption go unpunished because the symbolic boundaries between public and private spheres seem to be increasingly blurred. Trials are rare, and abuses, crimes, and extortion go unpunished. These social mechanisms, through their repetition, tend to skew social norms; the country seems to be developing, over time, a certain tolerance for corruption. Thus, those who plunder the country have asserted their right to dispose of property to the point of immorality and depravity.

This echoes what Jean Casimir emphasized in his book *The Haitian Nation and the State*. From 1791 onward, the public administration established by Europe was increasingly oriented toward the metropolitan, colonial, and modern state, seeking to render the sovereign people invisible. This administration consistently acted as a state designed to accommodate itself and respond to the demands of foreign powers, thus remaining unaccountable to the population.

The rule of law, the guarantor of better governance, struggles to find its place in internal and external power dynamics and in a liberal economy devoted to the outside world. Beyond the need for new regulations to combat corruption, we must also hope for a political approach capable of producing new social norms and restoring moral order. This approach will be led by actors, leaders endowed with "strong moral, philosophical, and religious convictions, distinguished by a high degree of personal autonomy, giving them the capacity to act in accordance with their own principles, independently of prevailing social values and any desire for recognition" (Michel Trestchenko: A Fragile Veneer of Humanity). These men and women exist in the country.

Anne-Edline François, lawyer

POSTFRAME

PETRO CARIBE: THE TRIAL OF THE CENTURY

When a nation's history becomes too heavy to bear in silence, when injustice reaches incomprehensible proportions, art must intervene. It is in this spirit that, after reading Judge Jean Sénat Fleury's book, "*Petro Caribe: The Prosecutor Speaks*", we decided to write a dramatic adaptation inspired by the book. *"Petro Caribe: The Public Prosecutor Speaks"* is a seminal work that documents one of the biggest financial scandals in Haitian history: Overbilling, embezzlement, fraud, theft, abuse of power, influence peddling, criminal conspiracy, and more. Organized crime is just one of the themes explored by Judge Fleury in this gripping fictional novel. His portrayal of the Haitian administrative machine reveals a state apparatus riddled with gangsters, where billions of dollars are siphoned off by the high-ranking officials who govern Haiti.

This work is not simply a judicial report. It is the beating heart, the core of evidence and indictments that inspired us to write this powerful dramatic work: *Petro Caribe: The Trial of the Century*. This three-act play, of which we offer here a substantial summary, does not spring from the pure imagination of a playwright, but from the burning soil of Haiti's recent history. It is the staging of a collective expectation, the theatrical catharsis of a thirst for justice too long quenched by impunity. To understand this play is to understand the narrative force of judicial truth when it is brought to the stage; it is to grasp how the facts established in investigative reports can be transformed into a modern tragedy with Shakespearean overtones, where fallen kings are confronted with their own depravity.

The dramatic narrative revolves around a landmark trial: the Petro Caribe embezzlement trial. This colossal sum, exceeding four billion dollars, was intended to build the country's future but instead fueled the appetite of corrupt elite. The play does more than simply expose the dishonest actions of the accused; it gives a face, a voice, and a soul to all the stakeholders in this national tragedy. On one side, there is the prosecution, embodied by Government Commissioner Guy Antoine, a figure of integrity and rigor, bearing the weight of the accusation and the hopes of an entire nation. His nocturnal monologues, faced with stacks of files, reveal the man behind the magistrate, aware that with his closing arguments, he is writing a pivotal chapter in Haitian judicial history. He is the moral backbone of the play, the one through whom the voice of the state and the victims finds its legal force and oratorical power.

Facing him are the accused : former president Michel Joseph Martelly, his jovial facade cracking under stress; former prime minister Laurent Salvador Lamothe, calculating and defensive; Jean-Max Bellerive, overwhelmed, consumed by a guilt that will eventually break; and a whole cohort of ministers and directors, whose arrogance or evasion characterizes the group portrait. The play is intelligent enough not to portray them as caricatured monsters, but as complex men, trapped in their lies and justifications. Their exchanges in the cell, the day before the trial, are remarkably dramatic, exposing cowardice, the rhetoric of justification ("others did it before me"), and the first cracks in the wall of denial.

Between these two poles, the play introduces a new, essential, and profoundly modern force: the people organized as judicial actors. The "Petro Challenger" collective, led by the emblematic figures of

Gilbert Mirambeau Jr., Emmanuela Douyon, and Juno Pierre, is not simply an ancient chorus commenting on the action. It is the driving force, the very origin of the trial. The play reminds us that without citizen mobilization, hashtags, and the incessant demonstrations shouting "kot kòb Petro Caribe a?" (Where did the Petro Caribe money go?), this legal confrontation would likely never have taken place. Their battle to be recognized as a civil party is not merely a procedural point; it is the symbol of the citizens' appropriation of justice. The court, in the play, thus becomes the arena where not only the State and its former leaders, but also civil society and those same leaders, clash.

The three-act structure perfectly matches the dramatic arc of the actual trial.

Act **I: The Night Before the Trial** sets the tone. It is a night of reckoning, feverish preparations, and final pressures. In his office, Maître Antoine broods over the enormity of his task, invoking the spirit of great trials of the past. In the street, the crowd vibrates with a restrained hope, ready to erupt. In the cell, the accused wage their first battle, the one against their own fears and their perception of the inevitable. This night is suspense in itself, a long take before the explosion.

Act **II: The Trial** plunges the viewer into the heart of the judicial machinery. The solemnity of the opening proceedings, the calling of the defendants, the verbal sparring between the prosecution and the defense; everything is rendered with meticulous attention to detail, demonstrating a keen understanding of the mechanisms of the law. The courtroom scenes are gripping. The prosecution's closing argument, presented by Maître Antoine, is not a mere enumeration of facts; it is an implacable narrative construction, moving from the macroeconomic context (the billions of dollars generated) to the micro-evidence (bank statements, contracts signed in a single day). Each figure is a resounding blow. Facing him, the defense, led by the experienced Me. Guilbaud and a host of other lawyers, employs the classic weapons of legal argument: challenging the materiality of the evidence, highlighting the lack of direct witnesses, invoking the difficult political climate, and the continuity of questionable practices between government agencies. The confrontation reaches its peak during the defendants' appearance in the dock. Martelly in denial and anger, Lamothe in technocratic justification, and finally Bellerive, whose confession ("I want to ask forgiveness from the Haitian people") shifts the dynamics of the courtroom and offers the play one of its most poignant and morally complex moments.

Finally, Act **III: The Verdict** is the culmination of all the tensions. The interwoven monologues during the deliberations are a brilliant dramatic device. Each character—the prosecutor, the citizen leader, the arrogant defendant, the repentant defendant, a victimized mother—reveals their innermost truth, their doubts, and their fears. This polyphony of consciences prepares the final verdict, delivered with a solemnity befitting the historical significance of the event. The sentence is final, and its reading is both a judicial and a theatrical act. The epilogue, set three years later, avoids naive optimism. It acknowledges concrete progress (hospitals, schools built with confiscated assets), but above all, it underscores the paradigm shift: it has been proven that impunity is not inevitable. The struggle, the characters conclude, must continue.

This play is therefore much more than a legal drama. It is a theatrical documentary, a civic tragedy, and a living memorial. It gives flesh and blood to legal articles, account numbers, and budget lines. It shows how a corruption trial can reach the level of a founding myth, where the pact between a people and its institutions is reenacted. The Petro Caribe trial, as staged, becomes the trial of impunity itself, the trial of a system that has existed for far too long.

The present work, *Petro Caribe: The prosecution's arguments* constitute the raw material, the factual backbone of this dramatic work. By reading the analyses, indictments, and evidence compiled here, the reader will understand where the playwright drew the strength of his dialogue, the veracity of his accusations, and the historical basis for each plot twist. The play, in turn, gives these legal texts a human and popular resonance. It takes them out of the courtroom and into the public square, into the symbolic space of the theater, the quintessential venue for debate and collective representation.

"*Petro Caribe: The Trial of the Century* " is an essential work. It is an act of remembrance, an educational tool, and a major contribution to a culture of accountability. It demonstrates that theater, far from being mere entertainment, can be a weapon of civic construction, a mirror held up to society so that it may see itself, judge itself, and perhaps transform itself. In this respect, this play and the book that inspired it are inseparable. They form a powerful diptych: one states the law, the other embodies its drama; one presents the facts, the other conveys the passions. Together, they tell the story of a country that, through one of the most difficult trials of its modern existence, attempts to rediscover the path to its own dignity.

Prof. Amerigo Bernadel

Partial List of Petrocaribe Projects/Funds

PROJECTS - AMOUNTS DISBURSED

PROJECTS	AMOUNTS DISBURSED
Construction of the Ministry of Commerce and Industry (MCI)	$14,721,556.27
Construction of Fifteen (15) Bridges in the Northwest	$20,483,189.60
Senate Projects Funded by the PetroCaribe Fund	50,000,000 HTG
The Chamber of Deputies' Projects	302 937 092.42 HTG
Institutional Strengthening of the CSCCA/PetroCaribe Fund	72 954 231 HTG
Trauma Center Construction Project	$6,370,100
Urban Renewal of the City of Saint-Marc (Phase I – Phase 2)	$8,619,030.10
Carrefour des Ruisseaux Redevelopment Project	$2,746,768.12
Construction of the Grande Rivière du Nord Public Market	$4,786,725
Construction of the Pignon Public Market	$6,488,266.94
Rehabilitation of 7 km of road in Lafiteau (mill road, 4 lanes)	$10,391,175
Construction of Community Infrastructure at the Jeremiah Wharf	$16,303,550

Urban Renewal and Residential Development Project in Bowenfield and Fort-National	314 260 515.55 HTG
Construction of the Jacmel Bridge (abandoned project)	$3,483,723.58
Rehabilitation of Hotel La Jacmélienne (abandoned construction site)	5,500,000 HTG
Construction of the premises for the Intervention and Law Enforcement Corps (CIMO)	$1,058,717.71
Construction of the Roche à Bateau and Chantal High Schools	79,882,460.58 HTG
Construction of the Bas-Limbé High School	38,090,218.76 HTG
Construction and Supervision of the Ranquitte High School	59 418 877 HTG
Construction of the Thomonde – Savanette – Cerca Carvajal High Schools	96,454,642.26 HTG
Additional Road Rehabilitation Works for Jacmel/La Vallée	$8,964,568.45
Urban Renewal Works and Construction of Socio-Community Infrastructure in Mirebalais and Las Cahobas	$16,823,483.79
List of Projects associated with the Territorial Development Program implemented by the PPTCE	$80,486,875.46
Construction of the Pilate High School	49,485,885 HTG
Construction of the Saut-D'Eau High School	60,078,513.12 HTG
Construction of the Anse-Rouge High School	18,756,686.57 HTG
Construction of a new high school in Hinche	60 463 485 HTG

Construction of the Roche à Bateau and Chantal High Schools	79,882,460.58 HTG
Construction of the Lower Limbé High School	38,090,218.76 HTG
Construction and Supervision of the Ranquitte High School	59 418 877 HTG
Construction of the high schools in Thomonde, Savanette, Cerca Carvajal	96,454,642.26 HTG
Construction of the Port Margot High School	38,179,084.72 HTG
Gros Morne Urban Renewal	54,720,796.23 HTG
Rehabilitation of the St-Michel School in Bon Repos	16,936,905.52 HTG
Maïssade Urban Renewal	32,157,843.87 HTG
St Louis du Nord Media Library	44,404,540.57 HTG
Construction of the Caracol High School	27,370,713.95 HTG
Construction of the Mont-Organisé and Capotille High Schools	98,970,970 HTG
Rehabilitation of the Mirebalais High School	3,969,000 HTG
Marchand Dessalines Urban Renewal	$4,204,955.58
Construction of citernes at Pointe à Raquette and Anse à Galets	$2,203,960.35
Dondon Urban Renewal	338 112 012 HTG
Urban Renewal of Saint-Raphaël	329 915 876 HTG

Sports Infrastructure Rehabilitation Projects	$27,787,385.59
Construction of the Port-de-Paix Media Library	27,644,341.80 HTG
Design and implementation of Territorial Development (Special Projects under the responsibility of UCLBT)	564,686,753.49 HTG
Economic and Social Assistance Fund (FAES) – Social Projects and Programs Financed by the PetroCaribe Fund	$71,612,680.23
Hospital Construction Project	$78,957,375 (MSPP)
Construction of the Delmas/Nazon Viaduct	$23,303,706.56
Construction of the Carrefour Viaduct (Haitian Navy)	$5,332,009.33
Street Rehabilitation Works in Pétion-Ville	$3,475,547.59
Construction of the Baie de l'Acul/Milot Road	$1,923,076.92
Rehabilitation of the Petite Rivière de Nippes/Petit Trou de Nippes road	$3,212,283
Execution of Works on the Battant River/Milot Section	$20,044,683.71
Additional work on the Laboule 12/Kenscoff section	$84,645.94 (83,576,303.98 HTG)
Construction of the Hyppolite Bridge (Cap-Haïtien)	$5,455,088.11
Construction on the Puilboreau/ Marmelade Intersection Road	$3,735,711.44
Street Adorning in Fort-Liberté	$2,009,000

Street paving in Ouanaminthe	$2,942,316.84
Rehabilitation of the Dufort/ Jacmel Crossroads Road	479,458,454.19 HTG
Construction of a bridge over the Rivière des Barres linking St-Louis du Nord and Anse à Foleur	$1,754,690.70
Dredging of the Port-au-Prince Bay Executions	$17,160,248.38
Rehabilitation of the Port-de-Paix/Port-Margot section	$5,000,000
Rehabilitation of the Borgne/ Petit Bourg de Borgne section	$633,199.52 (28,873,898 HTG)
Improvement of the Ennery/ Cap-Haïtien Road	$5,967,096.98
Construction of the Bridge over the Upper Cape River	2018 $753.44
Construction of Emergency Response Shelters at the Departmental Level	$1,747,272.48
Rehabilitation/Development of Public Squares (Saint-Anne – Geffrard – Occide Jeanty – Airport – Canapé Vert)	$5,791,970.33 (292,435,434.72 HTG)
Construction of the Port-de-Paix Hospital	$749,000 (38,784,643.10 HTG)
Rehabilitation of the Anse À Galets Health Center, La Gonâve	19,284,930 HTG
Purchase of Equipment for Notre-Dame Secours Hospital	$6,000,403.30
Reconstruction of the Tiburon parade ground (MSES/Construction)	7,949,176.55 HTG

Reconstruction of Place Fierté Cité Soleil (LE BATI Firm)	33 760 671 HTG
Reconstruction of the Place d'Armes and the Capois La Mort Memorial in Port-de-Paix (SOHACO Firm)	19,638,900 HTG
Sub-Programme for Combating Poverty and Social Exclusion (MAST/FAES)	$28,926,380.17
Poverty Reduction Program (FAES)	$28,500,000
Combating Poverty and Social Exclusion (MAST/FAES)	$1,841,620.63
Combating Poverty and Social Exclusion (MAST/FAES)	$12,344,680.53
Construction of the Fontamara Public Market (MPCE)	$4,102,879.88
Construction of the Cayes International Airport (MTPTC)	$7,242,448.64

Construction of the Southern University Campus (MPCE)	$8,000,000
Rehabilitation of the Colladère/Cerca Carvajal Road – 13 km (MPCE)	$7,481,232.06
Construction Road Jacmel/Vallée de Jacmel – 20 kms (MTPTC)	$8,983,704.13
Road rehabilitation Petit Trou de Nippes/ Petite Rivière de Nippes – 30 km (MTPTC)	$9,000,000
Rehabilitation of Route 44 in Côte de Fers (MTPTC)	$10,000,000
Sub-Programme for the Rehabilitation and Maintenance of Transport Infrastructure (MPTC)	$12,000,000
Price Stabilization Program (MEF)	$16,228,522.22
Hospital Construction and Rehabilitation (MSPP)	$20,000,000
Post-Earthquake Accommodation of January 12, 2010 (MPCE/UCLBP)	$5,000,000
Restoration of Sanssouci Palace (ISPAM)	$485,440.98

Rehabilitation of the Cul de Sac Plain Irrigation System (MARNDR)	$1,000,000
Rehabilitation of the Latannerie Irrigation System (MARNDR)	$1,000,000
Ban'm Limye Ban'm Lavi (BMPAD)	$2,500,000
Ti Manman Cheri	180,750,320
Kore Moun Andikape	10,879,837.20
Solidarity Voucher	163,935,350
Panye Solidarite	59,129,550
Kantin Mobil	33,112,548
Kore Peyizan	72,482,544
Kredi pou Fam m	19,709,850
Rehabilitation of the Delmas 2 Football Field	$500,000
Lahaie Dame-Marie Bridge Construction	$500,000
Construction of a media library in Saint-Louis du Nord	$702,128
Rehabilitation of the Dufort-Jacmel Crossroads Road	$553,910.88
Strengthening the Haitian National Police (PNH)/Healthcare within the PNH	$865,378.42
Construction of Food Security Storage Silos	795,164.23 $
Rehabilitation of Public Squares	$1,680,851
Price Stabilization Program	$3,771,478
Rehabilitation of the Pernier road	$6,000,000
Rehabilitation of the Tabarre road	$7,000,000
Construction and Rehabilitation of hospitals (HUEH, St-Michel de Jacmel, Simbi)	$12,000,000

Note: In the majority of projects, the CSCCA noted the following irregularities:

- Negotiated contracts signed outside of institutional norms and legal frameworks.
- Collusion, overbilling, and embezzlement.

- Disbursement of the advance payment to start the work even before the conclusion of the contract and the signing of the agreement.

- Use of funds for other purposes.

- Bonuses (bribes) in the distribution of contracts.

- Awarding contracts to two firms to perform the same work.

- Non-payment of the 2% advance payments collected for the benefit of the DGI.

- Advance payment for work starting above the 30% threshold is not guaranteed according to articles 83 and 83-1 of the law of June 12, 2009.

- No report (status) on the progress of the work.

- The deadline for completing the work was not met.

In summary, the projects financed by PetroCaribe via Haitian public institutions (BMPAD, MEF, MSPP, MPCE, MTIC, MTPTC, UCLBP, MJSAC, MARNDR, FAES, EDH, CNE, CACUSATH, SMCRS, SEEUR) and private contracting firms (AGRITRANS, BETREX, COMPHENER, ELMECEN, HADOM, ROFI, OECC, MTIC, UTE, HAYTRAC, AUTOMECA, SECOSA, IBT, V&F CONSTRUCTION, DOCE, ESTRELLA, J&J CONSTRUCTION, FIDEICOMMIS, CECOM, BETV-METRIC, HOGUYAN COMPANY LIMITED CONSTRUCTION, GRADES, HL CONSTRUCTION, TROPIC BUILD WORLDWIDE HOLDING, TRANSSAGRI, SUNTECH SOLAR/BESUCO, GTC, SOGENER, SECA, TECINA, SOGECOMAT, BDFK, FICONES, ANAPAAAH, EXPERT CONCEPT SA, CSA CENTRAL INC., CEEPCO HAITI SA, KITMAZOU, DIESEL NATIONAL COMPANY (DNC), P-JIMEX, SOGED, and

COMPAGNIE HAÏTIENNE DE MOTEURS are not managed efficiently, effectively, and transparently. According to reports from the Court of Auditors, manipulations have been calculated and meticulously planned to create a system of widespread corruption involving numerous actors. The intention is to manipulate the domestic justice system to obstruct any investigations that could lead to the prosecution of the alleged perpetrators.

Chronology

1. 2005: Launch of the Petro Caribe Program.
2. May 14, 2006: After the swearing-in ceremony for his second term, President René Préval, in the presence of Venezuelan Vice-President José Vicente Rangel, signs Haiti's accession to the *PetroCaribe Cooperation Agreement.*
3. May 15, 2006: Publication of the Decree ratifying the Petro Caribe Energy Cooperation Agreement signed between the Republic of Haiti and the Bolivarian Republic of Venezuela. (2006). Official Gazette of the Republic of Haiti, *Le Moniteur* No. 89.
4. January 4, 2008: Publication of the Law creating the Bureau for the Monetization of Development Assistance Programs. Official Gazette of the Republic of Haiti, No. 2, January 4. The Haitian State created the Bureau for the Monetization of Development Assistance Programs (BMPAD). Its mission is to ensure "the implementation of Conventions, Memoranda of Understanding, Grant and/or Loan Agreements concluded between the Haitian government and a donor or lender, within the framework of the Bureau for the Monetization of Development Assistance Programs." (Law of January 4, 2008, art. 3:4).
5. March 5, 2008: date of receipt of the first shipment of oil.
6. September 10, 2008: The Préval-Pierre-Louis government signed the resolution of September 10, 2008, for the amount of $197,500,000. This resolution concerns the first use of revenues generated by the Petro Caribe agreement, and this sum is allocated under the heading of emergency.

7. January 12, 2009: Robert Marcello, the coordinator of the National Commission for Public Procurement (CNMP), was kidnapped and murdered. The crime is linked to the PetroCaribe scandal. He was the first victim in the case.
8. November 11, 2009: Premier Michèle Duvivier Pierre-Louis resigned after refusing to authorize spending related to the Petro Caribe fund. This refusal led to a vote of no confidence against Ms. Pierre-Louis. She was replaced by Jean-Max Bellerive.
9. November 11, 2009: Jean-Max Bellerive is appointed Prime Minister of Haiti.
10. January 2010: Following the earthquake of January 12, 2010, Venezuela cancelled Haiti's debt of 395 million to the Bolivarian Republic.
11. February 11, 2010: Resolution adopted by the Council of Ministers for the use of Petro Caribe funds in the post-earthquake context in Haiti.
12. April 24, 2010: Second resolution adopted by the Council of Ministers for the use of PetroCaribe funds in the context of the emergency.
13. May 10, 2010: The World Bank cancels Haiti's $35 million debt to the institution.
14. May 12, 2010: Jean-Max Bellerive signs 16 negotiated contracts.
15. May 12, 2011: Jean-Max Bellerive, then Minister of Planning, signed a contract for the construction of ten sports parks, for US$445,000 per park. Another contract was signed on the same date for US$1.6 million.
16. May 14, 2011: René Préval leaves office and Michel Joseph Martelly is inaugurated as President of Haiti.
17. May 15, 2011: Jean-Max Bellerive resigns as Prime Minister. He will be replaced by Garry Conille.
18. September 6, 2011: A third contract covering eight sports parks was signed for a total amount of more than ten million dollars, or more than one million dollars per park.
19. 24 February, 2012: assassination of Alix Mary Junior Gassant, the director of a construction firm. He was the second victim in the Petro Caribe case.

20. February 24, 2012: Garry Conille resigns as Prime Minister.
21. May 4, 2012: Laurent Lamothe appointed as Prime Minister.
22. July 9, 2012: A fourth contract was signed for the construction of five sports complexes by Ms. Joséfa Raymond Gauthier, then Minister of Planning and External Cooperation.
23. August 19, 2012: an order declaring a state of emergency over the entire national territory was decreed for a period of one (1) month.
24. November 20, 2012: a socio-community infrastructure construction contract is signed for an amount of $18,411,135 to which is added one (1) amendment of $ 5,517,257.42, which brought the amount of the contract related to the project to $ 23,928,392.
25. January 11, 2013: A negotiated contract was signed between the Bureau of Monetization of Development Assistance Programs (BMPAD), the agency managing PetroCaribe funds, and the firm COMPHENER SA, represented by contractor Jovenel Moïse, for the purchase of supplies and the installation of 65 streetlights in the localities of Savanette and Mont Organisé for an amount of 4,949,389 gourdes or $116,058.34. This contract did not have the approval of the Superior Court of Accounts and Administrative Disputes and did not have a certificate of no-objection from the CNMP.
26. April 2, 2013: Committed citizens filed a complaint with the Port-au-Prince prosecutor's office against Michel Martelly for the 2.5 million US dollars received from Félix Bautista in November 2011 after his inauguration.
27. December 14, 2014: Laurent Lamothe resigns as Prime Minister.
28. July 5, 2015: a contract was signed for the installation of synthetic turf in sports parks, for an amount of 385 million gourdes.
29. January 22, 2016: Publication of the decree on the procedures of the Public Investment Program (PIP). With the decree of January 22, 2016, the Haitian government institutionalized project management by establishing the procedures of the

Public Investment Program (PIP). This instrument sets out the provisions for project management in general. The PIP includes resources from the public treasury, autonomous agencies, national funds, and donations from foreign governments such as Taiwan (MPCE, 2012). This means that project management policy is directly linked to the national budget.

30. February 7, 2016: Michel Martelly leaves power.
31. As of March 31, 2016, Haiti owed Venezuela an accumulated debt of $1.8 billion. The PetroCaribe accounts held a paltry $13.4 million. This minimal sum was insufficient to make debt payments. Consequently, from July 2015 to January 2016, Haiti was unable to make a single payment on its long-term debt. The country resorted to buying on credit.
32. August 17, 2016: Presentation of the report of the Ethics and Anti-Corruption Commission headed by Senator Youri Latortue.
33. July 12, 2017: Klaus Eberwein, former director of the Economic and Social Assistance Fund (FAES), reportedly "committed suicide" in a Florida hotel after agreeing to testify before the Senate committee investigating the use of PetroCaribe funds. It is claimed, however, that he was assassinated by those implicated in the PetroCaribe scandal.
34. October 26, 2017: The special Senate inquiry commission led by Senator Evalière Beauplan presents its 656-page report to the Senate.
35. November 17, 2017: In a press release, Mr. Laurent Lamothe's private secretariat stated that the three main charges relayed in the Beauplan report against the former prime minister were not subject to any rigorous verification, thus proving the negligence or even bad faith of the document's authors.
36. November 28, 2017: During a press conference, former Prime Minister Lamothe denounced the irregularities that plague the Beauplan report. "The Beauplan report is the biggest lie of the century," said Lamothe.
37. 1 , 2018: In a resolution, the Senate Assembly requested the Superior Court of Accounts and Administrative Disputes

(CSCCA) to conduct a thorough audit following two reports from the Senate's two committees. The CSCCA carried out three audits of nearly 400 projects implemented between 2008 and 2016. It presented the results by institution to define responsibilities.

38. February 26, 2018: "Petro Caribe Affair: MPs Make Their Voices Heard." Metropolehaiti.com.
39. March 2, 2018: the prosecution submitted its indictment. But this indictment has disappeared from the file.
40. April 14, 2018: date of receipt of the last oil shipment; a total of 219 shipments totaling 43.9 million barrels of fuel have been delivered and marketed in Haiti. In addition to this, there are six (6) shipments of asphalt and three (3) shipments of fuel oil, giving resulting in an accumulation of available resources of US$4,237,598,789.12.
41. May 14, 2018: Judge Paul Pierre recused himself for reasons of personal convenience.
42. August 2018: Haitian filmmaker Gilbert Mirambeau Jr launched the hashtag #PetroCaribeChallenge on Twitter.
43. 1 August, 2018: The two reports of the Senate's Ethics and Anti-Corruption Commission were sent to the Superior Court of Accounts and Administrative Disputes.
44. August 3, 2018: Two complaints were filed with the Investigating Cabinet against Dominican Senator Félix Bautista for his participation in the squandering of the PetroCaribe fund.
45. August 15, 2018: Haitian rapper K-Lib shares the hashtag #petrocaribechallenge by filmmaker Gilbert Mirambeau.
46. August 17, 2018: "Van Bèf Info Petro Caribe: Dimitri Vorbe is invited to the Haitian Senate."
47. August 24, 2018: A sit-in is organized in front of the Superior Court of Accounts and Administrative Disputes (CSCCA). The protesters demand that the judges shed light on the use of PetroCaribe funds.
48. September 9, 2018: Thousands of protesters march in Pétion-Ville in several streets of Port-au-Prince and those of the Commune of Delmas.

49. September 9, 2018: In the Commune of Trou du Nord (Northeast Department), a peaceful march was organized with the aim of "demanding accountability" for the management of PetroCaribe funds.
50. October 2018: A group of citizens from the civil society *Fondasyon Je Klere* filed a complaint with the investigating judge in charge of investigating the PetroCaribe scandal.
51. January 31, 2019: The Superior Court of Accounts and Administrative Disputes (CSCCA) submits a first 291-page audit report on the management of projects financed by PetroCaribe funds.
52. May 2, 2019: Publication of the second report by the Superior Court of Accounts and Administrative Disputes. The specific audit focuses on the management of PetroCaribe funds and the management of projects financed with those funds.
53. May 31, 2019: In front of press cameras, the president of the CSCCA, Pierre Volmar Desmesyeux, entrusts the 612 pages of the document constituting the second report of the Court relating to the investigation into the PetroCaribe affair to the president of the Senate Carl Murat Cantave.
54. September 9, 2019: *Mediapart*, a French news website, published an article entitled: "PetroCaribe, the development scam that is outraged in Haiti."
55. August 17, 2020: *France 24* devoted an entire article to the PetroCaribe affair, titled: "PetroCaribe Scandal: In Haiti, the Court of Auditors lambastes the government."
56. July 15, 2020: In a letter published on July 15, 2020, in the newspaper *Le Nouvelliste*, Olivier Martelly recalls that he served as President Martelly's advisor on youth and sports during his term. Appointed by presidential decree in June 2012 as "Coordinator of the Commission for Supporting Sports Infrastructure and Accompanying Haitian Youth (CACUSAJH)," he explains that his work consisted of "promoting sports activities for young people and monitoring the implementation of infrastructure projects decided upon by the government, which could contribute to the development of youth in the field of sports."

He emphasizes that these interventions were part of the "Football for Change" program.

57. August 20, 2020: *RFI* (Radio France International) highlights the demands and demonstrations of Haitians with their headline "Petro Caribe Funds: Haitians demand accountability from the political class."
58. August 27, 2020: Petro Caribe Case: The final audit report of the Superior Court of Accounts and Administrative Disputes (CSCCA) in light of positive Haitian law regarding the fight against corruption: the FKL considers the report relevant and paves the way for the organization of the trials that the Haitian people are waiting for.
59. November 20, 2022: Canada imposed sanctions on former President Joseph Michel Martelly as well as former Prime Ministers Laurent Lamothe and Jean Henry Céant.
60. On December 8, 2025, following a complaint filed in September 2024 by the organization *Together Against Corruption* (ECC), the ULCC accused former president Michel Martelly of false statements, omissions, and blatant inconsistencies. Martelly's financial declarations were incomplete, inconsistent, and deliberately misleading.

Bibliography

1. Alphonse, Roberson. "Petro Caribe: The World Bank criticizes, the government is incensed," *Le Nouvelliste*, December 4, 2013.
2. Antonin, Arnold. "Haiti, where is the PetroCaribe money?" Barril, December 27, 2018.
3. Barbière, Cécile. "Haiti would be better off without international aid", 2017.
4. Baggioni, Nadine. History of Haiti, the challenges of globalization from 1492 to the present day. CIDIHCA Editions.
5. Baulière, Arnousse. "Haiti: For an honest and responsible political power." A text published during the International Conference on Corruption held in Paris on June 8 and 9, 2019.
6. 246 Bayart, Jean-François. "The historicity of the imported state", Les Cahiers de CERI, no. 15.
7. Beauplan, Evalière and Col. Report of the Special Senate Commission of Inquiry into the Management of the Petro Caribe Fund, October 2017.
8. Blancpain, François. A century of financial relations between Haiti and France (1825-1922), Paris, l'Harmattan.
9. Boulet-Groux, Jonathan. "A deceptive calm has settled in Haiti," *Le Devoir*, February 20, 2019.
10. Call, CT (2008): The Fallacy of the "Failed State". Third World Quarterly, 8 (29), 1491 – 1507.
11. Cantave, T. (2012). Haiti today: Administrative reform or state reform and decentralization of decision-making powers. Haiti Perspectives, 2 (1), 67-70.
12. Chartrand, Luc. "A youth on the brink of revolution", *Radio Canada*, January 9, 2020.

13. Corten, A. (2011). The Weak State. Haiti and the Dominican Republic. Les mémoires d'encrier: Montreal.
14. Chapez, Jean. The international fight against money laundering and the financing of terrorism. French Yearbook of International Law, XLLZ-2003-CNRS, Editions, Paris.
15. Superior Court of Accounts and Administrative Disputes (January 2019). Specific audit of the management of Petro Caribe funds. Management of projects financed by Petro Caribe funds, Report 1.
16. Superior Court of Accounts and Administrative Disputes (2019, May). Specific audit of Petro Caribe fund management/ Report 2.
17. Superior Court of Accounts and Administrative Disputes (August 2020). Specific audit of the management of the Petro Caribe fund. Management of projects financed by Petro Caribe funds/ Report 3.
18. Cypri en, Maryse Saint-Pierre. Hugo Chávez and Petro Caribe: Oil as a weapon of the State and of South-South cooperation, Éditions L'Harmattan, 2023.
19. Cyprien, Maryse Saint-Pierre. Petro Caribe, an alternative to the classic AFD: A comparison between South/South and North/ South cooperation.
20. Decree of May 15, 2006, concerning the ratification of the PetroCaribe Energy Cooperation Agreement signed between the Republic of Haiti and the Bolivarian Republic of Venezuela. (2006). Official Gazette of the Republic of Haiti, No. [89] , September 18.
21. Decree of January 22, 2016 concerning the management of the public investment program. (2016). Official Gazette of the Republic of Haiti, No. 15, January 22.
22. Dommel, Daniel. Facing corruption. Karthala, Paris, 2003.
23. Dorismond, Edelyn, et al. (2018): "Petro Caribe, the epitome of survival politics", HPN, offering a perspective on the crisis.
24. Dubarry, Thibaut. "The putrescible Haitian scene of Petro Caribe: A song of the song of the last temptation of Christ

Mandela." A text published during the International Conference on Corruption held in Paris on June 8 and 9, 2019.

25. Emmanuel, RS (2021). Project management and public action in fragile states: An analysis of the management of Petro Caribe-funded projects in Haiti. University of Ottawa, Ottawa, Canada, 65 pages.
26. Émile, Etzer S. Haiti has chosen to become a poor country: The twenty reasons that prove it, Editions C, 2017.
27. Émile, Etzer. "Economic and financial costs of corrupt practices and lack of sanctions in the Haitian context: the case of Petro Caribe." A text published at the International Conference on Corruption held in Paris on June 8 and 9, 2019.
28. Gaillard, Roger. The Exterminating Republic (Part 5)· Le Grand Fauve, Port-au-Prince, Le Natal.
29. Gaudet, S. and Robert, D. (2018). The adventure of qualitative research. University of Ottawa Press.
30. Gilles, Alain. "The order of corruption in Haiti: a normal anomaly." A text published at the International Conference on Corruption held in Paris on June 8 and 9, 2019.
31. Goldwyn, DL and Gill, CR (2016). The waning of Petro Caribe? Central America and Caribbean energy in transition. Atlantic council, Adrienne Arsht Latin America Center.
32. *Haiti on the Move*: Petro Caribe: A historic opportunity wasted. (August 3, 2016).
33. *Haiti on the Move*: Petro Caribe: Power at the End of Millions. (August 5, 2026).
34. Hector, M. and Hurbon, L. (2009). Genesis of the Haitian state, 1804-1859. Paris: Maison des sciences de l'homme.
35. Holly, Daniel. On the State in Haiti, Paris L'Harmattan, 2011.
36. Honorat, Jean-Jacques. Haiti: The Failure, Economy and Politics of a Country in Tatters, Port-au-Prince, Le Natal, 1991.
37. Hubert Yves Barreau: Petro Caribe! When will the trial take place? *Le Nouvelliste*, September 20, 2018.
38. Huntington, Samuel. The Clash of Civilizations, Paris, Odile Jacob, 2000.

39. Jacqueline, Charles. “Dominican senator accused of ripping off Haiti sanctioned by Trump administration”, Miami Herald, June 12, 2018.
40. Johnson, Jake (2018). Works on corruption, often cited in analyses (see Cairn.info).
41. Jean, Moïse. Haiti, corruption and international law. Mediapart, December 10, 2019.
42. Jean-François, Sonel. “Petro Caribe Case: The Challenges Awaiting Haitian Justice,” *Le Nouvelliste*, April 10, 2019.
43. Jean-François, Sonel. “Objective conditions of the Petro Caribe trial.” A text published during the International Conference on Corruption held in Paris on June 8 and 9, 2019.
44. Joseph, Claude. “On the need to arbitrate between an effective fight against impunity and vindictive justice: The Petro Caribe report put to the test”, *Le Nouvelliste*, December 6, 2017.
45. Newspaper: Petro Caribe: the oil tap that unleashes anger in Haiti. El Tiempo, June 28, 2019.
46. Kim, Ives (2011). “New WikiLeaked Cables Reveal: How Washington and Big Oil Fought Petro Caribe in Haiti”, *Haïti Liberté.*
47. Klitgaard, Robert. Fighting Corruption (Translated from American English by Bernard Vincent, Paris, Nouveaux Horizons, 1995.
48. Lalime, Thomas. “Petro Caribe: A vast economic crime.” *Le Nouvelliste*, May 16, 2016.
49. Lalime, Thomas, “Lavalas or Tèt Kale: who squandered more public funds?” *Le Nouvelliste*, February 29, 2016.
50. Lamour, S. (2019). Irresponsibility, a skill of the dominant. International Journal of Development Studies, 239 (3), 7-29.
51. Laroche, Alix. “Haiti-Parliament: Petro Caribe Affair, a real bombshell in the Senate (August 25, 2018)”, *Haiti Press Network.*
52. Latortue, Youri et al. Report of the Senate Ethics and Anti-Corruption Commission on the management of the Petro Caribe fund, August 2016.
53. Latortue, Youri. Petro Caribe: My fight for accountability, Haiti, C3 Editions, 2018.

54. Lauture, Franck. "Mechanism for combating corruption and impunity: what role for Parliament?" A text published at the International Conference on Corruption held in Paris on June 8 and 9, 2019.
55. *Le Nouvelliste*: Petro Caribe: Justice is still walking on eggshells. (June 14, 2023).
56. Law of January 4, 2008, establishing the Bureau for the Monetization of Development Assistance Programs. (2008). Official Gazette of the Republic of Haiti, No. 2, January 4.
57. Lorenzi, Jean-Hervé. Who captures the State, Presses Universitaires de France, 2012.
58. Louis-Juste, Jean Anil (2003). "Social Crisis and International Community in Haiti", *Alterpresse.*
59. Madistin, Samuel. "Petro Caribe, CSCCA report, Agritrans' sin, the trial: clarifications by Samuel Madistin," *Le Nouvelliste*, March 19, 2019.
60. Madistin, Samuel. "Organizing a PetroCaribe trial within the framework of Haitian positive law." A text published during the International Conference on Corruption held in Paris on June 8 and 9, 2019.
61. Manigat, Mirlande. "The Consolidation Trial: a historical precedent (continued and concluded)", *Le Nouvelliste*, November 26, 2018.
62. Martinez, Holman Rodriguez. "Petro Caribe protest: the oil tap that unleashes anger in Haiti." *Courrier international*, June 28, 2019.
63. Mathon, Alix. Haiti, a case study, Port-au-Prince, Le Natal, 1985.
64. Mazouz, B. (2017). Project management in the public context. Presses de l'Université du Québec.
65. Médard, JF. (2006).The paradoxes of institutionalized corruption. International Review of Comparative Politics, 4 (13), 697-710.
66. Nesi, Jacques. "Petro Caribe: Haitians in Paris express their indignation!" *Haiti Liberté*, October 17, 2018.

67. Nesi, Jacques, Cadet Jean-Jacques. "The Petro Caribe Affair in Haiti: Corruption in the Global South. Between Politics and Science."
68. Nesi, Jacques. "Accountability: A Fool's Deal." A text published during the International Conference on Corruption held in Paris on June 8 and 9, 2019.
69. Nieto, Nubia. "Corruption as a global risk." A text published at the International Conference on Corruption held in Paris on June 8 and 9, 2019.
70. Olius, Gary. "Is the Report of the Special Senate Commission of Inquiry a political smokescreen?" *Le National*, November 15, 2017.
71. Olius, Gary. "Petro Caribe investigation beyond Attila's desire for revenge", *Le National*, April 19, 2018.
72. Olius Gary, Décembre Wilson, Joseph Claude, Jean Moïse. Petro Caribe Affair: Academics Question and Opinion, Haiti, C3 Editions, 2018.
73. Perreira, Brigitte. Ethics, governance and corruption. French Management Review, 2008, no · 186, pp. 53-77.
74. Peter Berger and Thomas Luckmann. The Social Construction of Reality, Éditions Méridiens Klincksieck, Paris, 1922.
75. Péan, Leslie (2006). Political Economy of Corruption, Volume 3, The Plunder, Maisonneuve et Larose, Paris, dealing with systemic corruption.
76. Péan, Leslie: "Will the Petro Caribe trials be stifled or brought to a conclusion?" A text published during the International Conference on Corruption held in Paris on June 8 and 9, 2019. *Alterpresse.org* (June 23, 2019).
77. Péan, Leslie. "The American occupation of Haiti and the true face of Sténio Vincent" (4 of 5) Friday, *Alterpresse*, July 26, 2013.
78. Pierre-Etienne, Sauveur. The Haitian Enigma. Failure of the Modern State in Haiti, Montreal, Mémoire d'Encrier/Les Presses de l'Université de Montréal.
79. Pierre, Luc Joseph. Haiti: The Origins of Chaos, Port-au-Prince, Imprimerie Deschamps, 1997.

80. Report of the Senate Ethics and Anti-Corruption Commission, August 2016.
81. Report of the Special Senate Commission on Petro Caribe funds (Sep. 2008 to Sept. 2016).
82. Reports from the Superior Court of Accounts and Administrative Disputes (CSCCA) on the management of Petro Caribe funds, January 2019.
83. Reports from the Superior Court of Accounts and Administrative Disputes (CSCCA) on the management of Petro Caribe funds, May 2019.
84. Reports from the Superior Court of Accounts and Administrative Disputes (CSCCA) on the management of Petro Caribe funds, August 2020.
85. Ruth, Stacy Emmanuel: The irresponsibility of the Haitian State in the management of projects financed by the Petro Caribe Energy Cooperation Agreement, University of Ottawa, 2021.
86. Senate of the Republic of Haiti. (2017). Final report of the Senate commission of inquiry into Petro Caribe funds covering the annual periods from September 2006 to September 2016.
87. Thomas, Frédéric. "The two roots of Haitian anger", *Le Monde Diplomatique*, February 1 · 2020.
88. Thomas, Frédéric. "Haiti the scandal of the century (1): The Petro Caribe dossier, February 20, 2019.
89. Thomas, Frédéric. "The Petro Caribe audit reveals another architecture of corruption in Haiti," *Le Monde*, June 12, 2019.
90. Thomas, Frédéric. Anti-corruption movements: issues and ambivalences. A text published at the International Conference on Corruption held in Paris on June 8 and 9, 2019.
91. Vivien Renaud. A last chance to seize to bring justice to the Haitian people, July 17, 2017.
92. Weil, Laurent. "On the importance of intelligent strategies and effective tools to fight corruption in Haiti." A text published at the International Conference on Corruption held in Paris on June 8 and 9, 2019.
93. Wilson, Laleau (2019). Haiti, Petro Caribe and its follies: Manifesto for an ethics of responsibility.

www.ingramcontent.com/pod-product-compliance
Lightning Source LLC
LaVergne TN
LVHW050908210926
848482LV00012B/372
* 9 7 9 8 9 0 5 2 8 0 2 4 5 *